The Animal That Therefore I Am

John D. Caputo, *series editor*

PERSPECTIVES IN
CONTINENTAL
PHILOSOPHY

JACQUES DERRIDA

The Animal That Therefore I Am
Edited by Marie-Louise Mallet

TRANSLATED BY DAVID WILLS

FORDHAM UNIVERSITY PRESS
New York ▪ 2008

The Animal That Therefore I Am was originally published in French as *L'animal que donc je suis* © 2006 Éditions Galilée.

Library of Congress Cataloging-in-Publication Data

Derrida, Jacques.
    [Animal que donc je suis. English]
    The animal that therefore I am / Jacques Derrida ; edited by Marie-Louise Mallet ; translated by David Wills.
        p.   cm.
    Includes bibliographical references (p.   ).
    ISBN-13: 978-0-8232-2790-7 (cloth : alk. paper)
    ISBN-13: 978-0-8232-2791-4 (pbk. : alk. paper)
    1. Animals (Philosophy)   I. Mallet, Marie-Louise.   II. Title.
B2430.D483A5513   2008
194—dc22   2008007491

This work has been published with the assistance of the National Center for the Book—French Ministry of Culture.

Ouvrage publié avec le soutien du Centre national du livre—ministère français chargé de la culture.

Contents

Foreword

MARIE-LOUISE MALLET

Jacques Derrida often expressed his intention to one day put together in a large work the texts he had written on "the animal." Although he had his heart set on such a project, various pressing tasks persistently pushed it aside. In 1997, for the ten-day Cerisy conference on his work whose title, "The Autobiographical Animal," he had expressly chosen, he wrote a long lecture or, rather, taking into account its approximately ten-hour duration, a kind of seminar. The introduction only was published in the conference proceedings, under the title of the whole lecture—"The Animal That Therefore I Am"—with the annotation "to be continued [*à suivre*]," announcing his intention to publish what followed.¹ Finally, in 2003, he decided to publish a text from near the end of the same lecture under the title "And Say the Animal Responded?" to be included among the unpublished texts he provided for the special issue of *Les Cahiers de L'Herne* that was to be dedicated to him.²

As Derrida himself recalled during his lecture, the question of "the animal" is very present in many of his texts. The insistence of this motif throughout his work derives from at least two sources. The first is no doubt a special and keen sensitivity, a certain aptitude for sentiments of "sympathy" with the aspects of animal life that have been most forgotten or scorned by philosophy. Whence the very great importance he gives to the question Bentham asks concerning animals: "Can they suffer?" Bentham's question is not whether they can reason or whether they can speak but whether they can suffer. This is a seemingly simple question but a

ix

very profound one for Jacques Derrida. He comes back to it several times in his texts. The suffering of animals never leaves him indifferent. Yet, and this is the second source, Bentham's question also seems to him to possess enormous philosophical relevance, being capable of surprising from behind—by means of the nonfrontal opposition of a digressive approach—the most constant and tenacious tradition of thinking in the history of philosophy. Even when that tradition defines the human as *zōon logon echon* or as *rational animal*, as an "animal" therefore, but one endowed with reason, it has always in fact opposed us to all the rest of animalkind, going so far as to erase all animality in us and, conversely, to define the animal, in an essentially negative way, as deprived of whatever is presumed to be "proper" to the human: "speech, reason, experience of death, mourning, culture, institutions, technics, clothing, lying, pretense of pretense [*feinte de feinte*], covering of tracks, gift, laughing, tears, respect, etc." And, Derrida emphasizes, "the most powerful philosophical tradition in which we live has refused the 'animal' *all of that*."[3] Philosophical "logocentrism," inseparable from a position of mastery, is in the first instance "a thesis regarding the animal, the animal deprived of the *logos*, deprived of the *can-have-the-logos*: this is the thesis, position or presupposition maintained from Aristotle to Heidegger, from Descartes to Kant, Levinas and Lacan," he writes elsewhere.[4] Moreover, the violence done to the animal begins, he says, with this pseudo-concept of "the animal," with the use of this word in the singular, as though all animals from the earthworm to the chimpanzee constituted a homogeneous set to which "(the hu)man" would be radically opposed. As a response to that first violence Derrida invents the word *animot*, which, when spoken, has the plural *animaux*, heard within the singular, recalling the extreme diversity of animals that "the animal" erases, and which, when written, makes it plain that this word [*mot*] "the animal" is precisely only a word. As a result, the different occurrences of this *animot* in his text function as so many alarm signals, wake-up calls designed to prevent the usage or unavoidability of the term *the animal*, in the singular, from soothing us into an all-too-ordinary and all-too-little-noticed dogmatic slumber.

Finally, the stakes of a deconstruction of the philosophical tradition that has maltreated animals in this way concerns more than just animals. Far from bringing about a simple reversal of perspective and, for example, restoring to "the animal" in general everything that the tradition has always deprived it of; far from substituting for the classical opposition the confusion of a no less deceptive failure to differentiate, such a deconstruction patiently multiplies the differences, bringing to our attention the fragility and porosity of the supposed frontiers of the "proper" upon which we have presumed for so long to found the traditional opposition between "man" and "animal." In so doing, however much it may disturb all those assurances concerning the "animality" of the animal "in general," it is no less disturbing for any assurance concerning the "humanity" of the human. As Derrida is careful to emphasize, it is less a matter of asking "whether one has the right to refuse the animal such and such a power . . . [than of] asking whether what calls itself human has the right rigorously to attribute to man, which means therefore to attribute to himself, what he refuses the animal, and whether he can ever possess the *pure, rigorous, indivisible* concept, as such, of that attribution."[5]

꒦

Given that, we can better understand why the question of "the animal" occupies such an important place in his thinking and why he was so attached to this book project. What that book would have been had he been given the time to bring it to fruition, alas, we shall never know. But it seems to us that we are being faithful to his wishes by collecting within this work, along with the two separately published pieces from the long Cerisy conference, those parts that have not yet seen the light of day. The latter fall within two categories: first, a long text that corresponds to the part of the lecture that was delivered between the two published fragments, and within which he follows from Plato to Levinas the "tracks," as it were, of similar recurring philosophical schemes concerning "the animal." This text, like all of Derrida's lectures, like every session of his regular teaching seminars as well, was written out perfectly and *in toto*. It has therefore been included without any modification other than minimal correction of typographical errors and the addition, in the form of notes, of certain references (or details of references) to works that he cites.

Second, one will find at the end of this work the last part of Derrida's lecture, which takes up the question of the animal in Heidegger. Its status is somewhat different and posed a number of specific problems in the context of its publication. The whole lecture, which began on July 15, 1997, continued the following day and, including discussion, lasted more than nine hours. The conference continued with the other programmed lectures, but participants were still expecting more: the question of the animal in Heidegger, which had been pointed to many times during the lecture, remained in abeyance. On the last day, therefore, July 20, at the end of the proceedings, Derrida agreed to improvise a response to that expectation. There remains only a recorded version of that improvisation, which was not written and was organized solely on the basis of a few notes and page references in Heidegger. We nevertheless believe that that sketch, however extemporaneous, has its place in this publication as the beginnings of what constitutes one of the major directions of his whole trajectory. We have provided here as faithful a transcription of it as possible, with our corrections limited to a few inevitable inconsistencies arising from the ad hoc oral presentation. We haven't sought to erase its viva voce character, its familiar and often playful tone—on the contrary, we regret only that we had inevitably to sacrifice the multiple variations of tone by means of which, no less than by means of the words, the sense was often conveyed. But while it is relatively easy to transcribe accurately every word uttered (sustained attention is all that is required), a type of interpretation comes into play once it is a matter of translating the rhythm, the silences, or the emphases of intonation constituting punctuation marks, and it is well known how much attention Derrida gave to such marks. In the end, had he been able to prepare this work for publication himself, he would no doubt have rewritten what is only a sketch, a simple outline [*silhouette*] as he says. But as he reminds us, the question of the animal in Heidegger had already been brought to light in many of his texts, in particular, in "The Ends of Man," "Geschlecht" and "Heidegger's Hand," *Of Spirit*, "Heidegger's Ear," and finally *Aporias*, all of which should therefore be read or reread.[6]

"If I had time and if we had the time together. . . . we don't have time. . . . if I had time I would try to show how. . . . we won't have time to go very far. . . . if we have the time to get there. . . . one should spend a long time on this. . . . I won't have time to do it. . . . if I had time, I would have liked to do justice. . . . I would have liked to insist on the moments of vertigo and circularity in this text. That's what would take time. . . . This exclamation mark is something I would have liked to follow throughout this enormous discourse, I'll do it, I hope, if I have the time and the strength: I'd like to do justice to this text." The reader of this transcription cannot fail to be struck by the return of this motif of the time one doesn't have, a motif that echoes for us today like the tolling of a bell. Well beyond the circumstantial reasons for that anxiety (the end of a colloquium, the little time remaining in fact, the fear, also, of taking up too much time and attention on the part of an audience that, nevertheless, was asking for nothing else), Jacques Derrida's readers and friends will recognize there an anxiety, an anguish, a "trembling" of the voice that they have often heard. "If I have the time and the strength": far from being satisfied with a work that was nevertheless immense, his thinking always forged ahead toward an uncertain future to come, in the first instance through this concern for "doing justice" to the text, the theme, the question, the motif, to what does not allow itself to be thematized, to the coming of the event. The most rigorous and intransigent "deconstruction" has always been motivated by that care, as much for justice as for precision [*justesse*].

In 1997 he still had a little time, but for a long time already, well before 1997, and very often after, this little sentence came back to him: "Life will have been so short." That future perfect today encounters its "absolute usage."

The Animal That Therefore I Am
(More to Follow)

In the beginning, I would like to entrust myself to words that, were it possible, would be naked.

Naked in the first place—but this is in order to announce already that I plan to speak endlessly of nudity and of the nude in philosophy. Starting from Genesis. I would like to choose words that are, to begin with, naked, quite simply, words from the heart.

And to utter these words without repeating myself, without beginning again what I have already said here, more than once. It is said that one must avoid repeating oneself, in order not to give the appearance of training [*dressage*], already, of a habit or a convention that would in the long term program the very act of thanking.

Some of you, and the thought of it moves me to tears, were already here in 1980, or again in 1992, at the time of the previous two conferences. Some even, among my dearest and most faithful friends (Philippe Lacoue-Labarthe and Marie-Louise Mallet) had already inspired, conceived of, and brought to fruition those two occasions, with the smiling genius that Marie-Louise radiates once again. Jean-Luc Nancy promised us he would be here again. Along with Philippe he opened the 1980 conference. I think of him constantly and he must know that his friends and admirers send him their very best wishes from here.[1]

To those I have just named I owe so much that the language of gratitude is insufficient. What I owe them remains infinite and indelible.

Without forgetting that, I wish, if you'll forgive me, to go back in time, back to an earlier moment still, to a time before that time.

And to speak starting from that point in time, so long ago, as one says,[2] a time that for me becomes fabulous or mythical.

Some of you here, Maurice de Gandillac, first of all, whom I wish to greet and thank in pride of place, know that about forty years ago, in 1959, our wonderful hosts here at Cerisy were already offering me their hospitality—and it was the moment of my very first lecture, in fact, the first time I spoke in public. If I were already to give in to what others might call the instinct of the autobiographical animal, I might recall that in 1959, as today, the theme was, in short, Genesis. The title of the conference was "Structure and Genesis," and it was my first ten-day Cerisy event. Following that I have greatly enjoyed returning for "Nietzsche" in 1972, "Ponge" in 1974, "Lyotard" in 1982. I don't think I have to say any more about that for you to be able, not so much to measure, for it is immeasurable, but rather to sense the immensity of my gratitude.

Everything I shall venture to say today will therefore be, once more, in order to express my thanks, in order to say "thanks to this place, to those who welcome us here and to you." I experience my returns to Cerisy as a wonderful and intense story that has parsed almost the whole of my adult life, everything I have tried to think about it out loud. If ever the animal that I am were one day to take it upon itself to write an autobiography (whether intellectual or emotional), it would have to name Cerisy again and again, more than once and in more than one way—in the renown of the proper name and of metonymy.

As for these ten days, the third in something like a series, they seemed to me unimaginable, even excluded in advance. Last time, in 1992, when Didier Cahen alluded to the possibility in the attic on the last evening, asking me what the theme of a third conference would be, I still remember dismissing such a hypothesis: "This guy is crazy," I exclaimed. He wasn't so crazy, but the whole idea remains, like everything that happens, and such is the condition for something to be able to happen, impossible to anticipate. It is only after the event, reading the titles of these three meetings (*Les fins de l'homme* [The Ends of Man], *Le passage des frontières* [The Crossing of Borders], *L'animal autobiographique* [The Autobiographical Animal]) with a feeling of uncanniness, that I perceived a sort of prescriptive arrangement, a preestablished if not harmonious order, a providential machine, as Kant would say, precisely, concerning the animal, "als ein Maschinen der Vorsehung," an obscure foresight, the process of a blind but sure prefiguration in the configuration: one and the same movement being outlined and seeking its end. The Ends of Man (title chosen by Philippe Lacoue-Labarthe and Jean-Luc Nancy without asking for my input, and I didn't ask to give it, although the title was also that of one of my texts), The Crossing of Borders, and The Autobiographical Animal (titles that I myself proposed to Marie-Louise and to our hosts at Cerisy): later I began to hear in them, in this series of three kick-offs, what no one, least of all myself, had ever calculated, and what no one would be able to reappropriate, namely, the outline or the temptation of a single phrase, a phrase offering more to follow [*qui se donnerait à suivre*].

It follows, itself; it follows itself. It could say "I am," "I follow," "I follow myself," "I am (in following) myself." In being pursued this way, consequentially, three times or in three rhythms, it would describe something like the course of a three-act play or the three movements of a syllogistic concerto, a displacement that becomes a *suite*, a result, in a single word.

If I am (following) this suite [*si je suis cette suite*], and everything in what I am about to say will lead back to the question of what "to follow" or "to pursue" means, as well as "to be after," back to the question of what I do when "I am" or "I follow," when I say "*Je suis*," if I am (following) this suite then, I move from "the ends of man," that is the confines of man, to "the crossing of borders" between man and animal. Passing across borders or the ends of man I come or surrender to the animal, to the animal in itself, to the animal in me and the animal at unease with itself, to the man about whom Nietzsche said (I no longer remember where) something to the effect that it was an as yet undetermined animal, an animal lacking in itself. Nietzsche also said, at the very beginning of the second treatise of *The Genealogy of Morals*, that man is a promising animal, by which he meant, underlining those words, an animal that is permitted to make promises (*das versprechen darf*). Nature is said to have given itself the task of raising, domesticating, and "disciplining" (*heranzüchten*) this animal that promises.

Since time, since so long ago, hence since all of time and for what remains of it to come we would therefore be in passage toward surrendering to the promise of that animal at unease with itself.

↭

Since time, therefore.

Since so long ago, can we say that the animal has been looking at us?[3]

What animal? The other.

I often ask myself, just to see, *who I am*—and who I am (following) at the moment when, caught naked, in silence, by the gaze of an animal, for example, the eyes of a cat, I have trouble, yes, a bad time[4] overcoming my embarrassment.

Whence this malaise?

I have trouble repressing a reflex of shame. Trouble keeping silent within me a protest against the indecency. Against the impropriety [*malséance*] that can come of finding oneself naked, one's sex exposed, stark naked[5] before a cat that looks at you without moving, just to see. The impropriety of a certain animal nude before the other animal, from that point on one might call it a kind of *animalséance*: the single, incomparable and original experience of the impropriety that would come from appearing in truth naked, in front of the insistent gaze of the animal, a benevolent or pitiless gaze, surprised or cognizant. The gaze of a seer, a visionary or extra-lucid blind one. It is as if I were ashamed, therefore, naked in front of this cat, but also ashamed for being ashamed. A reflected shame, the mirror of a shame ashamed of itself, a shame that is at the same time specular, unjustifiable, and unavowable. At the optical center of this reflection would appear this thing—and in my eyes the focus of this incomparable experience—that is called nudity. And about which it is believed that it is proper to man, that is to say, foreign to animals, naked as they are, or so it is thought, without the slightest consciousness of being so.

Ashamed of what and naked before whom? Why let oneself be overcome with shame? And why this shame that blushes for being ashamed? Especially, I should make clear, if the cat observes me *frontally* naked, face to face, and if I am naked faced with the cat's eyes looking at me from head to toe, as it were just *to see*, not hesitating to concentrate its vision—in order to see, with a view to seeing—in the direction of my sex. *To see*, without going to see, without touching yet, and without biting, although that threat remains on its lips or on the tip of the tongue. Something happens there that shouldn't take place—like everything that happens in the end, a lapsus, a fall, a failing, a fault, a symptom (and "symptom," as you know, also means "fall": case, unfortunate event, coincidence, what falls due [*échéance*], mishap). It is as if, at that instant, I had said or were going to say the forbidden, something that shouldn't be said. As if I were to avow what cannot be avowed in a symptom and, as one says, wanted to bite my tongue.

Ashamed of what and before whom? Ashamed of being as naked as a beast.[6] It is generally thought, although none of the philosophers I am about to examine actually mentions it, that the property unique to animals, what in the last instance distinguishes them from man, is their being

humans - so visually inclined. What about smell? about touch?

naked without knowing it. Not being naked therefore, not having knowledge of their nudity, in short, without consciousness of good and evil.

From that point on, naked without knowing it, animals would not be, in truth, naked.

They wouldn't be naked because they are naked. In principle, with the exception of man, no animal has ever thought to dress itself. Clothing would be proper to man, one of the "properties" of man. "Dressing oneself" would be inseparable from all the other figures of what is "proper to man," even if one talks about it less than speech or reason, the *logos*, history, laughing, mourning, burial, the gift, etc. (The list of "what is proper to man" always forms a configuration, from the first moment. For that very reason, it can never be limited to a single trait and it is never closed; structurally speaking it can attract a nonfinite number of other concepts, beginning with the concept of a concept.)

The animal, therefore, is not naked because it is naked. It doesn't feel its own nudity. There is no nudity "in nature." There is only the sentiment, the affect, the (conscious or unconscious) experience of existing in nakedness. Because it *is* naked, without *existing* in nakedness, the animal neither feels nor sees itself naked. And therefore it isn't naked. At least that is what is thought. For man it would be the opposite, and clothing derives from technics. We would therefore have to think shame and technicity together, as the same "subject." And evil and history, and work, and so many other things that go along with it. Man would be the only one to have invented a garment to cover his sex. He would be a man only to the extent that he was able to be naked, that is to say, to be ashamed, to know himself to be ashamed because he is no longer naked. And knowing *himself* would mean knowing himself to be ashamed. On the other hand, because the animal is naked without consciousness of being naked, it is thought that modesty remains as foreign to it as does immodesty. As does the knowledge of self that is involved in that.

What is shame if one can be modest only by remaining immodest, and vice versa? Man could never be naked any more because he has the sense of nakedness, that is to say, of modesty or shame. The animal would be *in* non-nudity because it is nude, and man *in* nudity to the extent that he is no longer nude. There we encounter a difference, a time or *contretemps* between two *nudities without nudity*. This contretemps has only just begun giving us trouble or doing us harm [*mal*] in the area of the knowledge of good and evil.

Before the cat that looks at me naked, would I be ashamed *like* a beast that no longer has the sense of its nudity? Or, on the contrary, *like* a man who retains the sense of his nudity? Who am I, therefore? Who is it that

I am (following)? Whom should this be asked of if not of the other? And perhaps of the cat itself?

I must immediately make it clear, the cat I am talking about is a real cat, truly, believe me, *a little cat*. It isn't the *figure* of a cat. It doesn't silently enter the bedroom as an allegory for all the cats on the earth, the felines that traverse our myths and religions, literature and fables. There are so many of them. The cat I am talking about does not belong to Kafka's vast zoopoetics, something that nevertheless merits concern and attention here, endlessly and from a novel perspective. Nor is the cat that looks at, concerning me, and to which I seem—but don't count on it—to be dedicating a negative zootheology, Hoffmann's or Kofman's cat Murr, although along with me it uses this occasion to salute the magnificent and inexhaustible book that Sarah Kofman devotes to it, namely, *Autobiogriffures*,[7] whose title resonates so well with that of this conference. That book keeps vigil over this conference and asks to be permanently quoted or reread.

An animal looks at me. What should I think of this sentence? The cat that looks at me naked and that is *truly a little cat*, *this* cat I am talking about, which is also a female, isn't Montaigne's cat either, the one he nevertheless calls "my [pussy]cat" [*ma chatte*] in his "Apology for Raymond Sebond."[8] You will recognize that as one of the greatest pre- or anti-Cartesian texts on the animal that exists. Later we will pay attention to a certain mutation between Montaigne and Descartes, an event that is obscure and difficult to date, to identify even, between two configurations for which these proper names are metonymies. Montaigne makes fun of "man's impudence with regard to the beasts," of the "presumption" and "imagination" shown by man when he claims, for example, to know what goes on in the heads of animals; especially when he presumes to assign them or refuse them certain faculties (330–31). On the contrary, he deems it necessary to recognize in animals a "facility" in forming letters and syllables. This capacity, Montaigne assures us with assurance, "testifies that they have an inward power of reason which makes them so teachable and determined to learn" (340). Taking man to task for "carv[ing] out their shares to his fellows and companions the animals, and distribut[-ing] among them such portions of faculties and powers as he sees fit," he asks, and the question refers from here on not to the animal but to the naïve assurance of man:

> How does he know, by the force of his intelligence, the secret internal stirrings of animals? By what comparison between them and us does he infer the stupidity that he attributes to them?

When I play with my cat [*ma chatte*], who knows if I am not a
pastime to her more than she is to me? (331)

[The 1595 edition adds: "We entertain each other with reciprocal
monkey tricks. If I have my time to begin or to refuse, so has she
hers."]

Nor does the cat that looks at me naked, she and no other, the one *I am
talking about here*, belong, although we are getting warmer, to Baudelaire's
family of cats,[9] or Rilke's,[10] or Buber's.[11] Literally, at least, these poets'
and philosophers' cats don't speak. "My" pussycat (but a pussycat never
belongs) is not even the one *who speaks* in *Alice in Wonderland*. Of course,
if you insist at all costs on suspecting me of perversity—always a possibility—you are free to understand or receive my emphasis on "really a little
cat" as a quote from chapter 11 of *Through the Looking Glass*. Entitled
"Waking," this penultimate chapter consists in a single sentence: "—it
really *was* a kitten, after all"; or as one French translation has it: "and,
after all, it really was a little black pussycat" [*et, finalement, c'était bel et
bien une petite chatte noire*].[12]
Although I don't have time to do so, I would of course have liked to
inscribe my whole talk within a reading of Lewis Carroll. In fact you can't
be certain that I am not doing that, for better or for worse, silently, un-
consciously, or without your knowing. You can't be certain that I didn't
already do it one day when, ten years ago, I let speak or let pass a little
hedgehog, a suckling hedgehog [*un nourrisson hérisson*] perhaps, before
the question "What is Poetry?"[13] For thinking concerning the animal, if
there is such a thing, derives from poetry. There you have a thesis: it is
what philosophy has, essentially, had to deprive itself of. It is the difference between philosophical knowledge and poetic thinking. The hedgehog of "What is Poetry?" not only inherited a piece of my name but also
responded, in its own way, to the appeal of Alice's hedgehog. Remember
the croquet ground where the "balls were live hedgehogs" ("The Queen's
Croquet Ground"). Alice wanted to give the hedgehog a blow with the
head of the flamingo she held under her arm, and it would "twist itself
round and look up in her face," until she burst out laughing.[14]
How can an animal look you in the face? That will be one of our concerns. Alice noticed next that "the hedgehog had unrolled itself and was
in the act of crawling away: besides all this, there was generally a ridge or
a furrow in the way wherever she wanted to send the hedgehog to." It was
a field on which "the players all played at once, without waiting for turns,
quarrelling all the while, and fighting for the hedgehogs."

We will be all the more silently attracted to *Through the Looking-Glass* because we will have to deal with a type of *mirror stage*—and to ask certain questions of it, from the point of view of the animal, precisely.

But my real cat is not Alice's little cat (certain translations say *le petit chat* for "kitten," or, as I have just quoted, *une petite chatte noire*), because I am certainly not about to conclude hurriedly, upon wakening, as Alice did, that one cannot speak with a cat on the pretext that it doesn't reply or that it always replies the same thing. Everything that I am about to entrust to you no doubt comes back to asking you to *respond* to me, you, to me, reply to me concerning what it is to *respond*. If you can. The said question of the said animal in its entirety comes down to knowing not whether the animal speaks but whether one can know what *respond* means. And how to distinguish a response from a reaction. In this respect we must keep in mind Alice's very Cartesian statement at the end:

> It is a very inconvenient habit of kittens (Alice had once made the remark) that, whatever you say to them, they *always* purr. "If they would only purr for 'yes,' and mew for 'no,' or any rule of that sort," she had said, "so that one could keep up a conversation! But how *can* you talk with a person if they *always* say the same thing?"
>
> On this occasion the kitten only purred: and it was impossible to guess whether it meant "yes" or "no."[15]

You can speak to an animal, to the cat said to be *real* inasmuch as it is an animal, but it doesn't reply, not really, not ever, that is what Alice concludes. Exactly like Descartes, as we shall later hear.

The letter counts, as does the *question* of the animal. The question of the animal response often has as its stakes the letter, the literality of a word, sometimes what the word *word* means literally. If, for example, the word *respond* appears twice in all the translations of Carroll that I consulted, it corresponds neither to any lexical term nor to any word as such in the original. The English no doubt implies responding without stating it, and this is surely a matter of economy. Where the translation says, without underlining the "always": *quoiqu'on leur dise, elles ronronnent toujours pour vous répondre*, the original simply says "whatever you say to them, they *always* purr." And where the translation says, without underlining the allusion to *pouvoir* ("can"): *Mais comment peut-on parler avec quelqu'un qui* répond *toujours pareil?* Carroll himself writes "But how *can* you talk with a person if they *always* say the same thing?"

That said, the sense of "response" seems to be implicit here; one can always maintain that the difference between the presence and absence of the word *response* doesn't count. Perhaps. Perhaps, on the contrary, one should take the matter very seriously, but that will only be later on.

In any case, isn't Alice's credulity rather incredible? She seems, at this moment at least, to believe that one can in fact discern and decide between a human *yes* and *no*. She seems confident that when it comes to man it is possible to guess whether yes or no. Let us not forget that the Cheshire Cat had told her, in the course of a scene that deserves a long meditation: "We're all mad here. I'm mad. You're mad." After that he undertakes to demonstrate to her this collective folly. It is the moment of a simulacrum of discussion, which comes to grief when they are unable to agree on the sense of the words, on what a *word* means, and in the end, no doubt, on what "word," what the term *word* could ever mean. "Call it what you like," the Cat ends up saying about the difference between growling and purring, before announcing that he will be present at the Queen's croquet game, where my poor hedgehogs will be badly treated [*mis à mal*].[16]

No, no, my cat, the cat that looks at me in my bedroom or bathroom, this cat that is perhaps not "my cat" or "my pussycat," does not appear here to represent, like an ambassador, the immense symbolic responsibility with which our culture has always charged the feline race, from La Fontaine to Tieck (author of "Puss in Boots"), from Baudelaire to Rilke, Buber, and many others. If I say "it is a real cat" that sees me naked, this is in order to mark its unsubstitutable singularity. When it responds in its name (whatever "respond" means, and that will be our question), it doesn't do so as the exemplar of a species called "cat," even less so of an "animal" genus or kingdom. It is true that I identify it as a male or female cat. But even before that identification, it comes to me as *this* irreplaceable living being that one day enters my space, into this place where it can encounter me, see me, even see me naked. Nothing can ever rob me of the certainty that what we have here is an existence that refuses to be conceptualized [*rebelle à tout concept*]. And a mortal existence, for from the moment that it has a name, its name survives it. It signs its potential disappearance. Mine also, and that disappearance, from this moment to that, *fort/da*, is announced each time that, with or without nakedness, one of us leaves the room.

But I must immediately emphasize the fact that this shame that is ashamed of itself is more intense when I am not alone with the pussycat in the room. Then I am no longer sure before whom I am so numbed with shame. In fact, is one ever alone with a cat? Or with anyone at all? Is this cat a third [*tiers*]? Or an other in a face-to-face duel? These questions will return much later. In such moments, on the edge of the thing, in the imminence of the best or the worst, when anything can happen, where I can die of shame or pleasure, I no longer know in whose or in what direction to throw myself. Rather than chasing it away, chasing the cat away, I am in a hurry, yes, in a hurry to have it appear otherwise. I hasten to cover the obscenity of the event, in short, to cover myself. One thought alone keeps me spellbound: dress myself, even a little, or, which amounts to the same thing, run away—as if I were chasing[17] myself out of the room—bite myself, therefore, bite my tongue, for example, at the very moment when I ask myself "Who?" But "*Who* therefore?" For I no longer know who, therefore, I am (following) or who it is I am chasing, who is following me or hunting me. Who comes before and who is after whom? I no longer know which end my head is. Madness: "We're all mad here. I'm mad. You're mad." I no longer know how to respond, or even to respond to the question that compels me or asks me who I am (following) or after whom I am (following), but am so as I am running [*et suis ainsi en train de courir*].

To follow and *to be after* will not only be the question, and the question of what we call the animal. We shall discover in the follow-through the question of the question, that which begins by wondering what *to respond* means and whether an animal (but which one?) ever replies in its own name. And by wondering whether one can answer for what "I am (following)" means when that seems to necessitate an "I am inasmuch as I am *after* [après] the animal" or "I am inasmuch as I am *alongside* [auprès] the animal."

Being *after*, being *alongside*, being *near* [près] would appear as different modes of being, indeed of *being-with*. With the animal. But, in spite of appearances, it isn't certain that these modes of being come to modify a preestablished being, even less a primitive "I am." In any case, they express a certain order of *being-huddled-together* [être-serré] (which is what the etymological root, *pressu*, indicates, whence follow the words *près*, *auprès*, *après*), the being-pressed, the being-with as being strictly attached, bound, enchained, being-under-pressure, compressed, impressed, repressed, pressed-against according to the stronger or weaker stricture of what always remains pressing. In what sense of the neighbor [*prochain*] (which is not necessarily that of a biblical or Greco-Latin tradition) should I say that I am close or *next to* the animal, and that I am (following) it, and in what type or order of pressure? Being-with it in the sense of being-close-to-it? Being-alongside-it? Being-after-it? *Being-after-it* in the sense of the hunt, training, or taming, or *being-after-it* in the sense of a succession or inheritance? In all cases, if I am (following) *after* it, the animal therefore comes before me, earlier than me (*früher* is Kant's word regarding the animal, and Kant will be one of our witnesses to come). The animal is there before me, there next to me, there in front of me—I who am (following) after it. And also, therefore, since it is before me, it is behind me. It surrounds me. And from the vantage of this being-there-before-me it can allow itself to be looked at, no doubt, but also—something that philosophy perhaps forgets, perhaps being this calculated forgetting itself—it can look at me. It has its point of view regarding me. The point of view of the absolute other, and nothing will have ever given me more food for thinking through this absolute alterity of the neighbor or of the next(-door) than these moments when I see myself seen naked under the gaze of a cat.

ℑ

What is at stake in these questions? One doesn't need to be an expert to foresee that they involve thinking about what is meant by living, speaking, dying, being, and world as in being-in-the-world or being-within-the-world, or being-with, being-before, being-behind, being-after, being and following, being followed or being following, there where *I am*, in one way or another, but unimpeachably, *near* what they call the animal. It is too late to deny it, it will have been there before me who is (following) after it. *After* and *near* what they call the animal and *with* it—whether we want it or not, and whatever we do about this thing.

I'll be obliged to return more than once to the malaise of this scene. I beg your forgiveness for it. I shall do all I can to prevent its being presented as a primal scene: this deranged theatrics of the *wholly other they call "animal,"* for example, *"cat."* Yes, the wholly other, more other than any other, which *they* call an animal, for example, a cat, when it looks at me naked, at the instant when I introduce myself, present myself to it— or, earlier, at that strange moment when, before the event, before even wanting it or knowing it myself, I am passively presented to it as naked, I am seen and seen naked, before even seeing *myself* seen by a cat. Before even seeing myself or knowing myself seen naked. I am presented to it before even introducing myself. Nudity is nothing other than that passivity, the involuntary exhibition of the self. Nudity gets stripped to bare necessity only in that frontal exhibition, in that face-to-face. Here, faced with a cat of one *or* the other sex, or of one *and* the other sex. And faced with a cat that continues to see me, to watch me leave when I turn my back on it, a cat that, from that moment on, because I no longer see it seeing me still, from behind, I therefore risk forgetting.

I have just attributed passivity to nudity. We could nickname this denuded passivity with a term that will come back more than once, from different places and in different registers, namely, *the passion of the animal,* *my* passion *of* the animal, my passion of the animal other: seeing oneself seen naked under a gaze behind which there remains a bottomlessness, at the same time innocent and cruel perhaps, perhaps sensitive and impassive, good and bad, uninterpretable, unreadable, undecidable, abyssal and secret. Wholly other, like the every other that is every (bit) other found in such intolerable proximity that I do not as yet feel I am justified or qualified to call it my fellow, even less my brother. For we shall have to ask ourselves, inevitably, what happens to the fraternity of brothers when an animal appears on the scene. Or, conversely, what happens to the animal when one brother comes after the other, when Abel is *after* Cain who is *after* Abel. Or when a son is *after* his father. What happens to animals, surrogate or not, to the ass and ram on Mount Moriah?

What does this bottomless gaze offer to my sight [*donne à voir*]? What does it "say" to me, demonstrating quite simply the naked truth of every gaze, when that truth *allows me to see and be seen* through the eyes of the other, in the *seeing* and not just *seen* eyes of the other? I am here thinking of those seeing eyes, those eyes of a seer whose color must at the same time be *seen and forgotten.* In looking at the gaze of the other, Levinas says, one must forget the color of his eyes; in other words, see the gaze, the face that gazes before seeing the visible eyes of the other. But when he reminds us that the "best way of meeting the other, is to not even notice the color of his eyes,"[18] he is speaking of man, of one's neighbor as man, kindred, brother; he thinks of the other human and this, for us, will later be revealed as a matter for serious concern.

As with every bottomless gaze, as with the eyes of the other, the gaze called "animal" offers to my sight the abyssal limit of the human: the inhuman or the ahuman, the ends of man, that is to say, the bordercrossing from which vantage man dares to announce himself to himself, thereby calling himself by the name that he believes he gives himself. And in these moments of nakedness, as regards the animal, everything can happen to me, I am like a child ready for the apocalypse, *I am (following) the apocalypse itself,* that is to say, the ultimate and first event of the end, the unveiling and the verdict. I am (following) it, the apocalypse, I identify with it by running behind it, after it, after its whole zoo-logy. When the instant of extreme passion passes, and I find peace again, then I can speak calmly of the beasts of the Apocalypse, visit them in the museum, see them in a painting (but for the Greeks "zoography" referred to the portraiture of the living in general and not just the painting of animals); I can visit them at the zoo, read about them in the Bible, or speak about them as in a book.

If I began by saying "the wholly other they *call* 'animal,' and, for example, 'cat,'" if I underlined the call [*appel*] and added quotation marks, it was to do more than announce a problem that will henceforth never leave us, that of appellation—and of the *response* to a call.

Before pursuing things in that direction, let me entrust to you the hypothesis that crossed my mind the last time my gaze met that of a cat-pussycat that seemed to be imploring me, asking me clearly to open the door for it to go out, as she did, without waiting, as she often does, for example, when she first follows me into the bathroom then immediately regrets her decision. It is, moreover, a scene that is repeated every morning. The pussycat follows me when I wake up, into the bathroom, asking for her breakfast, but she demands to leave that said bathroom as soon as it (or she) sees me naked, ready for everything and resolved to make her wait. However, there I am naked under the gaze of what they call "animal," and a fictitious tableau is played out in my imagination, a sort of classification after Linnaeus, a taxonomy of the *point of view of animals*. Other than the difference mentioned earlier between poem and philosopheme, there would be, at bottom, only two types of discourse, two positions of knowledge, two grand forms of theoretical or philosophical treatise regarding the animal. What distinguishes them is obviously the place, indeed, the body of their signatories; that is to say, the trace that that signature leaves in a corpus and in a properly scientific, theoretical, or philosophical thematics. In the first place there are texts signed by people who have no doubt seen, observed, analyzed, reflected on the animal, but who have never been *seen seen* by the animal. Their gaze has never intersected with that of an animal directed at them (forget about their being naked). If, indeed, they did happen to be seen seen furtively by the animal one day, they took no (thematic, theoretical, or philosophical) account of it. They neither wanted nor had the capacity to draw any systematic consequence from the fact that an animal could, facing them, look at them, clothed or naked, and in a word, without a word, *address them*. They have taken no account of the fact that what they call "animal" could *look at* them, and *address* them from down there, from a wholly other origin. That category of discourse, texts, and signatories (those who have never been seen seen by an animal that addressed them) is by far the one that occurs most abundantly. It is probably what brings together *all* philosophers and all theoreticians *as such*. At least those of a certain "epoch," let's say, from Descartes to the present, but I shall soon say why the word *epoch* and even this historicism leaves me quite uneasy or dissatisfied. Clearly all those (males and not females, for that difference is not insignificant here) whom I shall later situate in order to back up my remarks, arranging them within the same configuration—for example Descartes, Kant, Heidegger, Lacan, and Levinas—belong to this quasi-epochal category.[19] Their discourses are sound and profound, but everything in them goes on as if they themselves had never been looked at, and especially not naked, by an animal that addressed them. At least everything goes on as though this troubling experience had not been theoretically registered, supposing that it had been experienced at all, at the precise moment when they made of the animal a *theorem*, something seen and not seeing. The experience of the seeing animal, of the animal that looks at them, has not been taken into account in the philosophical or theoretical architecture of their discourse. In sum they have denied it as much as misunderstood it. From here on we shall circle round and round this immense disavowal, whose logic traverses the whole history of humanity, and not only that of the quasi-epochal configuration I just mentioned. It is as if the men representing this configuration had seen without being seen, seen the animal without being seen by it, without being seen seen by it; without being seen seen naked by someone who, from deep within a life called animal, and not only by means of the gaze, would have obliged them to recognize, at the moment of address, that this was their affair, their lookout [*que cela les regardait*].

But since I don't believe, deep down, that it has never happened to them, or that it has not in some way been signified, figured, or metonymized, more or less secretly, in the gestures of their discourse, the symptom of this disavowal remains to be deciphered. It could not be the figure of just one disavowal among others. It institutes what is proper to man, the relation to itself of a humanity that is above all anxious about, and jealous of, what is proper to it.

As for the other category of discourse, found among those signatories who are first and foremost poets or prophets, in the situation of poetry or prophecy, those men and women who admit to taking upon themselves the address that an animal addresses to them, before even having the time or the power to take themselves off [*s'y dérober*], to take themselves off with clothes off or in a bathrobe, I as yet know of no *statutory representative* of it, that is to say, no subject who does so as theoretical, philosophical, or juridical man, or even as citizen. I have found no such representative, but it is in that very place that I find myself, here and now, in the process of searching.

That is the track I am following, the track I am ferreting out [*la piste que je dépiste*], following the traces of this "wholly other they *call* 'animal,' for example, 'cat.' "

Why rename that appellation? Why say "the wholly other they *call* 'animal,' for example, 'cat'?" In order to recall a scene of name calling, beginning at the beginning, namely, in Genesis—and at least a type of new beginning, a second beginning in what is distinguished in Bereshit as the *second* narrative. For one must indeed specify that that story is a second "Heading" ("Entête" in Chouraqui's translation).[20] The man who, in that rendering, calls the animals by name is not only Adam, the man of the earth, the husbandman [*glébeux*]. He is also Ish preceding Ishah, man before woman. It is the man Ish, still alone, who gives names to the animals created before him: "The husbandman cried out the name of each beast," one translation (Chouraqui) says; another (Dhormes): "Man called all the animals by their names."

Let me insist: it is only recorded thus in the *second* narrative. If one believes what is called the *first* narrative, God creates man in his image but he brings male and female into the world at the same time, in a single stroke. Naming will thus have been the fact of man as a couple, if it can be put that way. The original naming of the animals does not take place in the first version. It isn't the man-woman of the first version but man *alone* and *before* woman who, in that second version, gives their names, his names, to the animals. On the other hand, it is in the so-called first version that the husbandman, created as God's replica, and created male-female, man-woman, immediately receives the order to subject the animals to him. In order to obey he is required to mark his ascendancy, his domination over them, indeed, his power to tame them. Having created the living animals on the fifth day (the beasts, that is to say animals for domestication, birds, fish, reptiles, and wild beasts) and having blessed them:

> Elohim said: "Let us make man in our image, in our likeness! Let them [note the sudden move to the plural] *have authority* [my italics] over the fish of the sea and the birds of the heavens, over the cattle, over all the wild beasts and reptiles that crawl upon the earth!" Elohim therefore created man in his image, in the image of Elohim he created him. Male and female he created them. Elohim blessed them and said, "Be fruitful and multiply, fill the earth and subdue it, *have authority* [my italics again] over the fish of the sea and the birds of the heavens, over every living thing that moves on the earth." (Dhormes)[21]

> Elohim said: "We will make Adam the husbandman—
> As our replica, in our likeness.
> They will *subject* [my italics] the fish of the sea, the flying creatures of the heavens,

The beasts, the whole earth, every reptile that crawls upon the earth."
   Elohim created the husbandman as his replica,
As a replica of Elohim he created him,
Male and female he created them.
Elohim blessed them. Elohim said to them:
"Be fruitful, multiply, fill the earth, conquer it.
Subject [my italics again] the fish of the sea, the flying creatures of the
   heavens,
Every living thing that crawls on the earth." (Chouraqui)[22]

That is the first narrative. God commands man-woman to command the animals, but not yet to name them. What happens next, in the second narrative? There occurs something, a single and double thing, twice at the same time, something that, it seems to me, gets little notice in most readings of this Genesis that is infinite in its second breath.

On the one hand, the naming of the animals is performed *at one and the same time,* before the creation of Ishah, the female part of man, *and,* as a result, before they perceive themselves to be naked; and to begin with they are naked without shame. ("The two of them are naked, the husbandman and his wife; they don't blanch on account of it."[23]) After a certain serpent—one we shall speak more of—comes by, they will perceive themselves to be naked, and not without shame.

On the other hand, and this is especially important, the public crying of names remains *at one and the same time* free *and* overseen, under surveillance, under the gaze of Jehovah, who does not, for all that, intervene. He lets Adam, he lets man, man alone, Ish without Ishah, the woman, freely call out the names. He lets him indulge in the naming all by himself. But he is waiting around the corner, watching over this man alone with a mixture of curiosity and authority. God observes: Adam is observed, within sight, he names under observation. In Chouraqui's translation: "He has them come toward the husbandman *in order to see* what he will call out to them."[24] He has them come forward; he summons them, the animals that, as the first narrative was saying, he had, moreover, created—and I firmly emphasize this trait, which is fundamental to what concerns us—he summons them in order to "subject" (Chouraqui) them to man's command, in order to place them under man's "authority" (Dhormes). More precisely, he has created man in his likeness *so that* man will *subject, tame, dominate, train,* or *domesticate* the animals born before him and assert his authority over them. God destines the animals to an experience of the power of man, *in order to see* the power of man in action, in order to see the power of man at work, in order to see man take power over all the other living beings. Chouraqui: "He has them come toward the husbandman *in order to see* what he will call out to them"; Dhormes: "He brings them to man *in order to see* what he will call them."[25]

"In order to see," which I have twice emphasized, seems to overflow with meaning. It is the same expression in both translations. God gives Ish alone the freedom to name the animals, granted, and that represents at the same time his sovereignty and his loneliness. However, everything seems to happen as though God still wanted to oversee, keep vigil, maintain his right of inspection over the names that would shortly begin to resound and by means of which Ish, Ish all alone, Ish still without woman, was going to get the upper hand with respect to the animals. God wanted to oversee but also to abandon himself to his curiosity, even allow himself to be surprised and outflanked by the radical novelty of what was going to occur, by this irreversible, welcome or unwelcome event of naming whereby Ish would begin to see them and name them without allowing himself to be seen or named by them. God lets him, Ish, speak on his own, call out on his own, call out and nominate, call out and name, as if he were able to say "*I* name," "*I* call." God lets Ish call the other living things all on his own, give them their names in his own name, these animals that are older and younger than him, these living things that came into the world before him but were named after him, on his initiative, according to the second narrative. In both cases, man is in both senses of the word *after* the animal. He follows him. This "after," which determines a sequence, a consequence, or a persecution, is not in time, nor is it temporal: it is the very genesis of time.

God thus lets Ish do the calling all alone; he accords him the right to give them names in his own name—but just in order to see. This "in order to see" marks *at the same time* the infinite right of inspection of an all-powerful God *and* the finitude of a God who doesn't know what is going to happen to him with language. And with names. In short, God doesn't yet know what he really wants: this is the finitude of a God who doesn't know what he wants with respect to the animal, that is to say, with respect to the life of the living as such, a God who sees something coming without seeing it coming, a God who will say "*I am that I am*" without knowing what he is going to see when a poet enters the scene to give his name to living things. This powerful yet deprived "in order to see" that is God's, the first stroke of time, before time, God's exposure to surprise, to the event of what is going to occur between man and animal, this time before time has always made me dizzy. As if someone said, in the form of a promise or a threat: "You'll see what you will see," without knowing what was going to end up happening. It is the dizziness I feel before the abyss opened by this stupid ruse, this feigned feint, what I have been feeling for so long [*depuis le temps*] whenever I run away from an animal that looks at me naked. I often wonder whether this vertigo before the abyss of such an "in order to see" deep in the eyes of God is not the same as that which takes hold of me when I feel so naked in front of a cat, facing it, and when, meeting its gaze, I hear the cat or God ask itself, ask *me*: Is he going to call me, is he going to address me? What name is he going to call me by, this naked man, before I give him woman, before I lend her to him in giving her to him, before I give her to him or before he gives her to himself by taking it upon himself, from under him, from at his side [*à ses côtés*]? Or even from his rib [*de sa côte*]?

Since time.

For so long now, it is as if the cat had been recalling itself and recalling that, recalling me and reminding me of this awful tale of Genesis, without breathing a word. Who was born first, before the names? Which one saw the other come to this place, so long ago? Who will have been the first occupant, and therefore the master? Who the subject? Who has remained the despot, for so long now?

⟁

Things would be too simple altogether, the anthropo-theomorphic reappropriation would already have begun, there would even be the risk that domestication has already come into effect, if I were to give in to my own melancholy. If, in order to hear it in myself, I were to set about overinterpreting what the cat might thus be saying to me, in its own way, what it might be suggesting or simply signifying in a language of mute traces, that is to say without words. If, in a word, I assigned to it the words it has no need of, no more than does the cat's "voice" in Baudelaire ("To utter the longest of sentences it has no need of words").

But in forbidding myself thus to assign, interpret or project, must I for all that give in to the other violence or *asinanity* [*bêtise*], that which would consist in suspending one's compassion and in depriving the animal of every power of manifestation, of the desire to manifest *to me* anything at all, and even to manifest to me in some way *its* experience of *my* language, of *my* words and of *my* nudity?

From the vantage of that time when the animals were named, *before original sin*, I shall mark, for the moment, still in the guise of an epigraph, the following reservation: the questions I am posing, my having confessed to feeling disarmed before a small mute living being, and my avowed desire to escape the alternative of a projection that appropriates and an interruption that excludes, all that might lead one to guess that I am not ready to interpret or experience the gaze that a cat fixes, without a word, on my nakedness, *in the negative*, if I can put it that way, as Benjamin suggests doing within a certain tradition, which we must speak of later. In fact that tradition assigns to nature and to the animality named by Adam a sort of "deep sadness" (*Traurigkeit*).²⁶ Such a melancholic mourning would reflect an impossible resignation, as if protesting in silence against the unacceptable fatality of that very silence: the fact of being condemned to muteness (*Stummheit*) and to the absence of language (*Sprachlosigkeit*), to stupor also, to that *Benommenheit* that Heidegger speaks of and that he defines, in a text that later I would like to read closely, as the essence of animality (*Das Wesen der Tierheit*). *Benommenheit* is a mute stupor, stupefaction, or daze. A new translation uses the word "absorption" [*accaparement*]²⁷ in order to attenuate, somewhat euphemistically, the potential violence of this qualification but also in order to render the sense of a type of encirclement (*Umring*) within which the animal, as *alogon*, finds itself, according to Heidegger, deprived of access in its very opening to the being of the entity as such, to being as such, to the "as such" of what is. It is true that, according to Benjamin, the sadness, mourning, and melancholy (*Traurigkeit*) of nature and of animality are born out of this muteness (*Stummheit, Sprachlosigkeit*), but they are also born out of and by means of the wound without a name: that of having *been given a name*. Finding oneself deprived of language, one loses the power to name, to name oneself, indeed to answer [*répondre*] for one's name. (As if man didn't also receive his name and his names!)

The sentiment of this deprivation, of this impoverishment, of this lack would thus be the great sorrow of nature (*das grosse Leid der Natur*). It is in the hope of requiting that, of redemption (*Erlösung*) from that suffering, that humans live and speak in nature—humans in general and not only poets as Benjamin makes clear. What is already more interesting is that this putative sadness doesn't just derive from the inability to speak (*Sprachlosigkeit*) and from muteness, from a stupefied or aphasic privation of words. If this putative sadness also gives rise to a lament, if nature laments, expressing a mute but audible lament through sensuous sighing and even the rustling of plants, it is perhaps because the terms have to be inverted. Benjamin suggests as much. There must be a reversal, an *Umkehrung* in the essence of nature. According to the hypothesis of this reversing reversal, nature (and animality within it) isn't sad because it is mute (*weil sie stumm ist*). On the contrary, it is nature's sadness or mourning that renders it mute and aphasic, that leaves it without words. (*Die Traurigkeit der Natur macht sie verstummen.*) What, for so long now, has been making it sad and as a result has deprived the mourner of its words, what forbids words, is not a muteness and the experience of a powerlessness, an inability ever to name; it is, in the first place, the fact of *receiving one's name*. This is a startling intuition. Benjamin says that even when the one who names is equal to the gods, happy and blessed, being named (*bennant zu sein*) or seeing oneself given one's proper name is something like being invaded by sadness, by sadness *itself* (a sadness whose origin would therefore always be this passivity of being named, this impossibility of reappropriating one's own name), or at least by a sort of obscure foreshadowing of sadness. One should rather say *a foreshadowing of mourning (eine Ahnung von Trauer)*. A foreshadowing of mourning because it seems to me that every case of naming involves announcing a death to come in the surviving of a ghost, the longevity of a name that survives whoever carries that name. Whoever receives a name feels mortal or dying, precisely because the name seeks to save him, to call him and thus assure his survival. Being called, hearing oneself being named, receiving a name for the first time involves something like the knowledge of being mortal and even the feeling that one is dying. To have already died of being promised to death: dying. (How could one, I ask in passing, refuse the animal access to the experience of death as such by depriving it thus of nomination?) But as I was suggesting just now, I am not (following) Benjamin when I find myself naked under the gaze of the animal, I am not ready to follow him in his wonderful meditation written right in the middle of the First World War, in 1916.

Why not? Among other reasons because his meditation lays out this whole scene of a grieving aphasia within the time frame of redemption, that is to say, after the fall and after original sin (*nach dem Sündenfall*). It would thus take place *since the time* of the fall. I situate this time of the fall at the purposive intersection of two traditions, because in the Genesis tale as much as in the myth of Prometheus (let's remember the *Protagoras* and the moment when Prometheus steals fire, that is to say, the arts and technics, in order to make up for the forgetfulness or tardiness of Epimetheus, who had perfectly equipped all breeds of animal but left "man naked [*gymnon*]," without shoes, covering, or arms), it is paradoxically on the basis of a fault or failing in man that the latter will be made a subject who is master of nature and of the animal. From within the pit of that lack, an eminent lack, a quite different lack from that he assigns to the animal, man installs or claims in a single stroke *his property* (the peculiarity [*le propre*] of a man whose property it even is not to have anything that is proper to him), and his *superiority* over what is called animal life. This latter superiority, infinite and par excellence, has as its property the fact of being at one and the same time *unconditional* and *sacrificial*.

That would be the law of an imperturbable logic, both Promethean and Adamic, both Greek and Abrahamic (Judaic, Christian, and Islamic).

Its invariance hasn't stopped being verified all the way to our modernity. Still, I have been wanting to bring myself back to my nudity before the cat, since so long ago, since a previous time, in the Genesis tale, since the time when Adam, alias Ish, called out the animals' names *before* the fall, still naked but before being ashamed of his nudity.

I am thus speaking from within that time frame [*depuis ce temps*]. My passion for the animal is awakened at that age. I admitted just now to being ashamed of being ashamed. I could therefore be surprised by my uneasiness, my shame at being ashamed, naked before the animal or animals, only by taking myself back to a time before the fall, before shame and the shame of being ashamed. Before evil [*le mal*] and before all ills [*les maux*]. Can one speak of the animal? Can one approach the animal? Can one from the vantage of the animal see oneself being looked at naked? From the vantage of the animal before evil and before all ills?

From within that time frame I am trying to speak to you, of myself in particular, in private or in public, but of myself in particular. That time would also be that which, in principle, supposing it were possible, separates autobiography from confession. Autobiography becomes confession when the discourse on the self does not dissociate truth from an avowal, thus from a fault, an evil, an ill. And first and foremost from a truth that would be due, a debt, in truth, that needs to be paid off. Why *would one owe* [devrait-on] truth? Why would it belong to the essence of truth to be due, and nude? And therefore confessed? Why this duty to pay off truth if hiding the truth, feigning truth, feigning also to hide, feigning to hide oneself or hide the truth, were not already the experience of evil and of ill, of a potential fault, of a culpability, of a sufferance [*passibilité*], of a debt—of deception and lying.

How and why would truth be due? And how and why caught, surprised from the first instant in a logic of debt and owing? Why would truth be what is due, that is to say, owed to veracity, to the revealing of oneself, to the truth of self as sincerity? Is there, and in particular in the history of discourse, indeed, of the becoming-literature of discourse, an ancient form of autobiography immune to confession, an account of the self free from any sense of confession? And thus from all redemptive language, within the horizon of salvation as a requiting? Has there been, since so long ago, room and sense for an autobiography before original sin and before all the religions of the book? Autobiography and memoir before Christianity, especially before the Christian institutions of confession? That has been in doubt for so long now, and a reading of the prodigious *Confessions* of European history, which have formed our culture of subjectivity from Augustine to Rousseau, would not suffice to dispel that doubt.

Between Augustine and Rousseau, within the same indisputable filiation, within the differentiated history of the *ego cogito ergo sum*, stands Descartes. He waits for us with his animal-machines. I presume that he won't interrupt the lineage that, for so long now, has tied the autobiographical genre to the institution of confession.

Since that time, since time: that means since the time that has passed, but also since the time before time. Since time, that is to say, since a time when there was not yet time, when time hadn't elapsed, if that is possible, before the verdict, the reckoning [*échéance*], or the fall [*déchéance*].

Although I must put off until later a patient reading and interpretation of the systematic and rich text that, in 1929–30, following *Being and Time*, Heidegger devoted to the animal, I note the following in anticipation of it here, having just spoken of time before time: one of the rare times, perhaps the only time (that needs checking) that Heidegger names the animal in *Being and Time*—a text that is also in its own way a treatise that seeks to be non-Christian, concerning a certain fall of the *Dasein*—it is in order to admit to and put off until later a difficulty (my hypothesis is this: whatever remains to be dealt with later will probably remain so forever; later here signifies never). What is that difficulty? That of knowing if the animal *has time*, if it is "constituted by some kind of time." According to Heidegger that "remains a problem" (*bleibt ein Problem*):

> It remains a problem in itself [or for itself, *bleibt ein Problem für sich*: remains an original problem, separate, to be treated separately] to define ontologically the way in which the senses can be stimulated or touched in something that merely has life [*in einem Nur-Leben-den*], and how and where the Being of animals [*das Sein der Tiere*], for instance [*zum Beispiel*], is constituted by some kind of "time."[28]

The being of animals is only an example (*zum Beispiel*). But for Heidegger it is a trustworthy example of what he calls *Nur-Lebenden*, that which is living but nothing more, life in its pure and simple state. I think I understand what that means, this "nothing more" (*nur*), I can understand it on the surface, in terms of what it would like to mean, but at the same time I understand nothing. I'll always be wondering whether this fiction, this simulacrum, this myth, this legend, this phantasm, which is offered as a pure concept (life in its pure state—Benjamin also has confidence in what can probably be no more than a pseudo-concept), is not precisely pure philosophy become a symptom of the history that concerns us here. Isn't that history the one that man tells himself, the history of the philosophical animal, of the animal for the man-philosopher? Is it a coincidence that the sentence is the last one preceding a section entitled "Die Zeitlichkeit des Verfallens" (the temporality of "reckoning," "fall," or "decay")?

↲

I suggested before that for certain of us, perhaps, for those who welcome us here, for those who have gratified me by coming back once more, this château has remained for me, for so long now, a château of haunted friendship. For nearly forty years. Indeed, friendship that is haunted, shadows of faces, furtive silhouettes of certain presences, movements, footsteps, music, words that come to life in my memory, on the terraces around us, among the trees, beside the lake, and in all the rooms of this mansion, beginning with this room. I enjoy more and more the taste of this memory that is at the same time tender, joyful, and melancholic, a memory, then, that likes to give itself over to the return of ghosts, many of whom are happily still living and, in some cases, present here. Others, alas, have died since that time, but they remain for me, just as when they were alive, close and present friends: Toyosaki Koitchi, Francis Ponge, Gilles Deleuze, Sarah Kofman. From here I can see them see and hear us.

However, if I am to believe a memory so swamped with memories, for so long now, a memory that is almost hallucinated, I find myself on the threshold of probably the most *chimerical* discourse that I have ever attempted, or that has ever tempted me in this château.

We thus have the scene of a chimera, the temptation of or attempt at a chimera in a haunted castle. Is it an animal, this chimera, an animal that can be defined as one, and only one? Is it more than or other than an animal? Or, as one often says of the chimera, more than one animal in one?

The animal, what a word!

The animal is a word, it is an appellation that men have instituted, a name they have given themselves the right and the authority to give to the living other.

At the point at which we find ourselves, even before I get involved, or try to drag you after me[29] or in pursuit of me upon an itinerary that some of you will no doubt find tortuous, labyrinthine, even aberrant, leading us astray from lure to lure, I'll attempt the operation of disarmament that consists in *posing* what one could call some hypotheses in view of theses; posing them simply, naked, frontally, as directly as possible, *pose* them as I just said, by no means posing in the way one indulgently poses by looking at oneself in front of a spectator, a portraitist, or a camera, but "pose" in the sense of situating a series of "positions."

First hypothesis: for about two centuries, intensely and by means of an alarming rate of acceleration, for we no longer even have a clock or chronological measure of it, we, we who call ourselves men or humans, we who recognize ourselves in that name, have been involved in an unprecedented transformation. This mutation affects the experience of what we continue to call imperturbably, as if there were nothing to it, the animal and/or animals. I intend to stake a lot, or play a lot on the flexible slash of this *and/or*. This new situation can be determined only on the basis of what is most ancient. We shall have to move continuously along this coming and going between the oldest and what is coming, in the exchange among the new, the "again [*de nouveau*]," and the "anew [*à nouveau*]" of repetition. Far from appearing, simply, within what we continue to call the world, history, life, etc., this unheard-of relation to the animal or to animals is so new that it should oblige us to worry all those concepts, more than just problematize them. That is why I would hesitate to say that we are *living through* that (if one can still confidently call *life* the experience whose limits come to tremble at the bordercrossings between *bios* and *zoē*, the biological, zoological, and anthropological, as between life and death, life and technology, life and history, etc.). I would therefore hesitate just as much to say that we are living through a historical turning point. The figure of the turning point implies a rupture or an instantaneous mutation whose model or figure remains genetic, biological, or zoological and which therefore remains, precisely, to be questioned. As for history, historicity, even historicality, those motifs belong precisely—as we shall see in detail—to *this* auto-definition, *this* auto-apprehension, *this* auto-situation of man or of the human *Dasein* as regards what is living and animal life; they belong to this auto-biography of man, which I wish to call into question today.

Since all these words, in particular *history*, belong in a constitutive manner to the language, interests, and lures of this autobiography, we should not be overhasty in giving them credence or in confirming their pseudo-evidence. I shall therefore not be speaking of a historical turning point in order to name a transformation in progress, an alteration that is at the same time more serious and less recognizable than a historical turning point in the relation to the animal, in the being-with shared by the human and by what the human calls the animal: the *being* of what calls itself man or the *Dasein with* what he himself calls, or what we ourselves are calling, what we are still daring, provisionally, to name in general but in the singular, *the animal*. However one names or interprets this alteration, no one could deny that it has been accelerating, intensifying, no longer knowing where it is going, for about two centuries, at an incalculable rate and level.

Given this indetermination, the fact that it is left hanging, why should I say, as I have more than once, "for about two centuries," as though such a point of reference were rigorously possible within a process that is no doubt as old as man, what he calls his world, his knowledge, his history, and his technology? Well, in order to recall, for convenience to begin with and without laying claim here to being at all exact, certain preexisting indices that allow us to understand and agree in saying "us" today. Limiting ourselves to the most imposing of these indices, we can refer to those that go well beyond the animal sacrifices of the Bible or of ancient Greece, well beyond the hecatombs (sacrifices of one hundred cattle, with all the metaphors that that expression has since been charged with), beyond the hunting, fishing, domestication, training, or traditional exploitation of animal energy (transport, plowing, draught animals, the horse, ox, reindeer, etc., and then the guard dog, small-scale butchering, and then experiments on animals, etc.). It is all too evident that in the course of the last two centuries these traditional forms of treatment of the animal have been turned upside down by the joint developments of zoological, ethological, biological, and genetic forms of *knowledge*, which remain inseparable from *techniques* of intervention *into* their object, from the transformation of the actual object, and from the milieu and world of their object, namely, the living animal. This has occurred by means of farming and regimentalization at a demographic level unknown in the past, by means of genetic experimentation, the industrialization of what can be called the production for consumption of animal meat, artificial insemination on a massive scale, more and more audacious manipulations of the genome, the reduction of the animal not only to production and overactive reproduction (hormones, genetic crossbreeding, cloning, etc.) of meat for consumption, but also of all sorts of other end products, and all of that in the service of a certain being and the putative human well-being of man.

All that is all too well known; we have no need to take it further. However one interprets it, whatever practical, technical, scientific, juridical, ethical, or political consequence one draws from it, no one can today deny this event—that is, the *unprecedented* proportions of this subjection of the animal. Such a subjection, whose history we are attempting to interpret, can be called violence in the most morally neutral sense of the term and even includes the interventionist violence that is practiced, as in some very minor and in no way dominant cases, let us never forget, in the service of or for the protection of the animal, but most often the human animal. Neither can one seriously deny the disavowal that this involves. No one can deny seriously any more, or for very long, that men do all they can in order to dissimulate this cruelty or to hide it from themselves; in order to organize on a global scale the forgetting or misunderstanding of this violence, which some would compare to the worst cases of genocide (there are also animal genocides: the number of species endangered because of man takes one's breath away). One should neither abuse the figure of genocide nor too quickly consider it explained away. It gets more complicated: the annihilation of certain species is indeed in process, but it is occurring through the organization and exploitation of an artificial, infernal, virtually interminable survival, in conditions that previous generations would have judged monstrous, outside of every presumed norm of a life proper to animals that are thus exterminated by means of their continued existence or even their overpopulation. As if, for example, instead of throwing a people into ovens and gas chambers (let's say Nazi) doctors and geneticists had decided to organize the overproduction and overgeneration of Jews, gypsies, and homosexuals by means of artificial insemination, so that, being continually more numerous and better fed, they could be destined in always increasing numbers for the same hell, that of the imposition of genetic experimentation, or extermination by gas or by fire. In the same abattoirs. I don't wish to abuse the ease with which one can overload with pathos the self-evidences I am drawing attention to here. Everybody knows what terrifying and intolerable pictures a realist painting could give to the industrial, mechanical, chemical, hormonal, and genetic violence to which man has been submitting animal life for the past two centuries. Everybody knows what the production, breeding, transport, and slaughter of these animals has become. Instead of thrusting these images in your faces or awakening them in your memory, something that would be both too easy and endless, let me simply say a word about this "pathos." If these images are "pathetic," if they evoke sympathy, it is also because they "pathetically" open the immense question of pathos and the pathological, precisely, that is, of suffering, pity, and compassion; and the place that has to be accorded to the interpretation of this compassion, to the sharing of this suffering among the living, to the law, ethics, and politics that must be brought to bear upon this experience of compassion. What has been happening for two centuries now involves a new experience of this compassion. In response to what is, for the moment, the irresistible but unacknowledged unleashing and the organized disavowal of this torture, voices are raised—minority, weak, marginal voices, little assured of their discourse, of their right to discourse, and of the enactment of their discourse within the law, as a declaration of rights—in order to protest, in order to appeal (we'll return to this) to what is still presented in such a problematic way as *animal rights*, in order to awaken us to our responsibilities and our obligations vis-à-vis the living in general, and precisely to this fundamental compassion that, were we to take it seriously, would have to change even the very cornerstone (and it is next to that cornerstone that I wish to do my business today) of the philosophical problematic of the animal.

It is in thinking of the source and ends of this compassion that about two centuries ago someone like Bentham, as is well known, proposed changing the very form of the question regarding the animal that dominated discourse within the tradition, in the language both of its most refined philosophical argumentation and of everyday acceptance and common sense. Bentham said something like this: the question is not to know whether the animal can think, reason, or speak, etc., something we still pretend to be asking ourselves (from Aristotle to Descartes, from Descartes, especially, to Heidegger, Levinas, and Lacan, and this question determines so many others concerning *power* or *capability* [pouvoirs] and *attributes* [avoirs]: being able, having the power or capability to give, to die, to bury one's dead, to dress, to work, to invent a technique, etc., a power that consists in having such and such a faculty, thus such and such a capability, as an essential attribute). Thus the question will not be to know whether animals are of the type *zōon logon echon*, whether they *can* speak or reason thanks to that *capacity* or that *attribute* of the *logos*, the *can-have* [pouvoir-avoir] of the *logos*, the aptitude for the *logos* (and logocentrism is first of all a thesis regarding the animal, the animal deprived of the *logos*, deprived of the *can-have-the-logos*: this is the thesis, position, or presupposition maintained from Aristotle to Heidegger, from Descartes to Kant, Levinas, and Lacan). The *first* and *decisive* question would rather be to know whether animals *can suffer*.

"Can they suffer?" asks Bentham, simply yet so profoundly.

Once its protocol is established, the form of this question changes everything. It no longer simply concerns the *logos*, the disposition and whole configuration of the *logos*, having it or not, nor does it concern, more radically, a *dynamis* or *hexis*, this having or manner of being, this *habitus* that one calls a faculty or "capability," this can-have or the power one possesses (as in the power to reason, to speak, and everything that that implies). The question is disturbed by a certain *passivity*. It bears witness, manifesting already, as question, the response that testifies to a sufferance, a passion, a not-being-able. The word *can* [pouvoir] changes sense and sign here once one asks, "Can they suffer?" Henceforth it wavers. What counts at the origin of such a question is not only the idea of what transitivity or activity (being able to speak, to reason, etc.) refer to; what counts is rather what impels it toward this self-contradiction, something we will later relate back to auto-biography. "Can they suffer?" amounts to asking "Can they *not be able*?" And what of this inability [*impouvoir*]? What of the vulnerability felt on the basis of this inability? What is this nonpower at the heart of power? What is its quality or modality? How should one take it into account? What right should be accorded it? To what extent does it concern us? Being able to suffer is no longer a power; it is a possibility without power, a possibility of the impossible. Mortality resides there, as the most radical means of thinking the finitude that we share with animals, the mortality that belongs to the very finitude of life, to the experience of compassion, to the possibility of sharing the possibility of this nonpower, the possibility of this impossibility, the anguish of this vulnerability, and the vulnerability of this anguish.

With this question—"Can they suffer?"—we are not undermining the rock of indubitable certainty, the foundation of every assurance that one could, for example, look for in the *cogito*, in *Je pense donc je suis*. But from another perspective altogether we are putting our trust in an instance that is just as radical, although essentially different: namely, what is undeniable. No one can deny the suffering, fear, or panic, the terror or fright that can seize certain animals and that we humans can witness. (Descartes himself, as we shall see, was not able to claim that animals were insensitive to suffering.) Some will still try—this is something else we will come to—to contest the right to call that *suffering* or *anguish*, words or concepts that would still have to be reserved for man and for the *Dasein* in the freedom of its being-toward-death. We will have reason to problematize that discourse later. But for the moment let us note the following: the response to the question "Can they suffer?" leaves no room for doubt. In fact, it has never left any room for doubt; that is why the experience that we have of it is not even indubitable; it precedes the indubitable, it is older than it. No doubt either, then, of there being within us the possibility of giving vent to a surge of compassion, even if it is then misunderstood, repressed, or denied, held at bay. Before the *undeniability* of this response (yes, they suffer, like us who suffer for them and with them), before this response that precedes all other questions, both ground and cornerstone of the problematic shift. Perhaps it loses all security, but in any case it no longer rests on the old, supposedly natural (ground) or historic and *artifactual* (cornerstone) foundation. The two centuries I have been referring to somewhat casually in order to situate the present in terms of this tradition have been those of an unequal struggle, a war (whose inequality could one day be reversed) being waged between, on the one hand, those who violate not only animal life but even and also this sentiment of compassion, and, on the other hand, those who appeal for an irrefutable testimony to this pity.

War is waged over the matter of pity. This war is probably ageless but, and here is my hypothesis, it is passing through a critical phase. We are passing through that phase, and it passes through us. To think the war we find ourselves waging is not only a duty, a responsibility, an obligation, it is also a necessity, a constraint that, like it or not, directly or indirectly, no one can escape. Henceforth more than ever. And I say "to think" this war, because I believe it concerns what we call "thinking." The animal looks at us, and we are naked before it. Thinking perhaps begins there.

ℑ

Here now, in view of another thesis, is the *second hypothesis* that I think must be deduced without hesitation. It concerns or puts into effect another logic of the limit. I would thus be tempted to inscribe the subject of this thesis in the series of three conferences that, beginning with The Ends of Man and followed by The Crossing of Borders, have been devoted to a properly *transgressal* if not transgressive experience of *limitrophy*. Let's allow that word to have a both general and strict sense: what abuts onto limits but also what feeds, is fed, is cared for, raised, and trained, what is cultivated on the edges of a limit. In the semantics of *trephō*, *trophē*, or *trophos*, we should be able to find everything we need to speak about what we should be speaking about in the course of these ten days devoted to the autobiographical animal: feeding, food, nursing, breeding, offspring, care and keeping of animals, training, upbringing, culture, living and allowing to live by giving to live, be fed, and grown, autobiographically. *Limitrophy* is therefore my subject. Not just because it will concern what sprouts or grows at the limit, around the limit, by maintaining the limit, but also what *feeds the limit*, generates it, raises it, and complicates it. Everything I'll say will consist, certainly not in effacing the limit, but in multiplying its figures, in complicating, thickening, delinearizing, folding, and dividing the line precisely by making it increase and multiply. Moreover, the supposed first or literal sense of *trephō* is just that: to transform by thickening, for example, in curdling milk. So it will in no way mean questioning, even in the slightest, the limit that we have had a stomachful of, the limit between Man with a capital *M* and Animal with a capital *A*. It will not be a matter of attacking frontally or antithetically the thesis of philosophical or common sense on which has been constructed the relation to the self, the presentation of self of human life, the autobiography of the human species, the whole history of the self that man recounts to himself, that is to say, the thesis of a limit as rupture or abyss between those who say "we men," "I, a human," and what this man among men who say "we," what he *calls* the animal or animals. I shan't for a single moment venture to contest that thesis, nor the rupture or abyss between this "I-we" and what we *call* animals. To suppose that I, or anyone else for that matter, could ignore that rupture, indeed that abyss, would mean first of all blinding oneself to so much contrary evidence; and, as far as my own modest case is concerned, it would mean forgetting all the signs that I have managed to give, tirelessly, of my attention to difference, to differences, to heterogeneities and abyssal ruptures as against the homogeneous and the continuous. I have thus never believed in some homogeneous continuity between what calls *itself* man and what *he* calls the animal. I am not about to begin to do so now. That would be worse than sleepwalking, it would simply be too asinine [*bête*]. To suppose such a stupid memory lapse or to take to task such a naive misapprehension of this abyssal rupture would mean, more seriously still, venturing to say almost anything at all for the cause, for whatever cause or interest that no longer had anything to do with what we claimed to want to talk about. When that cause or interest seeks to profit from what it simplistically suspects to be a biologistic continuism, whose sinister connotations we are well aware of, or more generally to profit from what is suspected as a geneticism that one might wish to associate with this scatterbrained accusation of continuism, at that point the undertaking becomes in any case so aberrant that it neither calls for nor, it seems to me, deserves any direct discussion on my part. Everything I have suggested so far and every argument I shall put forward today stands overwhelmingly in opposition to the blunt instrument that such an allegation represents.

There is no interest to be found in debating something like a discontinuity, rupture, or even abyss between those who call themselves men and what so-called men, those who name themselves men, call the animal. Everybody agrees on this; discussion is closed in advance; one would have to be more asinine than any beast [*plus bête que les bêtes*] to think otherwise. Even animals know that (ask Abraham's ass or ram or the living beasts that Abel offered to God: they know what is about to happen to them when men say "Here I am" to God, then consent to sacrifice themselves, to sacrifice their sacrifice, or to forgive themselves). The discussion is worth undertaking once it is a matter of determining the number, form, sense, or structure, the foliated consistency, of this abyssal limit, these edges, this plural and repeatedly folded frontier. The discussion becomes interesting once, instead of asking whether or not there is a limit that produces a discontinuity, one attempts to think what a limit becomes once it is abyssal, once the frontier no longer forms a single indivisible line but more than one internally divided line; once, as a result, it can no longer be traced, objectified, or counted as single and indivisible. What are the edges of a limit that grows and multiplies by feeding on an abyss? Here is my thesis in three versions:

1. This abyssal rupture doesn't describe two edges, a unilinear and indivisible line having two edges, Man and the Animal in general.

2. The multiple and heterogeneous border of this abyssal rupture has a history. Both macroscopic and microscopic and far from being closed, that history is now passing through the most unusual phase in which we now find ourselves, and for which we have no scale. Indeed, one can speak here of history, of a historic moment or phase, only from one of the supposed edges of the said rupture, the edge of an anthropo-centric subjectivity that is recounted or allows a history to be recounted about it, autobiographically, the history of its life, and that it therefore calls *History*.

3. Beyond the edge of the *so-called* human, beyond it but by no means on a single opposing side, rather than "The Animal" or "Animal Life" there is already a heterogeneous multiplicity of the living, or more precisely (since to say "the living" is already to say too much or not enough), a multiplicity of organizations of relations between living and dead, relations of organization or lack of organization among realms that are more and more difficult to dissociate by means of the figures of the organic and inorganic, of life and/or death. These relations are at once intertwined and abyssal, and they can never be totally objectified. They do not leave room for any simple exteriority of one term with respect to another. It follows that one will never have the right to take animals to be the species of a kind that would be named The Animal, or animal in general. Whenever "one" says "The Animal," each time a philosopher, or anyone else, says "The Animal" in the singular and without further ado, claiming thus to designate every living thing that is held not to be human (man as *rational animal*, man as political animal, speaking animal, *zōon logon echon*, man who says "I" and takes himself to be the subject of a statement that he proffers on the subject of the said animal, etc.), well, each time the subject of that statement, this "one," this "I," does that he utters an *asinanity* [bêtise]. He avows without avowing it, he declares, just as a disease is declared by means of a symptom, he offers up for diagnosis the statement "I am uttering an *asinanity*." And this "I am uttering an *asinanity*" should confirm not only the animality that he is disavowing but his complicit, continued, and organized involvement in a veritable war of the species.

Such are my hypotheses in view of theses on the animal, on animals, on the words *animal* [animal] or *animals* [animaux].

Yes, animal, what a word!

Animal is a word that men have given themselves the right to give. These humans are found giving it to themselves, this word, but as if they had received it as an inheritance. They have given themselves the word in order to corral a large number of living beings within a single concept: "The Animal," they say. And they have given it to themselves, this word, at the same time according themselves, reserving for them, for humans, the right to the word, the naming noun [*nom*], the verb, the attribute, to a language of words, in short to the very thing that the others in question would be deprived of, those that are corralled within the grand territory of the beasts: The Animal. All the philosophers we will investigate (from Aristotle to Lacan, and including Descartes, Kant, Heidegger, and Levinas), all of them say the same thing: the animal is deprived of language. Or, more precisely, of response, of a reponse that could be precisely and rigorously distinguished from a reaction; of the right and power to "respond," and hence of so many other things that would be proper to man.

Men would be first and foremost those living creatures who have given themselves the word that enables them to speak of the animal with a single voice and to designate it as the single being that remains without a response, without a word with which to respond.

That wrong was committed long ago and with long-term consequences. It derives from this word, or rather it comes together in this word *animal*, which men have given themselves as at the origin of humanity, and which they have given themselves in order to be identified, in order to be recognized, with a view to being what they say they are, namely, men, capable of replying and responding in the name of men.

I would like to try to speak of a certain wrong or evil that derives from this word, to begin with, by stammering some chimerical aphorisms.

The animal that I am (following), does it speak?

That is an intact question, virginal, new, still to come, a completely naked question.

For language is like the rest—it is not enough to speak of it.

From the moment of this first question, one should be able to sniff the trace of the fact that this animal seems to speak French here, and is no less asinine for it. "The animal that I am (following), does it speak?" This address could be a feint, like the switch from "I" to "it." The question could be the ruse or stratagem of what English calls a rhetorical question, one whose response is already taken for granted. The question will shortly be very much that of the response, and no doubt I shall try to imply that one cannot treat the supposed animality of the animal without treating the question of the response, and of what *responding* means. And what *being erased*[30] means. As we shall see, even those who, from Descartes to Lacan, have conceded to the animal some aptitude for signs and for communication have always denied it the power to *respond*—to *pretend*, to *lie*, to *cover its tracks* or *erase* its own traces.

But whether it is fictive or not, when I ask, "The animal that I am, does it speak?" the question seems at that moment to be signed, to be sealed by someone.

What does it seal? What claim does it make? Pretense or not, what does it seem to translate?

What this animal is, what it will have been, what it would, would like to, or could be is perhaps what I am (following).

But if I say that *I am (following) it* in French, in this and in no other language, that amounts less to claiming some national idiom than to recalling an irreducible ambiguity about which we shall have more to say: an animal's signature might yet be able to erase or cover its traces. Or allow it to be erased, rather, be unable to prevent its being erased. And this possibility, that of tracing, effacing, or scrambling its signature, allowing it to be lost, would then have considerable consequences. Having or not having traces at one's disposal so as to be able to dissimulate [*brouiller*] or erase them, in such a manner as, it is said, some (man, for example) can and some (the animal, for example, according to Lacan) cannot do, does not perhaps constitute a reliable alternative defining an indivisible limit. We will have reason to go back over these steps and tracks. The fact that a trace can always be erased, and forever, in no way means—and this is a critical difference—that someone, man *or* animal, I am emphasizing here, *can of his own accord* erase his traces.

It is a question of words, therefore. For I am not sure that what I am going to set about saying to you amounts to anything more ambitious than an exploration of language in the course of a sort of chimerical experimental exercise, or the testing of a testimony. Just to see. We can act as though I were simply trying to analyze a number of discursive modalities or usages—in order to put them to the test and to see, to keep an eye out for, what will come of it—that *they* (I insist on this "they"), what *humans* do with certain words, but also, and for some time yet, to track, to sniff, to trail, and to follow some of the reasons they adduce for the so confident usage they make, and which for the moment we are making together, of words such as, therefore, *animal* and *I*.

A critical uneasiness will persist, in fact, a bone of contention will be incessantly repeated throughout everything that I wish to develop. It would be aimed in the first place, once again, at the usage, in the singular, of a notion as general as "The Animal," as if all nonhuman living things could be grouped within the common sense of this "commonplace," the Animal, whatever the abyssal differences and structural limits that separate, in the very essence of their being, all "animals," a name that we would therefore be advised, to begin with, to keep within quotation marks. Confined within this catch-all concept, within this vast encampment of the animal, in this general singular, within the strict enclosure of this definite article ("the Animal" and not "animals"), as in a virgin forest, a zoo, a hunting or fishing ground, a paddock or an abattoir, a space of domestication, are *all the living things* that man does not recognize as his fellows, his neighbors, or his brothers. And that is so in spite of the infinite space that separates the lizard from the dog, the protozoon from the dolphin, the shark from the lamb, the parrot from the chimpanzee, the camel from the eagle, the squirrel from the tiger, the elephant from the cat, the ant from the silkworm, or the hedgehog from the echidna. I interrupt my nomenclature and call Noah to help insure that no one gets left on the ark.

Since I have come to the point of sketching out a taxonomy, excuse me the immodesty of a further confession. It won't be *oto*biographical, as I tried on a previous occasion with respect to a Nietzschean ear, although he, like Kafka, is more attuned than anyone else [*s'y entend comme pas un*] when it comes to animals. Instead it will be *zoo*tobiographical. This zoo-auto-bio-biblio-graphy will be brief. I allow myself or constrain myself to this indulgence precisely for mnemonic effect, in the name of the name of our meeting, The Autobiographical Animal. I shall indulge in it before dealing in a different mode with what ties the history of the "I am," the autobiographical and autodeictic relation to the self as "I," to the history of "The Animal," of the human concept of the animal. Since today I would like to run ahead of myself and sketch out other steps in moving forward, that is to say, in stepping out without too much retrospection and without looking twice, I won't go back over arguments of a theoretical or philosophical kind, or in what we can call a deconstructive style, arguments that for a very long time, since I began writing, in fact, I believe I have dedicated to the question of the living and of the living animal. For me that will always have been the most important and decisive question. I have addressed it a thousand times, either directly or obliquely, by means of readings of *all* the philosophers I have taken an interest in, beginning with Husserl and the concepts of *rational animal*, of life or transcendental instinct that are found at the heart of phenomenology (but, paradoxically, when it comes to the animal, Husserl, like Hegel, is not the most "Cartesian" of the philosophers I shall later speak of). Still, short of outlining a philosophical autobiography, short of retracing my steps along the paths of philosophy, I could have, or perhaps should have undertaken an anamnesic interpretation of all *my* animals. They certainly do not form a family, but they are the critters [*bêtes*] that I have been (following) from the start, for decades and from one ten-day conference to another. I won't do that, out of modesty or discretion, and because there are too many of them; it would be interminable and seen as indecorous in this august setting [*salon*]. But I do think I need to open other paths, two, perhaps, for whomever might wish, retrospectively, to follow such an exploration. I shall do so briefly, limiting myself strictly to the theme of our conference.

On the one hand, my animal figures multiply, gain in insistence and visibility, become active, swarm, mobilize and get motivated, move and become moved all the more as my texts become more explicitly autobiographical, are more often uttered in the first person.

I just said "animal figures." These animals are without doubt something other than figures or characters in a fable. As I see it, one of the most visible metamorphoses of the figural, and precisely of the animal figure, would perhaps be found, in my case, in "White Mythology." Indeed, that essay follows the movement of tropes and of rhetoric, the explanation of concept by means of metaphor, by prowling around animal language, between an Aristotle who withholds from the animal language and word and *mimesis*, and a Nietzsche who, if it can be said, "reanimalizes" the genealogy of the concept. The one who parodied *Ecce Homo* tries to teach us to laugh again by plotting, as it were, to let loose all his animals within philosophy. To laugh and to cry, for, as you know, he was mad enough to cry in conjunction with [*auprès de*] an animal, under the gaze of, or cheek by jowl with a horse. Sometimes I think I see him call that horse as a witness, and primarily in order to call it as a witness to his compassion, I think I see him take its head in his hands.

༕

Animals are my concern. Whether in the form of a figure or not.[31] They multiply, lunging more and more wildly in my face in proportion as my texts seem to become autobiographical, or so one would have me believe.

It is obvious. Even a little too obvious, beginning at the end, the end of "A Silkworm of One's Own," published this year. Already, in the iconography of "Socrates and Plato" at the Bodleian Library, the animals emerge on page after page, says the signatory of one of the postcards from July 1979, "like *squirrels*," "squirrels" "in a forest." As for the *monkey* of

"Heidegger's Hand," he takes, he grasps, but he will not give, or greet, and especially not think according to Master Heidegger. The *hedgehog* of "What is Poetry?" a letter written in the first person, bears in its quills, among other things, the heritage of a piece of my name. Which is signed "Fourmis" ["*Ants*"] in *Lectures de la différence sexuelle* (*Readings in Sexual Difference*).[32]

On the other hand, I note in passing that almost all these animals are welcomed, in a more and more deliberate manner, on the threshold of sexual difference. More precisely, of sexual differences, that is to say, what for the most part is kept under wraps in almost all of the grand philosophical-type treatises on the animality of the animal. This opening, on the threshold of sexual differences, was the very track left by the hedgehog and the (agrammatically) masculine ant, but more than that, in the most recent text, where it is precisely a matter of nakedness, with and without a veil, the thinking of what is naked, as it is said, like a worm,[33] "A Silkworm of One's Own." From beginning to end that threefold journal talks of the ambiguity of the sexual experience at its birth. It deals with veils of modesty and truth, while recalling one of the zootobiographical origins of my bestiary. After noting that "it was impossible to discern a sexual organ," the child recalls:

> There was indeed something like a brown mouth but you could not recognize in it the orifice you had to imagine to be at the origin of their silk, this milk become thread, this filament prolonging their body and remaining attached to it for a certain length of time: the extruded saliva of a very fine sperm, shiny, gleaming, the miracle of a feminine ejaculation, which would catch the light and which I drank in with my eyes. . . . The self-displacement of this little fantasy of a penis, was it erection or detumescence? I would observe the invisible progress of the weaving, a little as though I was about to stumble on the secret of a marvel, the secret of this secret over there, at the infinite distance of the animal, of this little innocent member, so foreign yet so close in its incalculable distance.

Later, the child continues: "the spinning of its filiation, sons or daughters—beyond any sexual difference or rather any duality of the sexes, and even beyond any coupling. In the beginning, there was the worm that was and was not a sex, the child could see it clearly, a sex perhaps but then which one? His bestiary was starting up."[34]

There is a rhythmic difference between erection and detumescence. It is no doubt at the heart of what concerns us here, namely, a sentiment of shame related to standing upright—hence with respect to erection in general and not only phallic surrection—and to the face-to-face. Let us leave that remark—notably, the role played by sexual difference in the matter of shame—to be followed up on or discussed later: Why would a man be at the same time *more and less* modest than a woman? What must shame be in terms of this "*at the same time*" of the "*more or less?*"

In calling up still more of my recent animal texts, or those of yesteryear, I take my cue from the title of our program. Indeed, that title obliges us to cross the animal with autobiography. I therefore admit to my old obsession with a personal and somewhat paradisaical bestiary. It came to the fore very early on: the crazy project of constituting everything thought or written within a zoosphere, the dream of an absolute hospitality and an infinite appropriation. How to welcome or liberate so many animal-words [*animots*³⁵] *chez moi?* In me, for me, like me? It would have amounted at the same time to something more and less than a bestiary. Above all, it was necessary to avoid fables. We know the history of fabulization and how it remains an anthropomorphic taming, a moralizing subjection, a domestication. Always a discourse *of* man, on man, indeed on the animality of man, but for and in man.

Rather than developing that fabulous bestiary, I gave myself a horde of animals, within the forest of my own signs and the memoirs of my memory. I was no doubt always thinking about such a company, well before the visitation of the innumerable critters that now overpopulate my texts. Well before the (masculine) ant, the hedgehog, or the silkworm of yesterday; well before the spider, bee, or serpents of "Freud and the Scene of Writing" (*Writing and Difference*) or of "White Mythology" (*Margins*); well before the wolves of the Wolfman in "Fors" (foreword to Nicolas Abraham and Maria Torok, *The Wolf Man's Magic Word*); well before the horse of *Spurs*, and especially before Kant's horse, about which it is said, in "Parergon" (*The Truth in Painting*), concerning his theory of free and dependent beauty, that, unlike birds or crustaceans, it is "bothersome" (the theory is straitjacketed by this horse, whether one takes it to be wild or broken in, exploited, tamed, "finalized" by man, by the subject of aesthetic and teleological judgements; relayed through the jennet [*genet*], the Spanish horse that runs through the middle of *Glas*; the horse from "Parergon" is, moreover, compared to the steer, the sheep, the pig, and the ass; there was also a quite different ass, the ass of multiple references to the *Ja Ja* of affirmation following the traces of Zarathustra); well before the mole from I forget where, *Specters of Marx*, I think; well before Florian's hare and Kant's black swan in *Politics of Friendship*, but also before those I secretly call "my friends the birds" of Laguna Beach in "Circumf-ession," where I also bring back on stage certain white hens sacrificed in the *Pardès* on the Day of Atonement of my Algerian childhood; and still yet before the fish of " + R" in *The Truth in Painting*, which plays upon "I" by means of the *Ich* of *Ichtus*, of Ish and Ishah, crossed with *Khi* by means of a chiasmus, and with a certain *Chi-mère* whose name decom-poses in *Glas*, where a certain eagle soars over the two columns; well be-fore all the dead-alive viruses, undecidably between life and death, between animal and vegetal, that come back from everywhere to haunt and obsess my writing; well before the reminder of all of Nietzsche's ani-mals in *Spurs* but also in "Otobiographies," including a certain "hypocrit-ical dog" (the Church) and the ears of a "phonograph dog"; well before Ponge's zooliterature in *Signsponge* (the swallow, the shrimp, the oyster); well before the sponge itself, that marine zoophyte that is wrongly held to be something vegetal, and about which I spoke in this very place, but which had also passed through my work earlier, again in "White Mythol-ogy," in relation to what Bachelard identified as the "metaphysics of the sponge." But since I wish ultimately to return at length to the treatment of the animal in Heidegger, permit me to create a special place in this short taxonomy, in the form of a reminder [*pense-bête*], for a note that appears in brackets. It is from *Of Spirit*. That short book deals abundantly and directly with the Heideggerian concept of the animal as "poor in world" (*weltarm*), an analysis I would like to pursue further tomorrow, looking closely at the seminar of 1929–30. The note in brackets in my text does not appear to relate to the development of the problematic of the animal. It brings to the fore the "gnawing, ruminant, and silent vorac-ity of . . . an animal-machine and its implacable logic." But there is only the resemblance to an animal-machine, Cartesian or otherwise. It is an animal of reading and rewriting. It will be at work in all the tracks we are heading down here, announcing them and ferreting them out in advance:

> [Pause for a moment: to dream of what the Heideggerian corpus would look like (*pour rêver à la figure* [also, "in the face of"—Trans.] *du corpus heideggerien*) the day when, with all the application and consistency required, the operations prescribed by him at one mo-ment or another would indeed have been carried out: "avoid" the word "spirit," at the very least place it in quotation marks, then cross through all the names referring to the world whenever one is speaking of something which, like the animal, has no *Dasein*, and therefore no or only a little world, then place the word "Being" everywhere under a cross, and finally cross through without a cross

all the question marks when it's a question of language, i.e., indirectly, of everything, etc. One can imagine the surface of the text given over to the gnawing, ruminant, and silent voracity of such an animal-machine and its implacable "logic." This would not only be simply "without spirit," but a figure of evil. The perverse reading of Heidegger. End of pause.][36]

This animal-machine has a family resemblance to the virus that obsesses, not to say invades everything I write. Neither animal nor nonanimal, neither organic nor inorganic, neither living nor dead, this potential invader is *like* a computer virus. It is lodged in a processor of writing, reading, and interpretation. But, if I may note this in generous anticipation of what is to follow, it would be an animal that is capable of deleting (thus of erasing a trace, something Lacan thinks the animal is incapable of). This quasi-animal would no longer have to relate itself to being *as such* (something Heidegger thinks the animal is incapable of), since it would take into account the need to strike out "being." But as a result, in striking out "being" and taking itself beyond or on this side of the question (and hence of the response) is it something completely other than a species of animal? Yet another question to follow up.

We are following, we follow ourselves. I shall not impose upon you a complete exposition of this theory of *animots* that I am (following) or that follow me everywhere and the memory of which seems to me inexhaustible. Far from resembling Noah's ark, it would become more like a circus, with an animal trainer having his sad subjects, bent low, file past. The multiple *animot* would still suffer from always having its master on its back. It would have it up to the neck [*en aurait plein le dos*] with being thus domesticated, broken in, trained, docile, disciplined, tamed. Instead of recalling the menagerie to which some who badmouth me might compare my autobibliography, I shall simply recall the idea, or rather the troubling stakes, of a philosophical bestiary, of a bestiary at the origin of philosophy. It was not by chance that it first imposed itself in the region of an undecidable *pharmakon*. Concerning the Socratic irony that "precipitates out one *pharmakon* by bringing it in contact with another *pharmakon*," that is to say, "reverses the *pharmakon*'s powers and turns its surface over," I tried (in 1968, thirty years ago, therefore) to imagine what the program of a Socratic bestiary on the eve of philosophy might be, and more precisely (I note this because this afternoon we shall speak more of it in the context of Descartes), how that would appear in a place where the demonic, the cunning, indeed, the evil genius has some affinity with the animal: a malign and hence perverse beast, at one and the same time innocent, crafty, and evil. Keeping to the program here, let me refer to the note that made explicit, right in the middle, in the very center, in the binding between the two parts of "Plato's Pharmacy," this alternating bordercrossing:

> Alternately and/or all at once, the Socratic *pharmakon* petrifies and vivifies, anesthetizes and sensitizes, appeases and anguishes. Socrates is a benumbing stingray but also an animal that needles [this is a reference to well-known texts]: we recall the bee in the *Phaedo* (91c); later we will open the *Apology* at the point where Socrates compares himself precisely to a gadfly. This whole Socratic configuration thus composes a bestiary. [Of course, since this is a matter of animal figures in Socrates' presentation of self, the question is indeed that of Socrates as "autobiographical animal."] Is it surprising that the demonic inscribes itself in a bestiary? It is on the basis of this zoopharmaceutical ambivalence and of that other Socratic *analogy* that the contours of the *anthropos* are determined.[37]

At the risk of being mistaken and of having one day to make honorable amends (which I would willingly accept to do), I'll venture to say that never, on the part of any great philosopher from Plato to Heidegger, or anyone at all who takes on, *as a philosophical question in and of itself*, the question called that of the animal and of the limit between the animal and the human, have I noticed a protestation *based on principle*, and especially not a protestation that amounts to anything, against the general singular that is *the animal*. Nor against the general singular of an animal whose sexuality is as a matter of principle left undifferentiated—or neutralized, not to say castrated. Such an omission is not without connection to many others that form, as we shall see, either its premise or its consequence. No one has ever called for changing philosophically this philosophical or metaphysical datum. I indeed said "philosophical" (or "metaphysical") datum, for the gesture seems to me to constitute philosophy as such, the philosopheme itself. Not that all philosophers agree on the definition of *the* limit presumed to separate man in general from the animal in general (although this is an area that is conducive to consensus and is no doubt where we find the dominant form of consensus). Despite that, through and beyond all their disagreements, philosophers have always judged and *all* philosophers have judged that limit to be single and indivisible, considering that on the other side of that limit there is an immense group, a single and fundamentally homogeneous set that one has the right, the theoretical or philosophical right, to distinguish and mark as opposite, namely, the set of the Animal in general, the Animal spoken of in the general singular. It applies to the whole animal kingdom with the exception of the human. Philosophical right thus presents itself as that of "common sense." This agreement concerning philosophical sense and common sense that allows one to speak blithely of the Animal in the general singular is perhaps one of the greatest and most symptomatic *asinanities* of those who call themselves humans. We shall perhaps speak of *bêtise* and of bestiality later, as that from which beasts are in any case exempt by definition. One cannot speak—moreover, it has never been done—of the *bêtise* or bestiality of an animal. It would be an anthropomorphic projection of something that remains the preserve of man, as the single assurance, finally, and the single risk of what is "proper to man." One can ask why the ultimate fallback of what is proper to man, if there is such a thing, a property that could never in any case be attributed to the animal or to God, thus comes to be named *bêtise* or bestiality.

Interpretive decisions (in all their metaphysical, ethical, juridical, and political consequences) thus depend upon what is presupposed by the general singular of this word *the Animal*. I was tempted, at a given moment, in order to indicate the direction of my thinking, not just to keep this word within quotation marks, as if it were a citation to be analyzed, but without further ado to change the word, indicating clearly thereby that it is indeed a matter of a word, only a word, the word *animal* [*du mot "animal"*], and to forge another word in the singular, at the same time close but radically foreign, a chimerical word that sounded as though it contravened the laws of the French language, *l'animot*.

ॐ

Ecce animot. Neither a species nor a gender nor an individual, it is an irreducible living multiplicity of mortals, and rather than a double clone or a portmanteau word, a sort of monstrous hybrid, a chimera waiting to be put to death by its Bellerophon.

Who was Chimera or what was Chimera?

Chimaera was, as we know, the proper name of a flame-spitting monster. Its monstrousness derived precisely from the multiplicity of animals, of the *animot* in it (head and chest of a lion, entrails of a goat, tail of a dragon). Chimaera of Lycia was the offspring of Typhon and Echidne. As a common noun *echidna* means serpent, more precisely, a viper and sometimes, figuratively, a treacherous woman, a serpent that one cannot charm or make stand up by playing a flute. *Echidna* is also the name given to a very special animal found only in Australia and New Guinea. This mammal lays eggs, something quite rare. Here we have an oviparous mammal that is also an insectivore and a monotreme. It only has one hole (*mono-trema*) for all the necessary purposes, urinary tract, rectum, and genitals. It is generally agreed that the echidna resembles a hedgehog. Along with the platypus, the five species of echidna make up the family of monotremes.

As the child of Typhon and Echidne, Chimaera interests me therefore because chimerical will be my address[38] and I shall gradually explain the reasons for it. In the first place, it concerns my old and ambivalent attachment to the figure of Bellerophon, who puts Chimaera to death. He deserves a ten-day conference alone. He represents, as is well known, the figure of the hunter. He follows. He is he who follows. He follows and persecutes the beast. He would say: I am (following), I pursue, I track, overcome, and tame the animal. Before Chimaera the animal in question was Pegasus, whom he held by the bit, a "golden bit given to him as a present by Athene." Holding him by the bit he makes him dance, he orders him to do some dance steps. I underline in passing this allusion to the choreography of the animal in order to announce that, much later, we will encounter a certain animal danceness[39] from the pen of Lacan. Pegasus, archetypal horse, son of Poseidon and the Gorgon, is therefore the half-brother of Bellerophon, who, descending from the same god as Pegasus, ends up following and taming a sort of brother, an other self: I am half (following) my brother, it is as if he says finally, I am (following) my other and I have the better of him, I hold him by the bit. What does one do in holding one's other by the bit? When one holds one's brother or half-brother by the bit?

There was also the matter of a dead animal between Cain and Abel. And of a tamed, raised, and sacrificed animal. Cain, the older brother, the agricultural worker, therefore the sedentary one, submits to having his offering of the fruits of the earth refused by a God who prefers, as an oblation, the first-born cattle of Abel, the rancher.

God prefers the sacrifice of the very animal that he has let Adam name—*in order to see*. As if between the taming desired by God and the sacrifice of the animal preferred by God the invention of names, the freedom accorded Adam or Ish to name the animals, was only a stage "*in order to see*," in view of providing sacrificial flesh for offering to that God. One could say, much too hastily, that giving a name would also mean sacrificing the living to God. The fratricide that results from it is marked as a sort of second original sin, in this case twice linked to blood, since the murder of Abel follows—as its consequence—the sacrifice of the animal that Abel had taken it upon himself to offer to God. What I am here venturing to call the second original sin is thus all the more linked to an apparition of the animal, as in the episode of the serpent, but this time it seems more serious and more consequential.

On the one hand, in fact, Cain admits to an *excessive* fault: he kills his brother after failing to sacrifice an animal to God. This fault seems to him unpardonable, not simply wrong but excessively culpable, *too* grave. But isn't a wrongdoing always excessive, in its very essence? As a form of default in the face of an imperative necessity [*le défaut devant le "il faut"*]? "Cain said to Jehovah: 'My fault is too great to bear'" (Dhormes). "My wrong is too great to carry" (Chouraqui).[40]

This excess will be paid for in two ways: by his flight, of course, for Cain is said to be "hunted," "expelled," tracked, persecuted ("you have expelled me," "you have chased me out," Cain says to God); but also by means of the flight of the one who feels pursued, by the shameful hiding of himself, by the veil of yet another nakedness, by the avowal of that veil ("I shall hide myself from before you. I shall be a fugitive and flee on earth and it will come to pass that whoever happens upon me will kill me" [Dhormes]; "I shall veil myself before you. I shall move and wander throughout the earth and whoever finds me will kill me" [Chouraqui]).[41] There is thus a crime, shame, distancing, the retreat of the criminal. He is at the same time put to flight, hunted, and condemned to shame and dissimulation. He must hide his nakedness under a veil. A little as though it followed a second original sin, this ordeal follows the murder of a brother, it is true, but it also follows the test to which he has been put by a God who prefers the animal offering of Abel. For God had put Cain to the test by organizing a sort of temptation. He had set a trap for him. Jehovah's language is indeed that of a hunter. As if he were a nomad shepherd farmer, such as Abel, "herder of cattle" [*pâtre d'ovins*], or "shepherd of small animals" [*pasteur de petit bétail*], as opposed to the sedentary agriculturist, the "cultivator of the ground" [*cultivateur du sol*], "the servant of the soil" [*serviteur de la glèbe*] that was Cain, who made his offering from the "fruits of the earth" or of the "soil." Having refused Cain's vegetable offering, preferring Abel's animal offering, God had exhorted a discouraged Cain not to lose face, in short, to be careful not to fall into sin, not to fall victim to the wrongdoing that was waiting for him around the corner. He encouraged him to avoid the trap of temptation and to once more tame, dominate, govern:

So Jehovah said to Cain: "Why do you feel anger and why is your visage downfallen? If you act well, will you not pick yourself up? If you do not act well Sin *lurks* at your door [I emphasize this word lurks (*est tapi*), referring to sin, like an animal lying in wait in the shadow, waiting for its prey to fall into the trap, a victim prey to temptation, a bait or lure]: its force is coming toward you but have dominion over it." (Dhormes)[42]

The word *lurk* also appears in the otherwise very different Chouraqui translation: "at the opening fault lurks; its passion is yours. Govern it."[43] By killing his brother Cain falls into the trap; he becomes prey to the evil *lurking* in the shadow like an animal.

However, *on the other hand*, the paradoxes of this manhunt follow one after the other as a series of experimental ordeals: "in order to see." Having fallen into the trap and killed Abel, Cain covers himself with shame and flees, wandering, hunted, tracked in turn like a beast. God then promises this human beast protection and vengeance. *As if* God had repented. *As if* he were ashamed or had admitted having preferred the animal sacrifice. *As if* in this way he were confessing and admitting remorse concerning the animal. (This moment of "repentance" of "retraction," "going back on oneself"—there is an immense problem of translation here, unlimited stakes in the semantics that I leave aside for the moment—is not the only such moment; there is at least one other at the time of the Flood, another animal story.[44]) So God promises seven vengeances, no more nor less. He vows to take revenge seven times on anyone who kills Cain, that is to say, the murderer of his brother, he who, after this second original sin, has covered the nakedness of his face, the face that he lost before Him.

This double insistence upon nudity, fault, and default at the origin of human history and within sight or perspective of the animal cannot not be associated once more with the myth of Epimetheus and Prometheus: first, man receives fire and technology to compensate for his nakedness, but not yet the art of politics; then, from Hermes this time, he receives shame or honor and justice (*aidos* and *dikē*), which will permit him to bring harmony and the bonds of friendship (*desmoi philias*) into the city (*polis*).

In comparing Genesis with the Greek myths once more, still within sight and perspective of the animal, of fault and of nakedness, I am not speculating on any hypothesis derived from comparative history or the structural analysis of myth. These narratives remain heterogeneous in status and origin. Moreover, I don't hold them to be causes or origins of anything whatsoever. Nor verities or verdicts. Simply and at least I hold them to be two symptomatic translations, whose internal necessity is confirmed all the more by the fact that certain characteristics partially overlap from one translation to the other. But translation of what?

Well, let us say of a certain "state," a certain situation—of the process, world, and life obtaining among these mortal living things [*vivants à mort*] that are the animal species, those other "animals" and humans. Its analogous or common traits are all the more dominant given that their formalization, to which we are devoting ourselves here, will allow us to see appear in every discourse concerning the animal, and notably in Western philosophical discourse, the same dominant, the same recurrence of a schema that is in truth invariable. What is that? The following: what is proper to man, his subjugating superiority over the animal, his very becoming-subject, his historicity, his emergence out of nature, his sociality, his access to knowledge and technics, all that, everything (in a nonfinite number of predicates) that is proper to man would derive from this originary fault, indeed, from this default in propriety, what is proper to man as default in propriety—and from the imperative necessity that finds in it its development and resilience. I'll try to show this better later, from Aristotle to Heidegger, from Descartes to Kant, from Levinas to Lacan.

Let us return to Bellerophon. He didn't trouble me only because he gained the upper hand with respect to his animal brother or half-brother (Pegasus), or only because he vanquished Chimaera and so confirmed his mastery as hunter-tamer. Rather, all of Bellerophon's exploits can be deciphered *from top to bottom* as a history of modesty, of shame, of reticence, of honor, to the extent that he is linked to modest decency (*aischunē* this time and not just *aidon*). That allows us to make explicit in advance the fact that the truth of modesty will, in the end, be our subject. The ordeals that constitute the story of Bellerophon are well known. They are all destined to put to the test his sense of modesty. Because he has resisted the shameless advances of Stheneboea, the wife of his host, Proetus, king of Argos; because he is accused by that shameless woman, also called Antea, of having sought to seduce her or take her violently during the hunt, he is condemned to death by her husband. But out of respect for the laws of hospitality, the latter cannot himself put his rival to death. He therefore sends Bellerophon to his father-in-law, king of Lycia, bearing a letter that, instead of recommending him to his future host, prescribes his execution. (This is the story, before the event, of Hamlet sent to England by his stepfather who entrusts to him a letter that is a death sentence. Hamlet escapes the trap. I make this allusion to Hamlet in order to recall in passing that that play is an extraordinary zoology: its animal figures are innumerable, which is somewhat the case all through Shakespeare—more to follow.) Bellerophon thus carries with him, without knowing it, a verdict in the form of a death-letter whose truth escapes him. He becomes its unconscious purveyor [*facteur*]. But his second host begins sheltering the postman before unsealing the letter; he is therefore obliged in turn, as if held by a potential bit, to respect the laws of hospitality and so defer the execution of the sentence. Instead he submits Bellerophon to a new series of hunting, war, and combat ordeals. It is in that context that the hunt of the Chimaera takes place. The Chimaera was said to be "invincible," of a divine race and in no way human (*theion genos, oud'anthrōpon*, says the *Iliad* in bk. 6, l. 180): a lion in front, a serpent behind, a goat in the middle, its breath spouting frightening bursts of flamboyant flame (*chimaira, deinon apopneiousa puros menos aithomenoio*).

As we shall understand, that is not how Descartes describes the Chimaera whose existence has to be excluded at the moment of "I think therefore I am," in part four of the *Discourse on Method* ("we can distinctly imagine a lion's head on a goat's body without having to conclude from this that a chimera exists in the world"[45]).

What is this "world?" We will later ask what "world" means. In passing we can consider whether we should take seriously the fact that in his description of the Chimaera Descartes forgets the serpent. Like Homer, he names the lion and goat, but he forgets the serpent, that is to say, the behind. The serpent (*drakōn*, dragon) is the animal's behind, the part that is at the same time the most fabulous, the most chimerical, like the dragon, and also the most cunning: the cunning genius of the animal, the evil genius as animal, perhaps. A question concerning the serpent again, concerning evil and shame.

The final episode is not recounted by Homer but by Plutarch. It again puts Bellerophon to the test of nakedness. It is the seventh and last test. Once more Bellerophon falls prey, if I might suggest, to women. In a movement of shame or modesty (*hyp'aischunēs*) before women he backs down from his outrage at the hounding persecution to which he is victim, perpetrated by his father-in-law Iobates. Having decided to destroy the city with the help of Poseidon, his father, he advances on it followed by a wave that threatens to engulf everything. But the women come at him, offering themselves to him shamelessly. Their behavior is doubly indecent, for they expose themselves in all their nakedness and they offer their bodies, prostituting themselves, for sale. They try to seduce him in exchange for being saved. Faced with this pornography Bellerophon weakens. He doesn't give in to their shameless advances, quite the contrary; he gives in to the impulse of his own shame and backs down before the immodesty of these women. He pulls back, retreats in shame (*hyp'aischunēs*) faced with the shameful conduct of these women. So the wave recedes and the city is saved. This movement of shame, this reticence, this inhibition, this retreat, this reversal is, no doubt, like the immunizing drive, the protection of the immune, of the sacred (*heilig*), of the holy, of the separate (*kadosh*) that is the very origin of the religious, of religious scruple. I have tried to devote several essays to analyzing that, relating it to what Heidegger calls *Verhaltenheit*, restraint, in his *Beiträge zur Philosophie* (*Contributions to Philosophy*). As I tried to do in "Faith and Knowledge," where I sought to account for all the paradoxes of the auto-immunitary, I might have been tempted today, had I the time, which I don't, to turn the spotlight once more on this terrible and always possible perversion by means of which the immune becomes auto-immunizing, finding there some analogical or virtual relation with auto-biography.

～

Autobiography, the writing of the self as living, the trace of the living for itself, being for itself, the auto-affection or auto-infection as memory or archive of the living, would be an immunizing movement (a movement of safety, of salvage and salvation of the safe, the holy, the immune, the indemnified, of virginal and intact nudity), but an immunizing movement that is always threatened with becoming auto-immunizing, like every *autos*, every ipseity, every automatic, automobile, autonomous, auto-referential movement. Nothing risks becoming more poisonous than an autobiography, poisonous for oneself in the first place, auto-infectious for the presumed signatory who is so auto-affected.

Ecce animot, as I was saying before this long digression. In order not to damage French ears too sensitive to spelling and grammar I won't repeat the word *animot* too often. I'll do it several times but each time that, henceforth, I say "the animal" [*l'animal*] or "the animals" [*les animaux*] I'll be asking you to silently substitute *animot* for what you hear. By means of the chimera of this singular word, the *animot*, I bring together three heterogeneous elements within a single verbal body.

1. I would like to have the plural *animals* heard in the singular. There is no Animal in the general singular, separated from man by a single, indivisible limit. We have to envisage the existence of "living creatures," whose plurality cannot be assembled within the single figure of an animality that is simply opposed to humanity. This does not, of course, mean ignoring or effacing everything that separates humankind from the other animals, creating a single large set, a single grand, fundamentally homogeneous and continuous family tree going from the *animot* to the *homo* (*faber, sapiens*, or whatever else). That would be an *asinanity*, even more

so to suspect anyone here of doing just that. I won't therefore devote another second to the double *asinanity* of that suspicion, even if, alas, it is
quite widespread. I repeat that it is rather a matter of taking into account
a multiplicity of heterogeneous structures and limits: among nonhumans,
and separate from nonhumans, there is an immense multiplicity of other
living things that cannot in any way be homogenized, except by means of
violence and willful ignorance, within the category of what is called the
animal or animality in general. From the outset there are animals and,
let's say, *l'animot*. The confusion of all nonhuman living creatures within
the general and common category of the animal is not simply a sin against
rigorous thinking, vigilance, lucidity, or empirical authority, it is also a
crime. Not a crime against animality, precisely, but a crime of the first
order against the animals, against animals. Do we consent to presume that
every murder, every transgression of the commandment "Thou shalt not
kill" concerns only man (a question to come), and that, in sum, there are
crimes only "against humanity"?

2. The suffix *mot* in *l'animot* should bring us back to the word,
namely, to the word named a noun [*nommé nom*]. It opens onto the referential experience of the thing *as such*, as what it is in its being, and therefore to the stakes involved in always seeking to draw the limit, the unique
and indivisible limit held to separate human from animal, namely, the
word, the nominal language of the word, the voice that names and that
names the thing *as such*, such as it appears in its being (as in the Heideggerian moment of this demonstration that we are coming to). The animal
would in the last instance be deprived of the word, of the word that one
names a noun or name.

3. It would not be a matter of "giving speech back" to animals but
perhaps of acceding to a thinking, however fabulous and chimerical it
might be, that thinks the absence of the name and of the word otherwise,
and as something other than a privation.

Ecce animot, that is the announcement of which I am (following) something like the trace, assuming the title of an autobiographical animal, in
the form of a risky, fabulous, or chimerical response to the question "But
as for me, who am I (following)?" which I have wagered on treating as
that of the autobiographical animal. That title, which is itself somewhat
chimerical, might surprise you. It brings together *two times two* alliances,
as unexpected as they are irrefutable.

On the one hand, it gives rise to the thought, in the informal form of a
playful conversation, a suggestion that would take witty advantage of

idiom, that quite simply there are those among humans, writers, and philosophers whose character implies a taste for autobiography, the irresistible sense of or desire for autobiography. One would say "(s)he's an autobiographical animal," in the same way that one says "(s)he's a theatrical animal," a competitive animal, a political animal, not in the sense that one has been able to define man as a political animal but in the sense of an individual who has the taste, talent, or compulsive obsession for politics: he who likes that, really likes doing that, likes politics. And does it well. In that sense the autobiographical animal would be the sort of man or woman who, as a matter of character, chooses to indulge in or can't resist indulging in autobiographical confidences. He or she who works *in* autobiography. And in the history of literature or philosophy, if it can be suggested in such a summary manner, there are "autobiographical animals," more autobiographical than others, animals for autobiography: Montaigne more than Malherbe, similarly Rousseau, the lyric and romantic poets, Proust and Gide, Virginia Woolf, Gertrude Stein, Celan, Bataille, Genet, Duras, Cixous; but also (the matter is structurally more rare and more complicated when it comes to philosophy) Augustine and Descartes more than Spinoza, Kierkegaard, playing with so many pseudonyms, more than Hegel, Nietzsche more than Marx. But because the matter is really too complicated (it is our theme, after all) I prefer to end the list of examples there. With the problems it poses, this connotation of the autobiographical animal must certainly remain present, even if tangential, to our reflections. It will weigh on them with its virtual weight.

But, *on the other hand,* I was not thinking in the last instance of that usage of the expression "autobiographical animal" in order to get to some bottom of the matter, if there is such a thing. It happens that there exist, between the word *I* and the word *animal,* all sorts of significant connections. They are at the same time functional and referential, grammatical and semantic. Two general singulars to begin with: the "I" and the "animal," both preceded by a definite article, designate an indeterminate generality in the singular. The "I" is anybody at all; "I" am anybody at all, and anybody at all must be able to say "I" to refer to herself, to his own singularity. Whosoever says "I" or apprehends or poses herself as an "I" is a living animal. By contrast, animality, the life of the living, at least when one claims to be able to distinguish it from the inorganic, from the purely inert or cadaverous physico-chemical, is generally defined as sensibility, irritability, and *auto-motricity,* a spontaneity that is capable of movement, of organizing itself and affecting itself, marking, tracing, and affecting itself with traces of its self. This *auto-motricity* as auto-affection and relation to itself is the characteristic recognized as that of the living and of animality in general, even before one comes to consider the discursive thematic of an utterance or of an *ego cogito*, more so of a *cogito ergo sum*. But between this relation to the self (this Self, this ipseity) and the *I* of the "I think," there is, it would seem, an abyss.

The problems begin there, we suspect, and what problems they are! But they begin where one attributes to the essence of the living, to the animal in general, this aptitude *that it itself is*, this aptitude to being itself, and thus the aptitude to being capable of affecting itself, of its own movement, of affecting itself with traces of a living self, and thus of *autobiograparaphing* itself as it were. No one has ever denied the animal this capacity to track itself, to trace itself or retrace a path of itself. Indeed, the most difficult problem lies in the fact that it has been refused the power to transform those traces into verbal language, to call to itself by means of discursive questions and responses, denied the power to efface its traces (which is what Lacan will deny it, and we will come back to everything that that implies). Let us set out again from this place of intersection between these two general singulars, the animal (*l'animot*) and the "I," the "I's," the place where in a given language, French, for example, an "I" says "I." Singularly and in general. It could be anyone at all, you or I. So what happens there? How can I say "I" and what do I do thereby? And in the first place, me, what am I (following) and who am I (following)?

"I": by saying "I" the signatory of an autobiography would claim to point himself out physically, introduce himself in the present [*se présenter au présent*] (*sui*-referential deixis) and in his totally naked truth. And in the naked truth, if there is such a thing, of his or her sexual difference, of all their sexual differences. By naming himself and answering for his name, he would be saying "I stake and engage my nudity without shame." One can well doubt whether this pledge, this wager, this desire or promise of nudity is possible. Nudity perhaps remains untenable. And can I finally show myself naked in the sight of what they call by the name of "animal"? Should I show myself naked when, concerning me, looking at me, is the living creature they call by the common, general, and singular name *the animal*? Henceforth I shall reflect (on) the same question by introducing a mirror. I import a full-length mirror [*une psyché*] into the scene. Wherever some autobiographical play is being enacted there has to be a *psyché*, a mirror that reflects me naked from head to toe. The same question then becomes whether I should show myself but in the process see myself naked (that is, reflect my image in a mirror) when, concerning me, looking at me, is this living creature, this cat that can find itself caught in the same mirror? Is there animal narcissism? But cannot this cat also be, deep within her eyes, my primary mirror?

The animal in general, what is it? What does that mean? Who is it? To what does that "it"[46] correspond? To whom? Who responds to whom? Who responds in and to the common, general, and singular name of what they thus blithely call the "animal"? Who is it that responds? The reference made by this what or who regarding me in the name of the animal, what is said in the name of the animal when one appeals to the name of the animal, that is what it would be a matter of exposing, in all its nudity, in the nudity or destitution of whoever, opening the page of an autobiography, says "here I am."

"But as for me, who am I (following)?"

[...]

2

"But as for me, who am I (following)?"

"But as for me, who am I (following)?"

Whether I address this question to you or ask it, in the first instance, of myself, it should concern only me, myself, me alone. And every response that I give to it will belong to a self-definition, as a first autobiographical gesture involving only the writing of my life, myself, me alone. Yet you well know that this question is so much older than me: "But as for me, who am I?" It shows all the wrinkles of a quotation and, from the beginning, has simply been waiting for a facelift. I repeat it, I can reproduce it mechanically, it has always been capable of being recorded, it can always be mimed, aped, parroted by these animals, for example, those apes and parrots about which it is said that they can imitate (even though Aristotle denied them mimesis) without understanding or thinking, and especially without replying to the questions they are asked. According to many philosophers and theoreticians, from Aristotle to Lacan, animals do not respond, and they share that irresponsibility with writing, at least in the terms in which Plato interprets the latter in the *Phaedrus*. What is terrible (*deinon*) about writing, Socrates says, is the fact that, like painting (*zōgraphia*), the things it engenders, although similar to living things (*ōs zōnta*), do not respond. No matter what question one asks them, writings remain silent, keeping a most majestic silence or else always replying in the same terms, which means not replying.[1] This famous passage from the *Phaedrus*, which interested me greatly in the past, just like the theme of the animality of writing, would have to be compared with that from *Alice in Wonderland*: as you will remember, we are told there that the cat does not answer because it always replies the same thing. Descartes says exactly the same thing, and it is always as if humans were less interested in emphasizing the fact that the animal is deprived of the ability to speak, a *zōon alogon*, than the fact that it is private and deprives humans of a response.[2] What counts when it comes to speech would be above all exchange, or the question-response coupling. And since I have just referred to the *Phaedrus*, let me note in passing that that grand work on writing, indeed, on autobiographical writing and on "Know yourself," is also a great work on the animal. From the beginning one watches Pegasus and the Chimera pass by, and on the same page Socrates speaks of the Delphic inscription (*to Delphikon gramma gnōnai emauton*) and in asking himself "Who am I?" doesn't exclude the possibility—this is in stark contrast to Descartes—of himself being a peculiar animal and of having to get to know himself as though he were a strange beast:

> Consequently I don't bother about such things [say goodbye (*khairein*) to them], but accept the current beliefs about them, and direct my inquiries, as I have just said, rather to myself, to discover whether I really am a more complex creature [*ti thērion*, "wild beast,"] and more puffed up with pride than Typhon [Typhon is the name of a smoking wind blown by a giant full of pride; to be *atuphhos* is, once one knows oneself, to be modest], or a simpler, gentler being [*zōon*, "animal"] whom heaven has blessed with a quiet, un-Typhonic nature.[3]

For the *Phaedrus* is also a sort of animal dialogue: it recalls Socrates' demonic voice (half-animal, half-divine); it evokes the yoking of two horses (the good and the bad); it questions the fact that the *zōon*, the living creature, can be called mortal as well as immortal (*thnēton/athanaton*; §246b); it invokes the myth of the cicadas, who used to be men and who were so intent on singing that they were capable of dying, having forgotten to eat and drink. When they came to report to Calliope and Urania, the cicadas remarked on the philosophers who spend their time doing honor to the music appropriate to those two Muses. "I philosophize" can mean that as a man I am a cicada, I recall what I am, a cicada who remembers having been a man. To remind myself of myself is to recall myself to singing and music.

ॐ

But can we, for our part, reply to the question "But as for me, who am I?" And what would ever distinguish the response, in its total purity, the so-called free and responsible response, from a reaction to a complex system of stimuli? And what, after all, is a citation?

"As to myself, what can I now say that I am? / But as for me, who am I?" We have all read this sentence, in the second of the *Meditations on First Philosophy*. We shall allow it to wait out the time of certain digressions, but I promise you that we shall shortly come back along this path of a great French tradition, namely, the Cartesian, the path of a genealogy that leads back to the putative father of French philosophy.

I am attributing to him this name of "father" for more than one reason. In the first place, in order to put us on the track of the presumed animality of the absolute father, of him who is killed or offered as a sacrifice in order to institute equality among brothers. In the second place, because I would like to set before you for discussion the hypothesis that certain versions of thinking concerning animality that seem to be the least Cartesian, the most heterogeneous vis-à-vis the mechanicism of the animal-machine, nevertheless belong to the filiation of the Cartesian *cogito*. They derive irresistibly from it, and sometimes do so by means of a symptomatic disavowal that I hold to be undeniable and that will require us to give a prominent place to a certain concept of the symptom. My examples or my exemplary referential *patrix* [*mes re-pères exemplaires*] will include Kant and Heidegger as well as Levinas and Lacan. There will, of course, be others, but in the time allowed to us I would at least like to recognize the latter places and types of discourse. I believe them to be at once paradigmatic, dominant, and normative. They constitute a general topology and even, in a somewhat new sense for this term, a worldwide anthropology, a way for today's man to position himself in the face of what he calls "the animal" within what he calls "the world"—so many motifs (*man, animal,* and especially *world*) that I would like, as it were, to reproblematize.

We will go back down all these paths more than once; in particular, when I try to explain to myself how, and account for what happened at the moment when, right in the middle of my declared title, as it was imprinted in me—*The Animal That I Am*—the idea came to me, just recently, to add this conjunction with a more or less syllogistic or expletive value: *The Animal That* Therefore *I Am*.

I've already said more than once that we would again pass by these paths. Such procedural steps [*démarche*] should be *followed*. And my only question today would be, if one wanted to reduce it to a word, the question, of which more to follow [*à suivre*], of the "to be followed": what is meant by "to follow," "more to follow," "to pursue" [*poursuivre*], even "to persecute." What does one do when one follows? What is it I am doing when I am (following)? When I am (following) *after* someone or something, after an animal that some hold to be something that is not necessarily someone? What does "to be after" mean? The steps to be consistently followed [*cette démarche suivie*] will indeed have to resemble those of an animal seeking to find or seeking to escape. Do they not resemble the running of an animal that, finding its way on the basis of a scent or a noise, goes back more than once over the same path to pick up the traces, either to sniff the trace of another or to cover its own by adding to it, precisely as though it were that of another, picking up the scent, therefore, of whatever on this track demonstrates to it that the trace is always that of another, demonstrating also that in following the consequence or direction of this double arrow (it is a matter of the scent, and the scent one smells is always the trace of another), the animal becomes inevitable, and, before it, the *animot*. To put it differently, one would have to ask oneself *first of all* what there is about scent and smell in man's relation to the *animot*—and why this zone of sensibility is so neglected or reduced to a secondary position in philosophy and in the arts. (I spoke many years ago in this very place, in the context of Freud and Kafka, of being before the law and the grand question of the erection of man, in particular, in the form of the upright stance and its ambiguous privilege, and of erection in another register, that, once more, of nudity.) One would have to ask oneself, *in the second instance*, after what a discourse on the trace of the other gets going (this discourse in the course of which and in coursing toward which I encountered Levinas in terms of what he has called a chiasmus) and why that discourse had to inscribe within itself the trace of another as animal, as *animot*, something I haven't stopped doing, but which Levinas, in this Cartesian tradition I just mentioned—and which, as it happens, is also, not by chance, a Greco-Judeo-Christiano-Islamic tradition—has never done, so far as I know.

The strategies of this *right (for more) to follow* [droit de suite] that I have just evoked resemble those of the hunt, whether the animal thereby follows its desire, what is desirable in its desire (or in its need, as will be said by those who wish, out of desire or need, to believe in an ironclad distinction between the two, desire and need, just as in the distinction between man and animal), or whether, while following its drive, the animal finds itself followed, tracked by the drive of the other. And we should not exclude the possibility that the same living creature is at the same time follower and followed, hunter knowing itself to be hunted, seducer and seduced, persecutor and fugitive, and that the two forces of the same strategy, indeed of the same movement, are conjugated not only in the same animal, the same *animot*, but in the same instant.

The animal in whose tracks therefore I am (following), and who picks up traces, who is it? Does it speak? Does it speak French? Imagine it signing a declaration, one trace among others, in the first person, *je, je suis.* That trace would already be the guarantee [*gage*] or undertaking [*engagement*], the promise of a discourse on autobiographical method. Whether it is pronounced, exposed as such, thematized or not, the "I" is always posed autobiographically. It refers to itself. The "I" shows itself, it speaks of itself and of itself as living, living in the present, in the living present, in the moment in which "I" is said, even were it to be already a dead thing speaking. The auto-biographical does not have to occur to an "I," living or dead, that would come to speak of itself. The auto-bio-graphical derives from the fact that the simple instance of the "I" or of the *autos* can be posed as such only to the extent that it is a sign of life, of life in presence, the manifestation of life in presence, even if the what, or who, male or female, that thereby gives this sign of life finds itself to have passed over to the side of death, and even says "I am on the side of death or rather on the other side of life." Even if this "I"—as is always possible—is quoted, mechanically repeated by a technique of reproduction or by Descartes' animal-machine. We are here analyzing this sign of life within the very structure of the auto-position of the *I* or of *ipseity* (even if this auto-position in neither a discursive nor a thematic utterance). We situate within the minimal phenomenological structure, in the simple appearing of the "I" in general, the trace of this manifestation of self, of this auto-presentation as living present (thing), this autobiographical guarantee, even if such a tracing can give rise to fantasy and to nonrigorous philo-sophical interpretations, even if it is in no way contradictory, far from it, with this "I am dead," which, as I tried to show in the past, was in some way implied in every *cogito ergo sum.*[4]

The animal that therefore I am (following), and whose language resembles French, lo and behold seems to sign a declaration. Which?

It would say what follows, namely, that henceforth I am (following), while reading, quoting myself, deciphering my traces.

I decline all responsibility. I respond no more, I no more answer for what I am saying. I reply that I am no longer responding. If autobiography were at least a genre, in the sense of an exercise fortified with all the assurances that a centuries-old institution can guarantee, you could right now recognize in that institution of the so-called "autobiographical" genre a signal merit: that of permitting whomever speaks of himself to find refuge—in order to decline all responsibility and all onus of proof—behind the artificial authority of a genre, behind the right to a genre whose literary pedigree, as we well know, remains problematic. It will, as we say, have caused much ink to flow. Discharged of every onus of proof, pure autobiography authorizes either veracity or mendacity, but always in accordance with a scene of witnessing, that is to say, an "I am telling you the truth" without shame, bareback, naked and raw [*à nu et à cru*]. As if, in speaking of oneself, I, me, my self were speaking of another, were quoting another, or as if I were speaking of an "I" in general, naked and raw.

With these words, "naked and raw," I have just seen an animal pass. Looking at me without blinkers. A mounted animal, like a horse, raw, naked down to its body hair [*à poil*].[5] The French expression—*monter un cheval à poil*, "to mount a horse bareback," that is, raw and without a saddle—is barely translatable.

And here we find ourselves already caught in a fleece, in the immense bushy enigma of body hair, of fur, coat, and skin, between Adam and Prom-Epimetheus, in the small pubic forest that seems to surround or protect—but from what?—the nudity of an intensely desirable zone in the body of certain living creatures, one that is also devoted to the reproduction of the species. The enigma of the pubic fleece led Freud, the Freud of *Femininity*, into what I tried to analyze elsewhere—in "A Silkworm of One's Own," I won't go back over that—as the fatality of a theoretical delirium. Like everybody else, Freud took woman to be a more naturally modest being than man. But modesty or shame is, naturally, such an aporetic movement, so self-contradictory, so exhibitionist within its very logic, that the most modest will always also be—this is the law of the symptom—the least modest. In the same movement the same ones will call woman the most modest and the most indecent. And, for the discourse that never resists placing the woman and child on the side of the animal, this is also the law that governs the nudity between what is called human and what I am calling the *animot*: the *animot* is more naked than the human, who is more naked than the *animot*.

I am still (following) in the same room.[6] The animal is looking at me. Should I avow, once more, at the risk of repeating myself, compulsively, thereby adding another shame to the double shame of the shame that I was talking about earlier, a certain reserve that you can always interpret as a phantasm? I am not going to admit to a fault, I am going to avow a shame without apparent fault, the shame of being ashamed of shame, ad infinitum, the potential fault that consists in being ashamed of a fault about which I'll never know whether it was one. I am ashamed of almost always tending toward a gesture of shame when appearing naked before what one calls an animal, a cat, for example, a seeing animal naked down to its hair, a sexed mammal (for they are not all sexed mammals—which is a distinction that few philosophers have taken into account, especially those within the Cartesian genealogy of a discourse on the animal in general—and they don't all have a face that faces me). I am therefore paralyzed by a movement of shame, of embarrassment and of modesty: the desire to go and get dressed as quickly as possible, even to turn my back so that such a cat doesn't see me naked, more precisely, though, so it doesn't see me face on with my sex organs exposed. In the context of what I have already told you, within the autobiographical exercise that I am frankly and shamelessly indulging in, I'll add that the matter is still more intense, and the malaise still more disturbing—fear as much as desire, fearful desire (but what is this fear? fear of what? of whom?)—the embarrassment even becomes intolerable whenever the fatality—I am indeed saying "fatality"—of two possible accidents comes to complicate the scene, or, if you prefer, the middle of the room [pièce]. The first is when another is in the room, when there is a third party in the bedroom or bathroom, unless the cat itself, whatever its sex, be that third party. Allow me to make things still more clear: all that becomes all the more acute if the third party is a woman. And the "I" who is speaking to you here dares therefore to posit himself, he signs his self-presentation by presenting himself as a man, a living creature of the masculine sex, even if he does so with all the necessary precautions, retaining an acute sense of the unstable complexity that he thinks he has to recall and lay claim to at every occasion, even suspecting that an autobiography of any consequence cannot not touch on this assurance of saying "I am a man," "I am a woman," I am a man who is also a woman.

Now this self, this male me, believes he has noted that the presence of a woman in the room warms things up in the relation to the cat, vis-à-vis the gaze of the naked cat that sees me naked, and sees me see it seeing me naked, like a shining fire with a cloud of jealousy that begins to float like the smoke of incense in the room. The other fatality of a possible accident (but is it an accident?), therefore, is that, besides the presence of a woman, there is a mirror [psyché] in the room. We no longer know how many we are then, all males and females of us. And I maintain that autobiography has begun there. What happens to me each time that I see an animal in a room where there is a mirror (not even to mention the animal that finds itself faced with a television that is showing it animals, in particular animals of the same species, for example, a cat seeing and hearing cats on television—somewhat later, tracking Lacan's traces, we will take up the question of the mirror stage in the animal)? I am not, therefore, wondering only about what takes place inside that cat's head; I am not questioning myself solely concerning the status of the discourse that would appeal for proof or witnessing about the animal in front of a mirror. To begin with, I am consciously taking stock [*je prends conscience*] of this massive fact: in the history of the grand canonical discourses on the animal, discourses of a philosophical type (from Aristotle to Descartes, from Kant to Hegel, to Heidegger, Levinas, or Lacan) as well as discourses of common sense, which at bottom are the same, well, not only does one tend to confuse all animal species under the grand category of "the animal" versus "man" (without taking into account differences between sexed and non-sexed animals, mammals and nonmammals, without taking into account the infinite diversity of animals, in particular, primates or those one calls anthropoids, given the enormous progress that has been made in primatological and ethological knowledge in general), but, in addition to that immense confusion, the question of whether an animal can see *me* naked, and especially whether it can see *itself* naked, is never asked. For it is certain that an enormous problematic field lies there, both for the so-called positive sciences of animal behavior (which perhaps, here and there, in their own way, have begun to clear the ground in that respect), and for philosophical thinking, which, I believe, has never touched on the matter. For my part, I have never picked up the least allusion to the experience of nakedness and the question of the mirror or the most elementary form of animal "reflection" in any of the authors I have just named (with the exception of Lacan—and we plan to read him closely on this point—who nevertheless places his interpretation of the animal imaginary and specular in the service of a zoo-logy that, according to me, still remains fundamentally Cartesian). For one of the structural differences among animals is drawn there, between those who have some experience of the mirror and those who don't have any at all. It is all the more complicated in view of the fact that the question doesn't reduce to one, already important and difficult in and of itself, concerning some "mirror stage" and self-identification in the development of animality in general, of this or that species or this or that individual in general. One would also have to know for certain something still more problematic: Where do the mirror and the reflecting image begin, which also refers to the identification of one's fellow being? Can one not speak of an experience that is already specular as soon as a cat recognizes a cat and begins to know, if not in the end to say, that "a cat is a cat?" Does not the mirror effect also begin wherever a living creature, whatever it be, identifies another living creature of its own species as its neighbor [*prochain*] or fellow [*semblable*]? And therefore at least wherever there is sexuality properly speaking, wherever reproduction relies on sexual coupling? One would therefore have to accept the additional but essential complication of extending this effect of specular recognition beyond the field of the properly visual image. Certain animals identify their partner or their fellow, they identify themselves and each other, by the sound of their voices or their songs. They recognize not only their master's voice or that of other animals, friends or enemies, but in the first place the voice of their congeneric fellows in cases of what one can call, without exaggeration, declarations of love or hate, peace or war, and of seduction or hunt, hence modalities of following, "I am (following)," or "I am following you." The narcissistic identification of one's fellow of the same species also works through the play of call and response between voices, of singing and sonic productions that are both coded and inventive. Wherever reproduction functions by means of sexual coupling (and that marks one of the important frontiers, subfrontiers, between so many animals or different species), well then, one has to register some mirror effect—visual, aural, indeed olfactory—some hetero-narcissistic "self as other." Especially when—and this is where one sees the intertwining of threads that until now seemed to be entangled without order or without law—this hetero-narcissism is erotic: once the specularity of one's fellow is understood to begin with sexual difference, on the eve of, but already involved in the technical stage of mirroring, of narcissistic or echographical mirroring, account has to be taken of the seductive pursuit without which there is no sexual experience, and no desire or choice of partner in general. Yet if one takes into account seductive pursuit or predatoriness, a seduction that is tenderly or violently appropriative, one can no longer dissociate the moment of sexual parade from an exhibition, or exhibition from a simulation, or simulation from a dissimulation, or the dissimulative ruse from some experience of nakedness, or nakedness from some type of modesty. Hence some sort of modesty or shame, in the sense of some sensitivity to nakedness, would no longer be limited to the human and foreign to the *animot*. Certain sexed animals would have access to it, certain nonhuman living creatures would have a right to it, and better still, would enter thereby into the order of the law, inseparable from the order of truth, to the extent that the latter is linked to the veil of modesty.

Once that displacement comes into effect, an immense and difficult question would then be raised concerning a sort of rhetoric of modesty. What right should be given to this double metonymy: on the one hand, that which would allow us to speak of modesty whenever there is a play of monstration/simulation/dissimulation, a ruse in the phenomena of *following* referred to as hunting or seduction, predatoriness or animal eroticism (phenomena that can be witnessed, attested to, and demonstrated, without necessarily requiring the behaviorist analyses that nevertheless remain so necessary, and whose extraordinary, subtle, and increasing richness so few philosophers take into account)? On the other hand, since every show of modesty is linked to a reserve of shame, to a reserve that attests to a virtual guilt, does one have the right to rely on this other metonymy in order to conclude that an animal modesty exists and therefore that animals have a sense of nakedness? Once the *animot* (the animality of certain animals) shows itself capable of undeniably guilty behavior, hiding or putting its tail between its legs after committing a fault, indeed, in times of sickness or at the point of death, both of which would be felt as faults, as what must not be shown (so many animals hide when they are ill or feel they are dying), does one have the right to infer from that animal debt, memory of a fault, shame, and hence modesty?

In other words, is every "hiding of oneself" (in the experiences of the hunt, of seduction, and of guilt) tied to the possibility of modesty, even when (and this is the metonymy in question) that modesty is not directed toward the genital organs? If we were provisionally to limit the field of this question to sexed animals, to the experience of life and death within sexual difference, how would we confront this metonymic difference, this difference of metonymy, which means that a living creature capable of modesty, of guilt, or of hiding or encrypting itself does not always and necessarily concentrate that modesty on the exposure of the genital organs? My hypothesis is that the criterion in force, the distinctive trait, is inseparable from the experience of holding oneself upright, of uprightness [*droiture*] as erection in general in the process of hominization. Within a general phenomenon of erection as passage to the straight verticality of the upright stance distinguishing the human from other mammals, one would still have to distinguish sexual erection from being-standing, and especially to distinguish in turn the alternating rhythm of erection and detumescence that the male is unable to dissimulate in the face-to-face of copulation (another overwhelmingly distinctive trait of human coupling). Wherever this difference in desire can no longer rely on spontaneous pretense or natural dissimulation, modesty is properly concentrated, that is to say, by arresting or concentrating the metonymy, on the phallic zone.

In short, it is in this place of the face-to-face that the animal looks at me; that is where I have difficulty accepting that what one calls an animal looks at me, when it looks at me, naked. That this difficulty [*mal*] does not exclude the announcement of a certain enjoyment [*jouissance*] is another question still, but one will understand that it is also the same thing, that thing that combines within itself desire, *jouissance*, and anguish. But I would prefer not, as Bartleby says, to appear naked before a cat, and then for our eyes to meet. What happens when, naked, one's gaze meets that of what they call an animal?

Before even beginning to dig into the burrow of words and images on the basis of which, in this château, I would dare address you, I dreamed for a long time. Of all sorts of possible scenes, possible and impossible worlds. I dreamed them, I dreamed of them, asking myself all along what an animal dream could be like and first of all whether the animal dreams. It is known that the animal, that certain animals dream. Nothing is known about their representations but it is understood, as a result of experimentation, that processes of an oneiric type traverse their sleep. Certain inhibitors simply had to be removed experimentally for moments of dreaming to be recorded. I also love to watch what they call an animal sleep, when such a living creature breathes with its eyes closed, for not all animals are seeing animals. I am saying "they," "what they call an animal," in order to mark clearly the fact that I have always secretly exempted myself from that world, and to indicate that my whole history, the whole genealogy of my questions, in truth everything I am, follow, think, write, trace, erase even, seems to me to be born from that exceptionalism and incited by that sentiment of election. As if I were the secret elect of what they call animals. I shall speak from this island of exception, from its infinite coastline, starting from it and speaking of it.

I love to watch them sleep, as though I were going to discover by surprise something essential. Since it indeed seems, if we are attuned to our common experience, to the most domestic, day-to-day observation of our dogs and cats, as well as to the conclusions of numerous qualified zoologists, that certain animals dream (I have just recalled that there are so-called objective, in fact encephalographically measurable signs of and criteria for that), then the general form of certain questions immediately emerges. In the first place, if certain animals dream—but not all, and not all in the same way—what sense is there in using this noun in the singular (the animal), and what right do we have to do so wherever an experience as essential as dreaming, and hence a relation among consciousness, subconscious, and unconscious, as well as representation and desire, separates so many animal species one from the other and at the same time brings together certain animals and what is called man? Should one not say "(the) animals," renouncing in advance any horizon of unification of the concept of the animal, to which one would be able to oppose in turn anything else identifiable whatsoever: man, for example, or even, much more significant, the nonanimal as nonliving, in fact, as dead [*le mort*]? The *animort*? In the second place, can one not transpose what I shall call the trial by dream to a nonfinite series of categories to which we will have to return (and not only during this session), a series whose law I won't, however, wait to point out? The question "Does the animal dream?" is, in its form, premises, and stakes, at least analogous to the questions "Does the animal think?" "Does the animal produce representations?" a self, imagination, a relation to the future as such? Does the animal have not only signs but a language, and what language? Does the animal die? Does it laugh? Does it cry? Does it grieve? Does it get bored? Does it lie? Does it forgive? Does it sing? Does it invent? Does it invent music? Does it play music? Does it play? Does it offer hospitality? Does it offer? Does it give? Does it have hands? eyes? etc.? modesty? clothes? and the mirror? All these questions, and a large number of others that depend on them, are questions concerning what is proper to the animal. They are immense in terms of their history, their presuppositions, the complexity of their stakes. Later I shall risk producing, on their side, a sort of key, which I'll have turn, not like some master key or pick[7] in a lock so as to open a cage or the door of a zoo, not with a view to liberating some animal race that is the victim of a confinement, of an encircling that is as old as humankind on its way to hominization, not even with a view to preparing a new declaration of the rights of the animal (I'll explain why shortly), but in a more musical sense, like a key or signature designed to register a set of regulated modulations, sharps and flats. I wish only to indicate a tonality, some high notes that change the whole stave.[8] How can the gamut of questions on the being of what would be proper to the animal be changed? How can a flat, as it were, be introduced in the key of this questioning to tone it down and change its tune?

I am dreaming, therefore, in the depths of an undiscoverable burrow to come.[9] I am dreaming through the dream of the animal and dreaming of the scene I could create here. Have been for some months. All my dreams came back to a sort of impasse, more precisely, to a sort of *schizis* brought about by a contradictory injunction. I dreamed that I gave myself incompatible commands, hence impossible tasks. How to have heard here a language or unheard-of music, somewhat inhuman in a way, yet not so as to make myself the representative or emancipator of an animality that is forgotten, ignored, misunderstood, persecuted, hunted, fished, sacrificed, subjugated, raised, corralled, hormonized, transgenetized, exploited, consumed, eaten, domesticated; rather, to have myself heard in a language that is a language, of course, and not those inarticulate cries or insignificant noises, howling, barking, meowing, chirping, that so many humans attribute to the animal, a language whose words, concepts, singing, and accent can finally manage to be foreign enough to everything that, in all human languages, will have harbored so many *asinanities* concerning the so-called animal. I am saying *asinanity* [*bêtise*] in order to name the sole human property whose expression is guaranteed in the semantics of the

French language. One can always speak of the *bêtise* of men, sometimes of their bestiality; there is no sense in speaking of the *bêtise* or bestiality of an animal [*bête*], no right to do so. That would be an anthropomorphism of the most stereotypical kind. In short, I was dreaming of inventing an unheard-of grammar and music in order to create a scene that was neither human, nor divine, nor animal, with a view to denouncing all discourses on the so-called animal, all the anthropo-theomorphic or anthropo-theocentric logics and axiomatics, philosophy, religion, politics, law, ethics, with a view to recognizing in them animal strategies, precisely, in the human sense of the term, stratagems, ruses, and war machines, defensive or offensive maneuvers, search operations, predatory, seductive, indeed exterminatory operations as part of a pitiless struggle between what are presumed to be species. As though I were dreaming, I myself, in all innocence, of an animal that didn't intend harm to the animal. But it is true—and it is even around such a truth that we are doing business here—that the dominant discourse of man on the path toward hominization imagines the animal in the most contradictory and incompatible generic terms [*espèces*]: absolute (because natural) goodness, absolute innocence, prior to good and evil, the animal without fault or defect (that would be its superiority as inferiority), but also the animal as absolute evil, cruelty, murderous savagery.

But as for me, the naked innocent one, the accused naked one [*nu prévenu*], presumed innocent and guilty at the same time, who am I, as I was asking just now? It is important that this question resonates here in the French language: *Qui suis-je?* or *Que suis-je?* Who or what am I (following)? Henceforth it is disturbed by an ambiguity that remains, within it, untranslatable, in what remains small, the small, the small word falling in the middle of this three-word interrogative proposition, namely, the little homonym *suis*, which, in the first person of the indicative conjugates more than one verb—*être*, to be, and *suivre*, to follow: *Qui suis-je?* "Who is it that I am (following)?" This little one, this dear little thing that enters as a third party and plays the part of the copula, saying *je suis, suis-je, qui je suis, que je suis*, without leaving us any assurance, coming between the subject and itself, between the subject and its complement, indeed between the subject and the object it worries, literally,[10] or about which it deludes itself by hunting in the mirror, where does it come from and where is it going?

I thought I had simply invented this innocent and at the same time perverse game of homonymy, this double usage of the little thing, of the powerful little word *suis*. I even thought I had justified it in advance. Not in general, of course, for that would be too crass, but on the subject of the animal. I invented it, in fact, because I thought that I had invented it and I don't remember having ever encountered it in the consequential form of the demonstration that I am undertaking: namely, that previously (before, but before what time, before time?), before the question of (the) *being* as such, of *esse* and *sum*, of *ego sum*, there is the question of following, of the persecution and seduction of the other, what/that I am (following) or who is following me, who is following me while I am (following) it, him, or her. It remains, if things are indeed as I think they are, that a certain conjuncture complicates the information given and deserves, no doubt, to be alluded to. While I had already caressed, in a sense, and even more or less polished everything that I am in the process of demonstrating for you, I fell less than ten days ago upon two citations that are more or less juxtaposed in an article by Michel Haar.[11]

The first is from a series of lines from Paul Valéry's "Silhouette of a Serpent." It interests me because the serpent from Genesis is speaking, and it says "I," naming thus, by designating itself, what will be for us one of the very forms of the question: ipseity, indeed *sui-referential egoity*, auto-affection and automotion, autokinesis, the autonomy that one recognizes in every animal: the very genesis of *zootobiography*. The serpent says "I," but doesn't say, as I do, the animal that I am. Listen to it hiss, for Valéry has it say, insisting on it, "I hiss":

Beast I am, but a sharp one,
Whose venom however vile
Can far out-vie the hemlock's wisdom[12]

That provided the occasion for me to reread this poem, differently. I must renounce doing it the justice it deserves here, in itself and in the complex intertwining of its voices. But if time allowed I would have liked to reflect on several of its motifs, that of disguise, in the first place. An "I" speaks, therefore, and presents itself as the "(stupid) beast [that] I am." Yet it speaks in order to denounce itself. It confesses. But it confesses also by presenting itself as "the most cunning of animals." This cunning master of nakedness dissimulated at the origin of desire begins by avowing: I am lying, I am an other, and here are the animal guises by means of which I disguise myself in "animal simplicity," showing and hiding at the same time what is in truth neither so much animal nor simple, nor, in any case, the identity of a single and simple animal:

The blue sky in its splendor sharpens
This wyvern who disguises me
In animal simplicity[13]

Let me remind you that the wyvern [*guivre*] is a fantastic animal (and every animal, as distinct from *l'animot*, is essentially fantastic, phantasmatic, fabulous, of a fable that speaks to us and speaks to us of ourselves, especially where a fabulous animal, that is to say, a speaking animal, speaks of itself to say "I," and in saying "I," always, *de te fabula narratur*). The wyvern, like the chimera, is an animal in three: there are still three, if it can be said, in the same piece, in the same body: body of a serpent, of course, but with piglet's feet and bat's wings.

The other motif I would have liked to analyze is that of the abyss, and thus of the vertigo that we could find recurrently concerning the animal, notably in Rilke and Heidegger. I am getting lost again in the chasm that I see opening, for my part, wherever I, wherever the "I" crosses gazes—to the point of drowning there—with the animal that sees me see it seeing me naked. In Valéry the abyss attracts the "I am," if you like, on two sides [*bords*], the side of the "I" or "me as self," and the side of being and of the "I am." The edge of being, and therefore of the being that I am, in the first place because what is here called the "animal abyss" is not a hole, a gulf, but too much being and the fact that there is being rather than nothing:

> Skies, his blunder! Time, his undoing!
> And the animal abyss agape! . . .
> What a collapse into origin,
> Glitters in place of total void![14]

The animal abyss, the vertigo of the beast that says "(stupid) beast [that] I am," brings to light not nonbeing but being, a spark in the place of nothingness, stand-in in place of the nothingness that I am [*étincelle au lieu de néant, lieu tenant du néant que je suis*]. If dizziness is still a function of emptiness, of a lack, defect, or privation, then it will make the head spin wherever there is something rather than where there is nothing. For in Valéry's terms the defect is being rather than nothingness. It is in this poem, which is uttered from the place of a snare, from the site of the *ego sum* of the serpent, that "most cunning of animals," that the famous stanza echoes out, turned or coiled upon itself:

> And loftiest of all my snares,
> You protect all hearts from knowing
> That the universe is merely a blot
> On the pure void of Non-being![15]

The being standing in place of nonbeing, this *milieu* that derives from nothingness, is me, the most cunning of animals, on the other side of vertigo, but of the same vertigo of the animal abyss, since it is I, the Self who self-reflects and says "(as for) me I am," and "beast I am." Listen to Me, this little word *Me* written here not just with a capital letter but wholly upper case at the beginning of the line, the three letters of the little word *Moi* so enlarged, as this pronoun or forename is presented as the first word from the Verb:

> Glitters in place of total void! . . .
> But the first syllable of his Word
> Was ME! . . . The proudest of the stars
> Uttered by the besotted maker,
> I am! . . . Shall be! . . . I illuminate
> How divinity was diminished
> By all the fires of the Seducer![16]

Everything leads one to think, therefore, that the all-powerful and seductive ruse of the serpent comes down to speaking as God in the place of God, of the besotted creator, miming Jehovah's "I am that I am," "I am what I am [*Ehieh acher ehieh*]," which is sometimes also formed in the future ("I am he who will be"), in terms of a promise to breach the purity of nothingness with a performative. Here the serpent says "Me! . . . I am! . . . I will be! . . . I am he who . . ." This show of force [*coup de force*] within the show of force produces nothing other and nothing less than being in the place of nothingness, namely the first impurity (the contamination of being, one might say, seriously perverting, for effect, Levinas's words). The show of force, the tour de force, consists in turning this ontological creation, creation itself, into an act of seduction. This self-engendering act of the "I am," this autobiographogenesis, is in its essence an act of seduction. Being becomes seduction, that is, the ruse of the most *rusé* of animals. "I am" becomes what it will have been, namely, the seduction of a seducer. One who says: I am He who is, who follows you and whom you are (following), who is (following) after you with a view to seducing you and to have it be that, coming after, you become one who follows me:

> Glitters in place of total void! . . .
> But the first syllable of his Word
> Was ME! . . . The proudest of the stars
> Uttered by the besotted maker,
> I am! . . . Shall be! . . . I illuminate
> How divinity was diminished
> By all the fires of the Seducer!

Later, "I am" is hissed out again, in mockery as the serpent repeats:

> I am He [theological, zoo-theo-morphic, auto-zoo-theo-morphic
> upper case] who modifies
> . . .
> In the depths of that very pleasure
> I'm the inimitable flavor
> You find that you alone possess![17]

"I am He who modifies" comes after a sort of hissing and mocking curse that vents in the direction of nomination itself, at the Name who creates beings, and who creates "stark naked humans" in his own likeness ("you are human, and stark naked, / Oh snow-white sanctimonious beasts!"[18]).

Why have I followed this thread of the onto-logical ruse as ruse of the animal that says "I am," "beast I am"? In order to draw attention to an opportunity that Michel Haar seems not to have noticed, for he shows no sign of having done so. Shortly after the quotation from "Silhouette of a Serpent" he cites some lines from Apollinaire in which the serpent is addressed, in "The Song of the Poorly Loved." But there it isn't the serpent who speaks in order to announce the being of an "I am" ("beast I am"), rather someone who, from the other side, speaking of himself while looking at the serpent, says "you follow me." Precisely not "you are" but "you follow me," "you are following me, persecuting me, pursuing me." What takes place here is but an exchange of places and a symmetrical swapping of sites of utterance, the substitution of following for being, of "you follow me" for "I am." As though the serpent were a face-to-face other. But it is nothing of the kind. The one who speaks addresses the serpent as if addressing himself, speaking reflexively to the other as to a shadow of oneself:

> And you who follow me crawling along
> God of my gods dead in autumn
> You measure how much sway
> The earth by right accords me
> My shadow my ancient snake[19]

This is the speech of a poorly loved one speaking of itself: the specular animalization of the autobiographical signature and of self-presentation would be merely one of the currents that should require us to relate "The Song of the Poorly Loved," in the context of one possible reading among many, to a great medieval tradition. Richard de Fournival's *Bestiaires d'amours* (*Bestiary of Love*) inscribes a large population of animal figures within the discourse of love. Yet its specular or narcissistic organization doesn't fulfill only the role prescribed by the explicit reference to Aristotelian mimesis that opens the volume, the mimesis that precisely remains, according to Aristotle, proper to the human. Since I am unable to undertake as close a reading of the *Bestiaires d'amours* as it deserves, I shall simply draw to your attention a sample passage that animalizes the image of self, as if the poet were confiding in us as an autobiographical animal. He confesses, but, being the Christian that he is, he also confesses the sin of confession, avowing the narcissism that is involved in writing on oneself, even in order to avow and to show oneself in one's nakedness. Naked as a beast. And then, being a writer who is fascinated by what he himself writes, by his self-distancing [*autotélique*] relation to himself, he compares himself to a tiger or, rather, to the female tiger who, being so taken by her own image in the mirror, would forget about her young offspring:

> Yes indeed I was captured more through my sight than the tiger is captivated before a mirror, for however enraged she may be when her young are stolen from her, if she happens upon a mirror she is forced to fix her eyes upon it. And she takes so much pleasure in looking at the great beauty of her beautiful form that she forgets to pursue the ones who have stolen her young from her, and she stays there as if caught in a trap.[20]

When one has to confess to the narcissism of confession, one admits that guilt, and even the lie and perjury, are lodged within veracity itself, within the heart of promise, in the naked and intransitive simplicity of the "I am," which already conceals its transitive interest, the following of an "I am following": I am (following) someone else, I am followed by someone else, I pursue a desire or a project, I hunt and chase myself at the same time, I do, me.

But as for me, the guilty innocent one, the accused presumed innocent and guilty at the same time, I who confesses even to the sin of confession, who am I (following), as I was asking before? It is important that this question resonate here in the French language: *Qui suis-je?* or *Que suis-je?* Who or what am I (following)?

✣

Let us come back to the original moment, to the first version of this sentence, which in French is already a translation: "But as for me, who am I, now that . . ." The little word *suis* doesn't come from Descartes' pen, at the moment he is writing, in Latin, the second of the *Meditationes de prima philosophia*, following the fiction of the *genium aliquem malignum*, that is, the evil demon [*Malin Génie*], a cunning genius as the most cunning of the animals, which we could, in turn, summon to appear in the vicinity of our zoobiographical genesis.

The young Duc de Luynes, son of Louis XIII's minister, introduced the little word *suis* when he imported into French, by means of his translation, a text that did without any explicit recourse to the verb *to be*. The word *suis*, or rather *sum*, remained silent in Latin: "Quid autem nunc, ubi suppono *deceptorem* aliquem potentissimum, & si fas est dicere, malignum, data opera in omnibus, quantum potuit, me delusisse?" which, once translated—at which time the little word *suis* makes its presence felt—becomes: "But as for me, whom am I [*qui suis-je*], now that I am supposing that there is some supremely powerful and, if it is permissible to say so, malicious deceiver, who is deliberately trying to trick me in every way he can?"[21] The relation between the two versions, as well as the event of the "am I," cannot be docilely read as an effect of translation between an original and a second version, a source and a target language. The translation is a return to Descartes' mother tongue and, what is more, according to Baillet he checked the translation:

> Under the pretext of looking over these versions he took the liberty himself of correcting and clarifying his own thinking. As a result, having found several places where he considered that he hadn't made his sense clear enough in Latin for all manner of persons, he undertook to clarify things in the translation by means of several minor changes, something that is easy to recognize once one compares the French with the Latin.[22]

Let us not forget that in the logical sequential order [*séquence conséquente de l'ordre*] of the reasons he gives, Descartes had already suspended his confidence in the definition of self as "man" and even as "rational animal." As he sees it, such definitions are not indubitable. I believe that one has to attach the greatest importance to that moment of suspension. It is not a matter of purely rhetorical precaution, and we will question its modern heritage, especially in Heidegger. Having affirmed "But I do not yet have a sufficient understanding of what I am, even as I am certain that I am [*moi qui suis certain que je suis; nondum vero satis intelligo, quisnam sim ego ille, qui jam necessario sum*]," Descartes eliminates any previous affirmations or beliefs that are not "certain and unshakeable [*indubitables*]." He eliminates them all of a sudden, so as not to waste time, he says, by compounding the questions. It is a lesson that I should take to heart, but as you can see, if one doesn't give oneself the necessary time, one always ends up running the risk of limiting the number of necessary questions. For the sake of such time saving, of giving or not giving oneself time, of the simplicity of a direct trajectory in any case, Descartes will, with all due rigor, do without his definition of the human in the combined terms of animality and rationality, of man as rational animal. There is in his gesture a moment of rupture with respect to the tradition, a rupture for which Descartes is not given credit often enough, not even by Heidegger, who, in his "Letter on 'Humanism,'" calls into question the definition of man as rational animal. In his eyes not a single philosopher within the tradition is excluded from what he reads as a "metaphysical interpretation," which, while not false, remains "conditioned by metaphysics" and by all the successive versions of humanism up to the moment when, in 1946, he is writing the following, in a context and according to a gesture to which we will have to return:

> The first humanism, Roman humanism, and every kind that has emerged from that time to the present, has presupposed the most universal "essence" of the human being to be obvious. The human being is considered to be an *animal rationale*. This definition is not simply the Latin translation of the Greek *zōon logon echon*, but rather a metaphysical interpretation of it. This essential definition [*Diese Wesensbestimmung*] of the human being is not false. But it is conditioned by metaphysics. The essential provenance of metaphysics, and not just its limits, became questionable [*frag-würdig*] in *Being and Time*.[23]

We shall have to return to this gesture of Heidegger. But for the moment let us keep in mind that Descartes the Roman was already saying, in his own way, in Latin, something that similarly made things questionable. According to a trajectory that differs in highly significant ways but that, in the end, is perhaps less irreducible than it seems, the *Meditations* suspends this definition of man as rational animal. Here, then, is how Descartes cuts things off when, in one blow, to economize, to save time, he eliminates everything that isn't "certain and indubitable":

> What then did I formerly think I was? A man. But what is a man? Shall I say a 'rational animal'? No; for then I should have to inquire what an animal is, what rationality is, and in this way one question would lead me down the slope to other harder ones, and I wouldn't like to waste the little time and leisure that remains to me by using it to disentangle subtleties of this kind. (*M*, 17)

If I want to hold onto and present what I am, and who I am, it is necessary to begin, therefore, by suspending this common definition of the "rational animal." "I am," in the purity of its intuition and thinking, excludes animality, even if it is rational. In the passage that follows this bracketing of the rational animal, Descartes proposes abstracting from his "I am," if I can put it this way, everything that recalls life. He had previously declared the need to keep separate from this "I am" everything that could be "something else" other than me: "But I do not yet have a sufficient understanding of what this 'I' is [*ce que je suis*], that now necessarily exists [*moi qui suis certain que je suis*]. So I must be on my guard against carelessly taking something else to be this 'I'" (ibid.). Descartes' prudence not only incites him to abstract from the "I am" his own living body, which, in a way, he objectivizes as a machine or corpse (these are his words); so much so that his "I am" can apprehend and present itself only from the perspective of this potential cadaverization, that is to say, from the perspective of an "I am mortal," or "already dead," or "destined to die," indeed "toward death": "Well the first thought to come to mind was that I had a face, hands, arms, and the whole mechanical structure [*toute cette machine*] of limbs which can be seen in a corpse, and which I called the body" (ibid.).

He goes further: each time that, in the name of experience, he has to evoke these signs of life or animation—therefore of animality—constituted by the auto-affection or auto-motion of feeling *oneself*, feeding *oneself*, moving *oneself*, he relates them to a living soul that, as such, and in order to remain objectivizable, can only be a body, "something tenuous [*extrêmement rare and subtile*], like a wind or fire or ether, which permeated my more solid parts" (ibid.). Descartes is, moreover, surprised (with a surprise that will motivate his whole interpretation of the union of soul and body) by a soul that is in no way like a pilot in his ship. While not ignoring the necessity and difficulty of that gesture, I won't follow it here, careful as I am to clearly delineate a very particular sequence, namely, that which, in order to define access to a pure "I am," must suspend or, rather, detach, precisely as detachable, all reference to life, to the life of the body, and to animal life. A little further along Descartes posits thinking as the only undetachable thing within the "I am": "Thinking? At last I have discovered it—thought; this alone is inseparable [*ne peut être détachée*] from me. I am, I exist—that is certain. But for how long? For as long as I am thinking" (18). The presence to itself of the present of thinking, the presence that presents itself to itself in the present, that is what excludes everything detachable constituted by life, the living body, animal life.

"But what then am I?" Descartes then wonders on the next page. Response: "a thing that thinks" (19). And what happens immediately thereafter concerning the animal itself within the famous analysis of the piece of wax that closely follows "I am a thing that thinks"? This piece of wax has just been "taken from the hive" says Descartes, removed, therefore, from the bees, but "it has not yet quite lost the taste of the honey" (20). Yet everything about the piece of wax that doesn't derive distinctly from "the scrutiny of the mind alone" (21), everything that falls within the ambit of the senses, everything that is known by means of the exterior senses, and even "'common' sense," (as they call it, Descartes makes clear, "that is, the power of imagination"), all that, all that sensible exteriority is something that animals are capable of. The least animal is capable of it: "for what distinctness was there in my earlier perception? Was there anything in it which wouldn't fall in the same way within the sense of the least animal?" (22). What is it then that escapes the sense of "the least animal?" Extension, the intelligible rather than sensible wax, as is well known. But is it insignificant that Descartes then denotes that intelligible extension as a denuded body, an undressed body, according to the figure of nakedness stripped bare, that of a pure body, in the sense of purely extended, and hence purified because I, as mind, as a human mind, would have divested it of its sensible finery [*parures*] or facing [*parements*]; namely, of what, in it, remains animal or exposed to animality? As if it were non-nudity, sensible clothing that resided henceforth on the side of animality? As for the wax itself, in its essential attribute, namely, its intelligible extension, it remains invisible and untouchable! In order, therefore, to gain access to the *je suis* as human and not animal mind, it is necessary to undress the wax. Have you ever tried to undress wax? That would be the condition, in any case, for establishing "even more effectively the nature of my own mind": "But when I distinguish the wax from its outward forms—take the clothes off, as it were, and consider it naked—then although my judgment may still contain errors, at least my perception now requires a human mind" (22).

The animal that I am not, the animal that in my very essence I am not, Descartes says, in short, presents itself as a human mind before naked wax. And it is from the perspective of this "not," from the point of view of my not being an animal, from where I do what the least animal could not do, that Descartes is going to *set his sights on* [prendre en vue] the animal. To bring it into view, therefore, from the point of view that is his and from where the animal doesn't look at or concern him. Can we say all the same that he will have been an animal philosopher [*philosophe animalier*]?

(A parenthesis: one should, though I won't do it here, summon this naked wax to appear before the company of all the specters and phantoms that come to haunt Descartes' dreams, in the first place, in the *Second Meditation*:

> And this might lead me to conclude without more ado that knowledge of the wax comes from what the eye sees, and not from the scrutiny of the mind alone. But then if I look out of the window and see men crossing the square, as I just happen to have done, I normally say that I see the men themselves, just as I say that I see the wax. Yet do I see any more than hats and coats which could conceal specters or counterfeit men who move only thanks to clockwork [*ressorts*]? I *judge* that they are men. And so something which I thought I was seeing with my eyes is in fact grasped solely by the faculty of judgment which is in my mind. (21)

Then, at the end of the *Sixth Meditation*, where, between waking and sleeping Descartes worries, once again in the context of man, of the "real man," about the simulacrum and spectral pretence:

> If, while I am awake, anyone were suddenly to appear to me and then disappear immediately, as happens in sleep, so that I could not see where he had come from or where he had gone to, it would not be unreasonable for me to judge that he was a ghost [*spectre*], or a vision [*fantôme*] created in my brain, rather than a real man. (61–62)

The specter to be conjured by judgment is, as you will have noted, always the mechanical simulacrum of the "real man," that is to say, spectral man as animal-machine, this animal-machine that we are getting closer to in order to try to flush him out by another means.)

I suppose that a historian of philosophy might one day wonder, as a historian of painting or sculpture might, whether within the classification of genres there existed the category of animal philosopher. There are animal painters and sculptors. One also speaks of animal literature, as though animality defined not only a kingdom, species, or genus, but an artistic genre. Why not a philosophical genre? Why could one not speak of an animal philosophy? And would there be essential reasons for this lacuna, if a lacuna is what it is? Descartes did all he could to avoid being an animal philosopher.

Right in the middle of my announced title, such as it first imprinted itself within me, "the animal that I am (following)," the idea came to me, just recently as I was saying, to inscribe a conjunction with a more or less syllogistic or expletive value, the animal that *therefore* I am. I might have been commemorating Mallarmé's *Igitur*. Perhaps insufficient attention has been paid to the zoology that obsessively resides in that poem. As is well known, *Igitur* refers quite deliberately, and precisely in line with Mallarmé's intentions, to Genesis, just after the creation of the animals and before that of man, who will be commanded to tame and name the other living creatures ("Igitur perfecti sunt coeli et terra et omnis ornatus eorum"). Mallarmé's work (*Igitur or the Madness of Elbehnon*,[24] referring in Hebrew to the sons of Elohim, the creative powers of Jehovah) recalls first of all, through the mirrors that reflect hour by hour throughout the text, "the infinite chance of conjunctions" (92), the memory of Hamlet the narcissist's race. At the moment he says "the account of my life I have to render you" (97), Igitur allows his self—his specular "perception" (97) of self, as he says, or again "consciousness" (97) of self, his *cogito*, in short, his *cogito sum*—to be haunted by a whole zoomorphic clan, by a "spider's ruff" (97), "spidery thread" (95), a "beating of absurd wings" (94), a "flutter" (96), all sorts of winged creatures that bring to mind bats but also "monsters" and chimeras. The word *chimera* occurs on at least four occasions in order to punctuate the relation to self of a phantom, precisely what is called the "scansion [*scandement*] of my measure" (97), or, a second time, the scansion of the "progress of my character" (96). And it is in fact a spectral drama of a mortal's autobiography that is caught in its mirror or surprised in its sepulcher in full genesis, before man and in the midst of chimerical animals.

But I wasn't thinking primarily of *Igitur* when I inserted this "therefore" in the middle of *the animal that I am*. This "therefore" is an *ergo*. And the expletive conjunction is designed not to commemorate but in the form of a summons issued to Descartes.

Furtive, placed in the very center (four letters between four or five words[25]) of a proposition that the signatory-subject relates to himself, at least affecting thereby to exhibit himself, index turned in the direction of one who says "I," this slight prosthesis, therefore, would not be designed solely to underline a sequence or the consequence of what follows. It would not in the first place call for following or pursuing, or even citing, in order to celebrate it, the *ergo sum*, the *donc je suis* of someone who, from the *Discourse on Method* to the *Meditations*, no doubt cleared the path of autobiographilosophical narration, of self-presentation as philosophical presentation, yet of someone who doubted to the level of hyperbole but never doubted—within a so-called mechanicist tradition that was also that of La Mettrie and so many others—that the animal was only a machine, even going so far as to make of this indubitability a sort of condition for doubting, that of the *ego* as such, as *ego dubito*, as *ego cogito*, and therefore as *ego sum*. The relation to itself of the soul and of thinking, that very being of the thinking substance, implied the concept of an animal-machine deprived of what would be, in short, nothing less than the *ego* as *ego cogito, je pense*. Such an automaton would be deprived of a "me" or "self," and even more of any capacity for reflection, indeed of any mark or autobiographical impression of its own life. Taking this grand mechanicist—and what is also called materialist—tradition back to the drawing board should not involve a reinterpretation of the living creature called "animal" only, but also another concept of the machine, of the semiotic machine, if it can be called that, of artificial intelligence, of cybernetics and zoo- and bio-engineering, of the *genic* in general, etc.

A question of a word. One will return to it often, in a thousand different ways; it will be as much a matter of the question of the word as of a question of words. And of knowing what a word, and what the word *word* means. Of knowing whether one can answer for it.

By inserting the hinge of this little *word* in French, the animal that *therefore* I am, I would like for my part to revive the memory, modestly, in a very limited way, of a letter by René Descartes, a letter dating from March 1638, the year following the *Discourse on Method*. Not, therefore, the grand theatrical chain of *cogito ergo sum*, nor the fifth part of the *Discourse on Method* concerning monkeys, magpies, and parrots, automata that would never be able to "answer" or, even if they could "utter words," would be incapable of doing so "by *witnessing* [my italics] to the fact that they are thinking what they are saying." An equivocal value for *witnessing*, an attestation that Descartes perhaps misuses immediately thereafter, when he concludes:

> On the other hand, men born deaf and dumb, and thus deprived of their speech-organs as much as the beasts or even more so, normally invent their own signs to make themselves understood by those who, being regularly in their company, have the time to learn their language. This *witnesses* [my italics] not merely to the fact that the beasts have less reason than men, but that they have no reason at all. . . . it would be *incredible* [my italics again] that a superior specimen of the monkey or parrot species should not be able to speak as well as the stupidest child—or at least as well as the child with a defective brain—if their souls were not completely different in nature from ours. And we must not confuse speech with the natural movements which *witness to* [my italics again] passions and which can be imitated by machines as well as by animals. Nor should we think, like some of the ancients, that the beasts speak, although we do not understand their language.[26]

Other than the word *credible* ("it would be incredible"), I have twice emphasized "witnessing." It seems to have been chosen with calculated insistence by a Descartes who thereby introduces, from another point of view—namely, of the *Discourse* he is writing—this auto-biographilosophy "in French, my native language," so that it would be accessible to all those who use only their "natural reason" (*D*, 151) and, as he makes clear elsewhere, "intelligible in part even to women."[27] I call your attention to this French word "witnessing [*témoignage*]" for more than one reason. First, because it is a key word for what is commonly called autobiography, often held to be a testimony. All autobiography presents itself as a testimony: I say or write what I am, saw, see, feel, hear, touch, think; and vice versa, every testimony presents itself as autobiographical truth: I promise the truth concerning what I, myself, have perceived, seen, heard, felt, lived, thought, etc. Second, because Descartes indeed seems to use the word *witnessing* in an equivocal and dogmatic way at the very moment when, on the one hand, he is affirming that "we see" (testimony, therefore) that magpies and parrots cannot "witness to the fact that they are thinking what they are saying," and where, on the other hand, still translating testimony into proof, he concludes that "this witnesses not merely to the fact that the beasts have less reason than men, but that they have no reason at all. . . . it would be incredible that a superior specimen of the monkey or parrot species should not be able to speak as well as the stupidest child."

Among all the "one sees / we see" that appeal so often to an evidence that is presumed to be commonly shared, even to good sense, this French word *témoignage* seems all the more ambiguous within this—almost the first—French autobiographilosophy, once one compares its usage with that in the *Meditations* some years later, more particularly, in comparing the original version of the *Meditations* written in Latin, as I recalled earlier, and the French translation by the Duc de Luynes. For this translation, as submitted to Descartes, thrice uses the single verb *témoigner* in order to translate three different Latin verbs, which refer to a discursive or logical mode that is each time different.

1. *On the one hand*, there is the mode of attestation properly speaking, even if *testatur*, translated as *témoigne* in the *Fourth Meditation*, has only a very confused testimonial sense: "the will to deceive is undoubtedly evidence of [*testatur*] malice or weakness, and so cannot apply to God" (*M*, 37). I quote this sentence in order to introduce the question of knowing whether what one calls the animal can, any more than God, seek to deceive and whether it is capable, of its own accord, of evil or malice. Lacan, for example, thinks the animal can pretend, certainly, but not deceive,

which is to say, according to his argumentation, that it could not lie, pretend to pretend, mislead by telling the truth (this will later raise serious stakes for us). The question of evil, of radical evil, seems inseparable from the traditional double figure of the animal, either as incarnating innocence, the incapacity for malicious desire, or, on the contrary, being demonic, satanic, apocalyptic.

2. *On the other hand*, in the same *Fourth Meditation*, the word *témoignent* is used to render the mode of demonstrative argument [*arguunt*]: "my errors (for these are the only evidence of [*arguunt*] some imperfection in me)" (*M*, 39).

3. Finally, in the *Sixth Meditation*, *témoignent* translates the mode of proof, of what is properly *probation* [probant]. There, it is precisely a matter of the "'common' sense [*sensus communis*]," which, through the intermediary of the brain, "presents the same signals to the mind [*menti idem exhibit*], even though the other parts of the body may be in a different condition at the time. This is established by [*comme le témoignent*] countless observations, which there is no need to review here [*ut probant innumera experimenta, quae hic recensere non est opus*]" (*M*, 59–60).

Whenever someone invokes an infinity of experiences that "witness to," or which one can testify to, but which "there is here no need to review," an animal I know well feels his ear cocking. Why would there be no need to review them?

One would have to follow this lexicon or semantics of witnessing with more of a nose, but also with an eye to its consequences throughout Descartes' discursive chain and order of reasons. As I was suggesting just now, the testimonial experience that, by definition, knows no limit within the field of discourse is, by destination, autobiographical. It has a vocation for autobiography. Moreover—something that would be at the same time ambitious and modest—everything I wish to confide in you here today derives from the testimonial mode. I would like to keep myself within the limits, however obscure, I admit, of a confession, one that will relate, directly or indirectly, not an infinity of experiences but this or that experience about which I'll say, contrary to the gesture of Descartes to which I have just referred, that there is a need to relate them here: *quae hic recensere opus est.*

This formula of the animal that *therefore* I am (following), which should not depict the immobile representation of a self-portrait but rather set me racing breathless after a round of traces, engaged in a kinetics or cynegetics, the cinematography of a persecution, a chase in pursuit of this animal that therefore I am or that I am supposed to be following as I relate my experiences, resonates less, as I was saying just now, with the grand moments of *je pense donc je suis* (in the *Discourse* or in the *Meditations*) than with what seems to lie in wait around the corner of a famous letter from March 1638. There, as Descartes again picks up and develops the hypothesis of the automatons, a year after the arguments of the *Discourse*, with the allegation regarding nonresponse inscribed this time within the structure of question and answer ("never, unless it be by chance, do these automatons *respond* [my italics], either with words or even with signs, concerning what is asked of them"[28]), he employs his demonstration, as always, in the service of a critique of infantile prejudice. What is puerile, and faulty, in his eyes, is not a spontaneous belief but a judgment that thinks it can be based on such an immature opinion. Moreover, the said spontaneous belief is not in question concerning "the resemblance between most of the actions of animals and our own" (for such a resemblance is incontestable, even in the eyes of Descartes, who never contests it as such). What is subject to critique here, according to him, what one should be wary of as one would be wary of an infantile opinion, is the passage from outside to inside, belief in the possibility of inducing from this *exterior* resemblance an *interior* analogy, namely, the presence in the animal of a soul, of sentiments and passions like our own. That is the prejudice of children or of "feeble minds." Descartes therefore shows himself to be very prudent. He doesn't cast doubt on the resemblance between animal and human but on the judgment or opinion that is induced from it. And it is there that he advances the hypothesis of a world inhabited at first by a man who is presumed never to have seen an animal—"would never have seen any animals other than men." This purely methodological fiction could be extracted, temporarily, from such a Cartesian reasoning in order to point us in the direction of two other questions, both of which open onto their own ends, not the ends of man but the ends of the animal.

1. First, a phenomenological end of sorts, an eidetic end. Can one, even in the name of fiction, think of a world without animals, or at the very least a world poor in animals, to play without playing with Heidegger's formula, discussion of which awaits us, according to which the animal is "poor in world" (*weltarm*)? Does animality participate in every concept of the world, even of the human world? Is being-with-the-animal a fundamental and irreducible structure of being-in-the-world, so much so that the idea of a world without animals could not even function as a methodological fiction? What would being-with-the-animal mean? What is the company of the animal? Is it something that occurs, secondarily, to a human being or to a *Dasein* that would seek to think itself before and

without the animal? Or is being-with-the-animal rather an essential structure of *Dasein*? And in that case, how is it to be interpreted and what consequences are to be drawn from it? Those are the questions that we will encounter again in dealing with Heidegger's text on the world and the animal, the animal that is poor in world (*weltarm*) and the *Dasein* that is world-forming (*weltbildend*). As we shall see, this question will be nothing other than that of the being-world of the world. What is the world? What does one call "world"? And is the presence of life, of animal life, essential or not to the mundanity of the world? The scope of this question will be clearer later on.

2. The horizon of the ends of the animal is not only a fiction in the service of phenomenology or of the eidetic analysis of a structure of the world or of *Dasein*. It is, if you'll permit me to say it, the horizon of a real hypothesis. For what brings this hypothesis of Descartes to the surface, even if it lasts only a moment and retains a sort of pedagogical or methodological value, is also a spectacle that is more plausible today than in the seventeenth century. This spectacle can develop only as the symptom of a desire or phantasm: the tableau of a world *after* animality, after a sort of holocaust, a world from which animality, at first present to man, would have one day disappeared: destroyed or annihilated by man, either purely and simply—something that seems almost impossible even if one feels we are heading down the path toward such a world without animals—or by means of a devitalizing or *disanimalizing* treatment, what others would call the denaturing of animality, the production of figures of animality that are so new that they appear monstrous enough to call for a change of name. This science fiction is more and more credible, having begun with taming and domestication, dressage, neutering, and acculturation, and is being pursued with medico-industrial exploitation, overwhelming interventions upon animal milieus and reproduction, genetic transplants, cloning, etc.

Let us leave those questions open and come back to Descartes' fiction. The man who "would never have seen any animals other than men" would nevertheless be capable, as *homo faber* or *technicus*, as engineer, of manufacturing automatons that resemble humans for some, and animals (a horse, a dog, a bird, says Descartes) for others, resembling them enough to be mistaken for them. They would walk, eat, even *breathe*—let's keep in mind this important point. They would "imitate" (Descartes' word) "as much as was possible, all the other actions of the animals they resembled, without excluding even the signs we use in order *to witness to* [again!] our passions, such as crying out when struck, or fleeing when there is a lot of noise around them."

Descartes does not, for his part, give any sign here that he paid attention to his own choices, to the examples of animals chosen by him, and especially not to the examples of imitated signs that he chose. The latter are both signs of *reaction* (I am saying "reaction" as one says "reaction to stimuli," and not "response," for everything is in play in the distinction between reaction and response), and in particular of reaction to harm. For Descartes does not seem to attribute any significance to the signs themselves, to the category of signs that he chooses. They are signs of reaction, and, as if by chance, they both manifest a misfortune, the pain or fear of a hunted animal, in essence persecuted, chased, maltreated; they are signs of an animal passion that are to be compared to signs of human passion ("without excluding even the signs we use in order to witness to our passions, such as crying out when struck, or fleeing when there is a lot of noise around them"). In the *princeps* passage, if we can call it that, of *Discourse on Method*, the passage that upholds the argument repeated in this letter, Descartes already spoke, as if by chance, of a machine that simulates the living animal so well that it "cries out that you are hurting it" (*D*, 140). That doesn't necessarily mean that René Descartes was insensitive to the suffering of animals. But here, he certainly wants to remain indifferent to the philosophical or ethical relevance of Bentham's question ("Can they suffer?"). Can they suffer? Perhaps, Descartes seems to say; yet, he would add, that is neither the question nor the interest of this hypothesis. And, moreover, the suffering of one's passion is not a true passion. For it is simply a matter of knowing whether the automatons in this hypothesis can allow us to conclude that there is a "true passion," a "true sentiment." The answer [*réponse*] is well known: no, and precisely because these automatons are incapable of *responding*. For immediately after evoking the possible resemblance between the signs we use "in order to witness to our passions," and those of automatons manufactured by a man who is henceforth having difficulty distinguishing between real living creatures and those who would merely have the external appearance of the same, Descartes proposes two criteria (he calls them two "methods"[29]) for discerning the true from the false, the authentic from the mimetic simulacrum of the automaton. These two means are those of the *Discourse on Method*. It is a question of two criteria that we will have to keep well in mind, for they will govern the *whole* tradition of discourses that I would like to outline later, all the way to Heidegger and Lacan: (1) nonresponse, the inability to respond, to respond to our questions, hence to hear our question marks; (2) a lack, defect, or general deficit, a deficiency that is nonspecific except to say that it is a lack that is incommensurable with lack, with all our lacking, all the deficiencies or impoverishments, all the privations that can affect us, even in cases of debility or madness. What the animal lacks, in its very perfection, what its defect is, is incommensurable with what is lacking in human imperfection, which in turn draws from this lack, from this incomparable defect, its superiority. I would add to these two traits, which I would like to emphasize in the passage that I am going to read, the following one, which in my eyes does not count less, in my eyes and from the point of view of the eye. It concerns the theoretical animal, if I can call it that, the objectivizing staging of the animal of theory, the animal as it is seen, and not the animal that sees, the animal as a thing to be observed, object for a human who says "I," "I am," or "we," "we are." Descartes appeals to a man who sees an animal that doesn't see him. I am going to italicize several words in passing within this fragment that belongs to the staging of this programmer [*informaticien*] of artificial intelligences who is unable to discern, among his own automatons, between true and false passions, because the signs resemble each other so:

> without excluding even the signs we use in order to witness to our passions, such as crying out when struck, or fleeing when there is a lot of noise around them, etc., with the result that he would often be prevented from discerning among the real men those who had merely the external appearance of them; and whom experience would have taught that, in order to recognize them, there are but the two means that I have explained on page 57 of my *Method*: of which one is that never, unless it be by chance, do these automatons *respond* [my italics], either with words or even with signs, concerning what is *asked* [my italics] of them [*ce dont on les* interroge]; and the other that although the movements that they make are often more regular and more certain than those of the wisest men, they nevertheless *lack* [my italics] several things that they should do in order to imitate us, more than would the most senseless of men. I say that we must consider what judgment this man would make of the animals that are among us were he to *see* [my italics] them.[30]

Further down on the same page we find a literal reference to the animal that is seen, the animal exposed to theoretical spectacle, object for a human who says "I am," spectacle for a specular subject who reflects his essence and who does not find, or does not want to find himself reflected in the image of the animal that he looks at but that doesn't look at him. There we have something *certain and indubitable*:

> Now there is no doubt that this man, *seeing* the animals that are among us [I am emphasizing according to the same formula as

above: *seeing* the animals that are nevertheless *among us*], and noting in their actions the same two things that make them different from ours, which he would have a habit of noticing in his automatons, would not *judge* [my italics] that there was in them any *true senti-ment*, or any *true passion* [my italics], as there is in us, but simply that they were automatons.[31]

The scene and logic of the argument seem to me more strange than has been most often noted. Here we have a character, a man, and this man is a man who, having learned, fictitiously, to manufacture impeccable au-tomatons, would conclude *in reality*, by means of a judgment, that the animals are *in truth*, for their part, automatons, automatons of flesh and blood. And why is this so? Because they *resemble* automatons that *resemble* humans. And this conclusion, let us never forget, follows from a judg-ment. By definition it can in no way be a sentiment, perception, or affect; it is an inferred judgment, an act of understanding tied to the will, an infinite will, as always in Descartes, which extends beyond the ends of understanding. This judgment is at the same time a judicative proposition and a verdict, a sentence [*arrêt*] concerning where the animal stops, the limit at which it comes to a halt, must stop or be arrested, namely, on the threshold of the response, before the response, on this side of a certain essence of the response. But let us leave there that other abyss of the *autos* and ipseity, of autokinesis and automotion, to whose heart, between the law of nature (reaction) and the law of freedom (response and responsibil-ity), we must surrender.[32]

Why has this well-known argumentation been found so shocking, and why does it continue to shock the shared good sense that it nevertheless exposes and translates? The reason is that it comes to interrupt long his-torical debates, an enormous play of intricate theses and antitheses, which here I have had to decide to treat through recourse to paralepsis. An inter-minable conversation already involved all those, from Plutarch to Por-phyry and Montaigne, most often against Aristotle and the Stoics, who never stopped debating in every way the questions that Descartes finally settled, with the cavalier gesture of a "French cavalier," with so much authority. Concerning the simple question of the response, for example, concerning the simple and abyssal question of knowing what "respond-ing" means, in the first place between human and animal, there had al-ready been numerous responses before Descartes, who no doubt knew of them at the moment he brought the discussion to a close. When he takes up the argument of the *Discourse* again in this letter, it probably isn't by chance that Descartes adds a detail—and that is at least one of the reasons why I preferred first to pay attention to the letter rather than to the canonical passage from the *Discourse*. In the latter text it is said that a machine simulating a monkey or "some other animal that lacks reason" (*D*, 139) could not, on the one hand, "declare [its] thoughts to others" as we do, or, on the other, even given the hypothesis of a perfected machine that would be endowed with speech (we could today think of a somewhat rudimentary answering machine), would it ever be able to "put together" words, "produce different arrangements of words so as to give an appropriately meaningful answer to whatever is said in its presence, as the dullest of men can do" (*D*,140). Yet even if Descartes could not have imagined in their refinements, capacity, and complexity all the powers of reaction-response that today we can, and tomorrow we should be better and better able to attribute to machines, and to another concept of the machine, he must have sensed the risk of his both vague and limited definition of the field of response ("whatever is said in its presence"). In the letter, it is no longer simply a matter of an inability, on the part of the animal, to respond to whatever is said in its presence, which could be a call, an order, a noise—to which, Descartes knew full well, the animal "responds" or reacts—but of responses to questions, questioning concerning "what is asked of them." As though the animal were certainly able to respond, to react to a call or an order, to the sign of its name, for example, but certainly not able, even by means of mechanically programmed words, to respond to a question. The question of the response is thus that of the question, of the response as response to a question that, at one and the same time, would remain unprogrammable and leave to the other alone the freedom to respond, presuming that were possible (a techno-historical field with a bright future, even though the programmation of question and response seems to foreclose the future). The Cartesian animal, like its descendants (once again I'll try to recognize there Kant, Heidegger, Lacan, and Levinas, which also means so many others), would remain incapable of responding to true questioning. For it lacks the power of real questions. What is this interest in a true question, that is the whole question, that which has been subsequently determined—no sooner said than done—as the question of the *logos*, of reason, being, and the other?

In deciding on the limit of the animal as limit to the response, Descartes himself responds, and offers a retort, to the repertoire [*argumentaire*] of a whole tradition. I shall mark just one of its points of reference, in Porphyry's inexhaustible survey of the ethics of vegetarianism in Antiquity, and of all the preceding philosophical debates (Pythagoreanism, Platonism, Stoicism, Epicureanism) that take place around relations of community, rights, duty, justice, etc., which do or do not bind men to other living creatures. At a particular moment in his marvelous and capacious *Peri apokhēs*, Porphyry insists on the *animot*'s capacity to listen to a voice and respond to it. *Upakouō*, precisely so ambiguously, has the following senses: I hear, I listen, I respond, I respond to a question but also to an invitation or a command, I obey, *I present* myself in response to a call, an interrogation, an order, a summons, or an injunction. *I present myself* is at the same time the first autobiographical gesture and the gesture of all the "Here-I-am's" in the history of the law. Now, even when it is mute, Porphyry's *animot* seems capable of what I *do* when I *say* upakouō. It is capable of doing what I say I am doing even if, for its part, it doesn't say so:

> It is reported [*istoreitai*] that even some voiceless [*tōn aphtoggōn*] animals readily respond to their masters [*upakouein tois despotais*], more so than a human friend would. A lamprey which belonged to the Roman Crassus would come to him when called by name [*onomasti kaloumene*], and had such an effect on him that he mourned when it died, though he had earlier borne with moderation the loss of three children. [Plutarch, one of Porphyry's very numerous sources, said "mourned more than Domitius Ahenobarbus upon the death of his three wives."]

A little later, Porphyry enlarges still more the field of response and recognizes it as belonging to the animal:

> Nor are animals unaware of the voice of humans [*anthropōn phone*], whether the humans are angry or friendly or calling, whether the voice is hunting or wanting something or giving something, in short, whatever it is doing: to every one they respond appropriately [*alla pasais oikieiōs upekousan*: they respond to everything in an appropriate manner].[33]

Other reasons have led to my preference for highlighting this letter by Descartes rather than, once again, his *Discourse on Method*. For the letter seeks itself to be a response, it presents itself in response to certain questions, a deferred or mediated response. Descartes writes to his interlocutor in order to propose that the latter transmit his response to his friend: "since that is what he wanted, I shall trouble you to pass on to him my responses."[34] Consequently, and especially within those responses, the question of the response of the automaton, or of the animal as automatic responder[35] and therefore without response (the "without response" that defines the death of the face in Levinas, to which we will return) is immediately preceded, in an apparently contingent manner, by a response to the subject of a *cogito*. Even if it is not necessarily signed by a dead person, this *cogito ergo sum* should not, all the same, have anything to do with the self-affirmation of a life, of an "I breathe" that would signify "I am living, I have breath in me [*animé*], I am animal." A properly phenomenological logic, precisely an *epochal* one, is employed in demonstrating that "I am" is deduced from "I breathe" only when it is implied that "I think" that I am breathing, or "I believe" or "I feel" (in Descartes' sense), "I think that I am breathing," and "therefore I am," even if the "I am breathing" is false, even if I am in fact not breathing or not living. "I breathe therefore I am," as such, does not produce any certainty. By contrast, "I think that I am breathing" is always certain and indubitable, even if I am mistaken. And therefore I can deduce "therefore I am" from "I think that I am breathing." What I am experiencing—phenomenologically, according to the definition of the Cartesian "I think"—is not that I am breathing but that I think that I am breathing. The indubitable conclusion is one that proves, but that proves absolutely only on the basis of what is experienced [*ce qui s'éprouve*] and what presents itself to oneself as thinking. We have to say that the sure conclusion of absolute certainty, whose consequence must follow without the least doubt, can follow only from an "I think." It proceeds, therefore, from "I think" to "I am," or from "I think that I am living" (even if it is false) to "I am," and not from "I am living" or "I am breathing" to "I am": "When one says 'I breathe, therefore I am,' if one wants to conclude that one exists from the fact that breathing cannot be without our existing, one doesn't conclude anything, because it would first have to have been proven that it is true that one is breathing, and that is impossible, unless one has also proved that one exists."[36] That amounts to saying that the expression "I am living (that is to say, as an animal) therefore I am" is assured of no philosophical certitude, no more than is the conclusion from which I have produced a title or signature, "the animal that therefore I am." I can save a sentence like "I think that I am an animal therefore I am" from doubt, but the sentence will have no privileged status; it will be equivalent to any other sentence beginning with "I think." And "I think" is something that an animal cannot utter. No more than "I" in general. Why? That is the whole question, the question of the question and the question of the response.

Without reconstituting this argument in all its intricate articulations—as I would have liked to do for the preceding argument concerning obedience or the response of nurses to an infant who cries in commanding or commands by crying (a scene that we will come back to in a note from Kant's *Anthropology*)—I propose that we retain at least this: the indubitability of existence, the autoposition and automanifestation of "I am" does not depend on being-in-life but on thinking, an appearance to self that is determined in the first place not as respiration, breath, or life, indeed, on a thinking soul that does not at first appear to itself as life. That is all I would like to retain as we embark on the itinerary that awaits us (notably along the path that leads from Descartes to Heidegger and to his neutralization of life), having it engage with the motifs that characterize the animal-machine. Such motifs appear to be many and varied, but they bring together in a single system nonresponse, a language that doesn't respond because it is fixed or stuck in the mechanicity of its programming, and finally lack, defect, deficit, or deprivation.

⟅

The trajectory that I am now getting ready to follow presupposes certain choices. I would like to try to justify its economy, at least. Today, and into the future, the perspective of a particularly dissymmetrical struggle has been opened, between those who don't consider themselves obligated by any respect for the rights of the animal as such and those who, on the contrary, seek to think through what such a respect for such rights could at least mean—rights not of the animal, perhaps, but of animals and, short of rethinking the very idea of right, of the history and concept of rights, which, until now, in its very constitution, has presumed the subjection, without respect, of the animal.

As you know, there has existed, since the date of its original version some twenty years ago, a *Universal Declaration of Animal Rights*. It includes ten articles and was made public in 1989 by the International League of Animal Rights. You have it in front of you.[37] A long history preceded it, at least two centuries long, from the time of Thomas Young and Jeremy Bentham. I shan't go back over it, no more than I will analyze all the questions posed by each article. But since this text presents itself as a legal one (even if, for the moment, it is assured of neither means nor force of application, and therefore does not possess the authentic status of a right, which in principle must always imply a means of constraint), since it appeals to fundamental yet problematic concepts, such as the animal in general, the "respect of animals by humans [as] inseparable from the respect of men for each other," freedom ("the right to live . . . in freedom in their own natural environment"), nature, life, and especially "the specific legal status of animals," since it presumes full light to have been shed on all the other concepts that we just hurriedly enumerated, we have grounds for questioning the status of this right [*droit*] and the subjects under the law [*sujets de droit*] that it presumes. My hypothesis is, therefore, as follows: within the history of rights or law and the concept of the legal subject, the subject of rights and duties, within the history of the concept of the subject that is inseparable from it, one particular sequence is decisive for our time. I am preparing to reconnoiter [*survoler*] that sequence, both from a great height and close up, from one peak to the next (Descartes to Lacan, Kant to Levinas, Heidegger to Descartes), in the way one would fly over the summits of a mountain range in the hope of sighting the animal (the *animot*) in its habitat. This sequence, analyzed according to the criteria I have announced, turns out to have determined a certain concept of the subject, which, while founding law and right, will have led at the same time to the denial of all rights to the animal, or rendered radically *problematic* any declaration of animal rights. In a very modest way, it is therefore a matter of marking some preliminary points of reference, which appear to be indispensable, in the very constitution of this problematic.

In spite of the strong sympathy that this Universal Declaration of Animal Rights elicits from me, I wonder whether it is justified in presenting itself as such, namely, as a declaration of rights, and whether "right" is the pertinent concept here. Must we pose the question of our relations with the *animot* in terms of "rights"? And what does that mean? For want of time I cannot tackle here the immense question of whether we can recognize the rights of subjects that are exempted from or incapable of duties. It is generally thought not, except in some exceptional cases. Such a possibility is not excluded in the history of the law, but it is a thorny problem, which I think I'll have to relegate to the margins for the moment. I plan to say just a little about it later on, concerning Kant. Yet even presuming we were to agree to recognize such rights, the Declaration of these rights remains eminently perfectible. The past has very much shown that to be the case already, with respect to human as well as animal rights. As with every right, this infinite perfectibility can have implications for the content as well as the founding concepts, for the implicit definitions or axioms of such a Declaration. Being content with an empirical enumeration that is limited to the very terms of the Declaration, for example, concepts of the animal itself, of the "oneness [*unité*]" of life, of the nervous system, of natural rights (Preamble), of the necessary, instantaneous, or cruel killing of an animal (Article 3), of use, exhibition (Article 5), genocide, biotope (Article 8), and, especially, of the specific legal status [*personnalité juridique*] of animals (Article 9).

If, in order to reintroduce these questions in a most preliminary manner, I have chosen to follow the post-Cartesian genealogy that comes down to us from "I think" or "I am," from "I say that I think therefore I am," from the place where, supervising thinking regarding the animal, this utterance in truth commands like a form of mastery over the animal, it is because one must at the same time honor the contract of this conference (autobiography, "I say that I think therefore I am," "I present myself such as I am"—in truth as regards the animal), and to take account of a tradition and filiation that, according to my hypothesis, I hold not only to be dominant in philosophy and as philosophy, in our world, in "modern times," but also to be, more precisely, the discourse of domination itself. And this domination is exercised as much through an infinite violence, indeed, through the boundless wrong that we inflict on animals, as through the forms of protest that at bottom share the axioms and founding concepts in whose name the violence is exercised, even when such forms of protest are channeled toward a Declaration of animal rights or an ecological or vegetarian culture with already such a rich and ancient history.

My hypothesis is, therefore, that this filiation governs, in the sense of being prevalent or hegemonic in, all domains that treat the question of the animal, indeed, where the animal itself is treated: zoology, ethology, anthropology, but first of all ontology, mastery by means of knowledge and (zoo-bio-genetic) technology, as well as ethics, politics, and law.

Before even beginning this survey, I shall note several traits that are common to the four philosophies that orient it, whose arrows will signpost its path, like intermittent signals, indicators only, which I might venture to call here, for the reasons already mentioned, perspicacious warning lights.[38] In spite of the immense differences and contradictions that separate them, which I would be the last to want to minimize, Kant, Heidegger, Levinas, and Lacan share, vis-à-vis what they call "the animal," a considerable number of what I'll call "beliefs," which, if you prefer, you might name axioms, prejudices, presumptions, or presuppositions. In any case I would like to show that they, like Descartes, think that in contrast to us humans—a difference that is determined by this fact—the animal neither speaks nor responds, that its capacity to produce signs[39] is foreign to language and limited or fixed by a program. Not one of them has ever taken into account the essential or structural differences among animal species. Not one of them has taken into account, in a serious and determinate manner, the fact that we hunt, kill, exterminate, eat, and sacrifice animals, use them, make them work or submit them to experiments that are forbidden to be carried out on humans. Apart from Lacan—but this, however, in no way changes the traditional axiomatics of his work—not one of them takes into account animal sexuality. Not one of them really integrates progress in ethological or primatological knowledge into his work. Of course, in the work of each these common traits are distributed according to different configurations (for which we shall account), but they always come down to the same thing, to this sameness, to the very same fact that I am [*à cela même que je suis*]. And this sameness, that very same fact remains unaffected, unless it be in a secondary and inessential way, by the following, which I here recall in the most general terms: (1) Descartes does not call his "I think, therefore I am" subjectivity (nevertheless, and this is what counts here, it concerns a foundation of the subject); (2) Kant's "I think" calls into question the whole repertoire of Cartesian ontology relating to the *cogito ergo sum* (nevertheless, it concerns an "I think" that, accompanying every representation, and this is what counts, defines the relation to self of reason, which is denied the animal); (3) Heidegger's *Dasein* is defined by a deconstruction of Cartesian subjectivity (nevertheless, and this is what counts, it concerns a matter of a *Dasein* anchored in an "I am" and in a *Jemeinigkeit*); (4) what Levinas names the "subject" is host or hostage (the "subject is host," the "subject is hostage," says Levinas, and it nevertheless concerns a human who relates to another human as to "us" as "brothers" or "neighbors" faced with an animal without a face and foreign to all ethics); (5) the Lacanian "subject," called as such, derives from a logic of the unconscious (nevertheless, and this is what still counts here, it concerns a human subject, and positive reference to Descartes is retained).

Other invariants: along with Descartes, Kant, Heidegger, Levinas, and Lacan—let's say, the signatory subjects who carry or are borne by those names—never evoke the possibility of being looked at by the animal that they, for their part, observe, and of which they speak. No more than Descartes does any of them evoke or take into account the problem of nakedness or modesty operating between animal and human. No more than Descartes do they think to distinguish animals one from another, and, like Descartes, they speak of "the animal" as of a single set that can be opposed to "us," "humans," subjects or *Da-sein*s of an "I think," "I am," along the line of a single common trait and on the other side of a single, indivisible limit. Their examples are always as meager as possible and are always aimed at illustrating a general identity of the animal and not structural differences between different types of animals. No more than Descartes do they recognize any minimal right, or any aptitude to response, as such, on the part of what they call "the animal."

As far as invariants and common traits go, I shall add yet another, which inspires [*anime*] everything and must therefore feed [*irriguer*] everything, namely, that at the heart of all these discourses *sacrifice* beats like a vital impulse. They represent four varieties of thinking sacrificial experience, four varieties of thinking that would not gather together around themselves in such a systematic and consequential way were it not for their reaffirmation of the necessity of sacrifice. Not necessarily of sacrifice as ritual sacrifice of the animal—even though, to my knowledge, none of them has ever denounced the same—but of sacrifice as fundamental, indeed, of a founding sacrifice, within a human space where, in any case, exercising power over the animal to the point of being able to put it to death when necessary is not forbidden. The fundamental place of sacrifice is marked in an explicit and thematic manner in the thinking of Kant, Heidegger, Lacan, and Levinas.[40] It seems unlikely that sacrificial pathos is Cartesian, and the sacrificed animal, it should be said, is not presumed to be an animal-machine. But in order to recall the depth of the Judeo-Christian and hence sacrificialist current in the Cartesian *cogito*, it would be sufficient to situate two of its tributaries. First, that which leads back, in spite of all of Descartes' denials, to the *cogito* of Augustine. If one wanted to deal with the autobiographical animal in the *Confessions*, one would have to convoke, before Nietzsche's or Kant's horses, Augustine's "good horse [*bonus equus*]." I can love him all I want, he says, but I couldn't wish to be like him, although I can wish to be like another human, love him from afar without knowing him, or love and admire an actor that I could not be. Augustine then wonders (and there would be so much to say about these examples of the actor and the horse at the heart of this immense autobiography): "How is it that I love in a human being what I would hate to be, when I also am human? Man is a vast deep [*grande profundum est ipse homo*]. . . . Yet it is easier to count his hairs than the passions and emotions of his heart."[41] This is the deep abyss that Augustine allows in his Christian brothers and fellow men but refuses the animal, whereas others will flock to the animal as to the dizziness of the abyss.

The other Christian tributary in Cartesian thinking is not foreign to the sacrificial scene that is in question here, on the way back from the lamb and the ram, for it concerns Descartes' attempt—which is, moreover, convincing—at what he considered to be a possible and necessary reconciliation between his interpretation of the relations among substances, souls, and bodies and the doctrine of eucharistic transubstantiation.

At the moment of bringing and including together, in a single embrace, Descartes, Kant, Heidegger, Levinas, and Lacan, as a single living body at bottom, indeed, as a single *corpus delicti*, the mobile system of a single discursive organization with several tentacles, I have the impression that I am myself trying to gain—as though wrestling, fishing, or hunting—a sufficiently expert or knowledgeable purchase [*prise*] on what might touch the nervous system of a single animal body. A little like someone who would claim to know which way to take hold of a cuttlefish or octopus, without hurting it too much, and especially without killing it, keeping it at a distance long enough to let it expel its ink. In order to displace its powers without doing anybody too much harm. Its ink[42] or power would here be the "I," not necessarily *the power to say* "I" but the ipseity of being *able to be* or *able to do* "I," even before any autoreferential utterance in a language.

I admit to that, to be trying to grasp it, to gain such a purchase on this concept. I admit to it in the name of autobiography and in order to confide in you the following: given the infinite complications that I am in the process of recalling, I have a particularly animalist perception and interpretation of what I do, think, write, live, but, in fact, of everything, of the whole of history, culture, and so-called human society, at every level, macro- or microscopic. My sole concern is not that of interrupting this animalist "vision" but of taking care not to sacrifice to it any difference or alterity, the fold of any complication, the opening of any abyss to come.

⋙

In guilt or in innocence, my grasp will begin today with the reprise of the Cartesian *cogito* by Kant's "I think." Following all the critiques that the theory of the animal-machine elicited during the Enlightenment, when Kant comes to reaffirm the difference constituted by the human as rational animal he does so on the basis of an "I." Although it is distributed throughout his work, this fundamental anthropocentrism is declared as such—as egological, tautological, and autographical—at the beginning of *Anthropology from a Pragmatic Point of View*. From the first words man is defined as he who can possess the representation of an "I" (*der Mensch in seiner Vorstellung das Ich haben kann*). It is a power, let us not forget. This capability, this power to have [*pouvoir-avoir*] the "I" takes the high ground; it erects, it raises (*erhebt*) man infinitely (*unendlich*) above all the other beings living on earth (*unendlich über alle andere auf Erden lebende Wesen*). This infinite elevation identifies a subject in the strict sense, for immediately after Kant emphasizes the fact that "I" signifies the unity of a consciousness that remains the same throughout all its modifications. The "I" is the "I think," the originary unity of the transcendental apperception that accompanies every representation. The subject that is man is a person, "one and the same person [*die selbe Person*]," therefore, who will be the subject of reason, morality, and the law. What exists in opposition to this person? Well, the thing (in consequence, one will find there the ancient Roman distinction between the rights of persons and the rights of things, something that should be recalled here). The person is an entirely different being (*ganz verschiedenes Wesen*), in rank and dignity (*durch Rang und Würde*), from these things (*Sachen*), which are irrational animals (*dergleichen die vernunflosen Thiere sind*). One has power and authority (*walten*) over these irrational animals because they are things. One can use them and lord over them as one pleases (*nach Belieben schalten und walten kann*). The force of this power over the irrational animals, the free authority of this *walten und schalten*, is not posited by Kant as an attribute or consequence—one among others—of the person's power to say "I." Power over the animal is the essence of the "I" or the "person," the essence of the human (this conforms, moreover, to the divine injunction that, from Genesis on, assigned to man such a destination, that of marking his authority over living creatures, which can be effected only through the infinitely elevated power of presenting himself as an "I," of presenting himself and just that, of presenting himself to himself, by means of a form of presence to himself that accompanies every presentation and representation. This presence to oneself, this self of the presence to itself, this universal and singular "I" that is the condition for the response and thus for the responsibility of the subject—whether theoretical, practical, ethical, juridical, or political—is a power, a *faculty* that Kant is prudent or bold enough not to identify with the power *to speak*, the literal power of *uttering* "I." This personal subject *is capable* of its selfness [peut *son égoïté*], is capable of doing it without saying it, if I can say so; it can affirm itself in its selfness and in its dignity, which is to say its *responsibility*, its power to respond, to answer for itself, before others and before the law, "even when he cannot yet say 'I' [*selbst wenn er das Ich noch nicht sprechen kann*]." He has this "I" in his thinking (*in Gedanken*), and that defines thinking itself as what gathers itself, there where it remains the same, gathered and present to itself through this power of the *I*, through the *I can* of this *I*, this *I can I* as an "I think" that accompanies every representation. Even where the ipseity of the I cannot speak itself and utter itself as such in the word *je, Ich, I, ego*, it *effects itself* in every language, provided it is human. In relation to the *ego*, Kant's gesture is here the same as Heidegger's will later be in relation to being, namely, the condition for experience of what is "as such," which, as we shall see, distinguishes human *Dasein* from the animal. Every human language has at its disposal this self "as such," even if the word for it is lacking. Here is Kant:

> All languages must think it when they speak in the first person [and at bottom it is this first person that is lacking from animal life, radically depriving it of any autobiographical relation to the self], even if they do not have a special word to express this concept of "I" [this

"egoness"—*diese Ichheit*—and it is better to translate Ichheit by "egoness (*egoïté*)" than by "I," as the French translation does, for it is not just a matter of positing an "I," my very own "I" here and now, but of acceding by means of language to what makes my "I" an "I," a being-I, one's egoness as such, one's universal being-ego, one's phenomenon of the being-ego in general, in the general singular].[43]

If Kant gives, to men and to languages that don't have a word for "I," credit for something for which he will never give credit to animals and their systems of signs, it is not just because the latter lack words in general (on account of the defect and fixity of their system of communication), but because the "I" that is in thinking before being in language is nothing other than thinking itself, the power to think, the understanding that is lacking in the animal: "For this faculty [*Vermögen*] (namely, to think) [*nämlich zu denken*] is *understanding* [*der Verstand*]."[44]

This would perhaps be the place or moment to clarify once more the both subtle and decisive stakes of this power of the "I." No doubt it will not simply be a case of the relation to self, nor even of a certain auto-motion, an auto-kinetic spontaneity that no one, not even the most negative of minds vis-à-vis the animal, not even Descartes, disallows in the animal. Let me repeat it, every living creature, and thus every animal to the extent that it is living, has recognized in it this power to move spontaneously, to feel itself and to relate to itself. However problematic it be, that is even the characteristic of what lives, as traditionally conceived in opposition to the inorganic inertia of the purely physico-chemical. No one denies the animal auto-affection or auto-motion, hence the self of that relation to the self. But what is in dispute—and it is here that the functioning and the structure of the "I" count so much, even where the word *I* is lacking—is the power to make reference to the self in deictic or autodeictic terms, the capability at least virtually to turn a finger toward oneself in order to say "this is I." For, as Benveniste has clearly emphasized, that is what utters and performs "I" when I pronounce or effect it. It is what says "I am speaking of me"; the one who says "I" shows himself in the present of his utterance, or at least of its manifestation. Because it is held to be incapable of this autodeictic or auto-referential self-distancing [*autotélie*] and deprived of the "I," the animal will lack any "I think," as well as understanding and reason, response and responsibility. The "I think" that must accompany every representation is this auto-reference as condition for thinking, as thinking itself; that is precisely what is proper to the human, of which the animal would be deprived.

Of course, the question is immense and abyssal. The critical reelabora-
tion that I would be tempted to submit it to does not consist in denying,
without speaking of the animal in general (which I'll never do), that many
animals in fact seem incapable of an auto-deixis or *literal* auto-reference,
as in the visible form of an adept manipulation of the specular image or
of the index finger turned back at oneself in order to speak or to manifest
in saying "this is I who is showing me myself, I'll answer for it." Yet, *on
the one hand*, it is not certain that this auto-deicticity is not at work, in
various forms, evidently, in every genetic system in general, where each
element of the genetic writing has to identify itself, mark itself according
to a certain reflexivity, in order to signify in the genetic chain; nor is it
certain that this auto-deicticity doesn't take on highly developed, differentiated, and complex forms in a large number of social phenomena that can
be observed in the *animot*. Who can deny that phenomena of narcissistic
exhibition in seduction or sexual combat, the "follow me who is (following) you" deployed in colors, music, adornments, parades, or erections of
all sorts derive from such an auto-deixis? One could go a long way in
multiplying these indices and examples, something I don't have time to
do. But conversely, and *on the other hand*, according to what constitutes
the logical matrix of my argument, it is not just a matter of giving back
to the animal whatever it has been refused, in this case the *I* of *automons-
tration*. It is also a matter of questioning oneself concerning the axiom
that permits one to accord purely and simply to the human or to the
rational animal that which one holds the just plain animal to be deprived
of. If autoposition, the *automonstrative autotely* of the "I," even in the
human, implies the "I" to be an other that must welcome within itself
some irreducible hetero-affection (as I have tried to demonstrate elsewhere), then this autonomy of the "I" can be neither pure nor rigorous;
it would not be able to form the basis for a simple and linear differentia-
tion of the human from the animal. Besides all the differences that are
reintroduced and taken into account in this way (among humans, among
animals, between humans and animals), the question of the "I," of "I am"
or "I think," would have to be displaced toward the prerequisite question
of the other: the other, the other me that I am (following) or that is following me. Which other? And how will the determination of the law of
the other, of heteronomy, permit the anthropocentrism whose logic we
are following to be either displaced or confirmed, its logic or the *logos*
(for its logic is an active interpretation of the logos, a logocentrism)? That
question awaits us still.

Within the immense network of consequences that one could draw, in Kant himself, from this anthropologism of the "I think" and of the concept of finitude that is fitted to it (a finitude that, paradoxically, Kant and Heidegger will deny the animal), I shall follow but two virtual trajectories.

The first would allow us to examine in more detail what I analyzed elsewhere in terms of the domestic animal in Kant. At the end of his *Anthropology* Kant once more marks a limit. This time it is no longer a question of the "I" but of sociality. Kant is very much tempted to go quite far, at first, in the direction of a comparison between animal and human society. To begin with, by pointing out that animality (*Thierheit*) still remains in its manifestations prior (*früher*) to pure humanity as well as more powerful (*mächtiger*), all the way to the formation of the republic, into every civil constitution (*bürgerliche Verfassung*), namely, into what represents the highest degree of the good tendencies of humankind with respect to its final end and destination (*Bestimmung*). Thus there exists this priority, this being-before (*früher*) of the animal (another way of saying that man is *after* the animal), and this superiority of powerfulness also. That priority and superiority are reversed only when a weakening (*Schwächung*) on the part of the animal makes it submit to man and to the domestication that renders it more useful to humans than the wild beast. The socialization of human culture goes hand in hand with this weakening, with the domestication of the tamed beast: it is nothing other than the becoming-livestock [*devenir-bétail*] of the beast. The appropriation, breaking-in, and domestication of tamed livestock (*das zahme Vieh*) are human socialization. As an individual, the human would, like the wild beast, also be ready to go to war against its neighbors in order to affirm its unconditional freedom. There is therefore neither socialization, political constitution, nor politics itself without the principle of domestication of the wild animal. The idea of an animal politics that claimed to break with this power to command beasts, to order the becoming-livestock of the beast, would be absurd and contradictory. Politics supposes livestock. That is why, while remaining seduced by it, Kant inscribes a limit to any comparison between animal and human society. He doubtless makes a concession: although the human is not destined to become part of a herd, like a domestic animal, its sociality resembles, however, that of a beehive (in line with an analogy with a rich history that survives all the way to Marx). In both cases it is a matter of being destined to become a member of a cooperative and civil society. The most simple and least artificial means of proceeding toward the organization of that society involves having a guide, master, sage (*Weiser*) in the hive—this is the monarchic principle of the bee. But the comparison (*Gleichnis*) stops there. For, in their multiplicity, hive insects commit to a war that, according to Kant, cannot be compared to human wars. They unleash their robber bees with a view to remaining in a bellicose state of nature, in a relation of ruse, violence, and exploitation of the strength of others, whereas human wars (which Kant implicitly praises in the end, as he often does) bring about a passage from the state of wild nature to the state of society. Kant seems less convincing and to belabor things more than ever when, for example, he writes the following, which, far from bringing the comparison to a close, on the contrary invites it, or so it seems to me:

> Here the comparison ends—[bees attack each other not as human beings do] but only to use by cunning or force *others'* industry for *themselves*. Each people seeks to strengthen itself through the subjugation of neighbouring peoples, either from the desire to expand or the fear of being swallowed up by the other unless one beats him to it [one would have to investigate this motif of speed in the technological competition between human societies as animal societies]. Therefore civil or foreign war in our species, as great an evil as it may be, is yet at the same time the incentive [*Triebfeder*: what excites the drive] to pass from the crude state of nature to the *civil* state.[45]

Yet what is it, in the last instance, that here distinguishes animal war, that which maintains animals in savage bestiality, from human war, which, on the contrary, would bring us out of the savage state, opening onto culture and social consciousness? What is it in the end that goes in the same direction as this "I think" that insures the humanity and animal rationality that I am? Well, paradoxically, it is nothing other than a mechanism, a machine, but this time a providential machination. The *Triebfeder* that raises humanity to the level of society and brings it out of the savage state by means of war, in contrast to the same war that keeps bestiality there, is *ein Maschinenwesen der Vorsehung*, a mechanical device of providence: not an animal machine but a providential god that sees further than the present of perception. This providential whatsit [*machin*] sees in advance both evil and what use evil can have. The thingamajig foresees the finality of these two wars, even though they are two wars and two wars based on animality (since the animal remains in the human, in human society, as older [*früher*] and stronger than the human who is *after* it): "War is like a mechanical device of Providence, where to be sure the struggling forces injure each other through collision, but are nevertheless still regularly kept going for a long time through the push and pull of other incentives [*durch den Stoss oder Zug anderer Triebfeder*]."[46]

One should analyze long and hard this contradiction and this inversion, this counterpulsionality—drive against drive, motive [*mobile*] against motive (*Triebfeder* against other *Triebfedern*)—which functions, yes, we must say "works" or "functions," *like a machine* for stabilizing and regularizing the course of a society and a history. And one may wonder whether this criterion of stability and regularity alone would not be just as pertinent for describing so-called animal or savage societies. As always, and as is the rule when one speaks of the animal, Kant is not far from denying, recanting, and contradicting what he says, even as it concerns contradiction. He is so close to doing so that in a little-remarked remark, a glaring note at the bottom of the page, he evokes, as an evolutionist, the possibility that one day, in a "third epoch," the chimpanzee might be able to say "I think" and so accede to understanding. And hence to the rank and dignity of the human. One has to wonder, therefore, how to interpret the intention of this *Maschinenwesen der Vorsehung*, this providential *deus ex machina*, this anthropotheocentric computer just referred to. Coming just before the passage that we have just read, the note exposes a subtle and painstaking interpretation of the child's cry at birth. Kant is as obsessed with it as Descartes was, especially when dealing with the animal. He will blithely affirm that the cry of the newborn signifies not a complaint but anger and indignation. The infant gives vent to an outburst of protestation. He doesn't cry about his pain but indicates that something is annoying, vexing, or frustrating him (*ihm etwas verdriesst*). Kant therefore asks about nature's intention (*Absicht*) in thus exposing this tiny, angry, rolled-up newborn to the voracity of a neighboring wolf or pig, which could be attracted by the screams of the little one while its mother is absent or weakened by her labor. If I can sum it up, Kant's response, which is at the same time extra-lucid and totally wild, is threefold. There are three different eras. First, prior to history, in a time before time, in the state of pure nature, the baby didn't cry at birth. Next, without our knowing how or why, says Kant, quite literally, on the day that parents accede to culture, nature makes the disturbing cry of the newborn possible, no doubt within the perspective of speech. Finally—and this is his third response—Kant proffers a remark that, he says, "can lead us far [*diese Bemerkung führt weit*]." Quite far, but how far? As far as the hypothesis of a *third era*, an era to come that would require a redistribution of the whole logic of this anthropocentrism, and by extension Kant's whole work. Here is the hypothesis:

> This remark leads us far—for example, to the thought that upon major upheavals in nature this second epoch might be followed by

a third, when an orang-utan or a chimpanzee developed the organs used for walking [a passage, therefore, to the erection of the upright stance with everything that ensues in terms of the face-to-face and face-to-face copulation], handling objects, and speaking (*zum Sprechen*) into the structure of a human being [*zum Gliederbau eines Menschen*], whose innermost part contained an organ for the use of understanding [*ein Organ für den Gebrauch des Verstandes*] and which developed through social culture [*durch gesellschaftliche Cultur*].[47]

Our interest in this extraordinary note is clear. Kant is no longer speaking of the animal in general, and he takes into account a structural difference between nonhuman types of animal. The note also marks an opening to an evolutionary process that is even "historical" (I'll leave this word within the quotation marks that I have tried to explain before), a macrodimensional periodization of hominization and beyond, which, while being somewhat improbable and described in naïve terms, at least frees up the attention of philosophers for the work of primatology to come. Such knowledge should oblige them to "deconstruct" their habitual discourse even if they do not of their own account discover, within that very discourse, incitations to do so.

That said, this note has the status of a reverie with no tomorrow. In that respect it resembles Levinas's cursory remark about Bobby—the "Kantian dog" so much cited and admired by Levinas's readers, and about which we'll say more—all the more so because the traverse of this dog remains without precedent, without consequence, and without a future within the discourse in which it appears, not to mention the internal limits to which we'll shortly return. It seems to me that Kant himself draws no consequence from his note on the future of the animal for the dominant organization of his discourse. Moreover, like the story of Bobby, the reference remains strongly anthropomorphic and anthropocentric. The future that is opened if not promised to the orangutan and chimpanzee retains the familiarity of a human structure (*zum Gliederbau eines Menschen*). From the point of view of this human structure, no law or right is currently recognized as pertaining to animality in general, including present-day primates. The animal is not a rational being, since it is deprived of the "I think" that is the condition for understanding and reason. In that way, deprived for the same reason of liberty and autonomy, it cannot become the subject of rights or duties, given the correlation between right and obligation that is proper to the subject as a free person. Kant envisages the rupture of such a correlation within the subjectivity of the subject in two cases: that of the serf who is subject to duties but enjoys no rights, and that of God, who has every right but is bound by no duty.[48] However, this double exception in no case applies to the animal, which has access to no rights or obligations and remains foreign to the kingdom of ends. The animal (and even the animal in man) cannot be taken to be an end in itself, but only a means. It belongs to the purely sensible order of existence that must always be *sacrificed* (this is always Kant's word when speaking of the subordination of interests and vital or sensible passions). In a word, and in order to cut straight to the chase, what the nonrational animal is deprived of, along with subjecthood, is what Kant calls "dignity [*Würde*]," that is to say, an internal and priceless value, the value of an end in itself, or if you prefer, a price above any comparable or negotiable price, above any market price.[49] There can be a negotiable market price for the animal, as for every means that is incapable of becoming an end in itself, whence the virtual cruelty of this pure practical reason. Accents of cruelty already mark Kant's discourse when he speaks of the imperative necessity of *sacrificing* sensibility to moral reason. But this sacrificial cruelty can become so much more serious, and virtually terrible, implacable, and ferocious when it comes to the animal that some, such as Adorno, have not hesitated to denounce it as an extreme violence, even a sort of sadism. It is perhaps also Kant with Sade, and the fact that Lacan didn't investigate in the direction of cruelty *against* the animal is perhaps not unrelated to a certain logic of his of which we shall speak more. In his *Philosophy of Music* (in the context of a remark concerning Beethoven that it would be interesting to delve deeper into if we had time), Adorno for his part does not hesitate to judge as "suspect," "so suspect [*so suspekt*]," Kant's notion of "dignity," which is given to the human only "in the name of autonomy." The capacity for autonomy, self-determination, moral autodestination (*Selbstbestimmung*), let us also say for auto-prescription and moral autobiography, is indeed what, in Kant, becomes the privilege or absolute advantage of the human (in the sense in which, we might say, the *autos* of automotion, reflexive *autotely*, is generally held to be the property of what lives in general). Inasmuch as it assures the dominance or mastery (*Herrschaft*) of man over nature, that capacity is in fact, Adorno makes clear, "directed against animals [*Sie richtet sie gegen die Tiere*]."[50] Adorno is not satisfied with identifying a desire for mastery over nature or, as is often said in relation to the Cartesian project, a general and neutral intention of the subject who presumes to dominate nature by means of science and technique. On the contrary, he interprets it as an act of war and a gesture of hate, an animosity, as though Kant were raising the stakes in a bid to add venom to a Cartesian project that, for its part, would remain essentially neutral and indifferent, funda-mentally indifferent to the animal-machine. (I don't believe it for a mo-ment. I think that Cartesianism belongs, beneath its mechanicist indifference, to the Judeo-Christiano-Islamic tradition of a war against the animal, of a sacrificial war that is as old as Genesis. And that war is not just one means of applying technoscience to the animal in the absence of another possible or foreseeable means; no, that violence or war has until now been constitutive of the project or of the very possibility of techno-scientific knowledge within the process of humanization or of the appro-priation of man by man, including its most highly developed ethical or religious forms. No ethical or sentimental nobility must be allowed to conceal from us that violence, and acknowledged forms of ecologism or vegetarianism are insufficient to bring it to an end, however more worthy they be than what they oppose.)

In any case, if we refer to the prejudice that holds the theory of the animal-machine to be neutral and indifferent, impassive, then accusing Kantian morality of being "directed against the animal" in an act of war precisely amounts to being interested in an interest, in a negative interest in the animal, an allergic passion, an instinctive [*pulsionnelle*] inflexion, identifying a significant aggravation of "Cartesianism" that becomes a sort of "hatred" of the animal: "wishing" harm to the animal. Later, Adorno will in fact speak of hate and revilement directed by the Kantian toward animality. In other words, the principle of pure practical reason, Kant's ethical project, would be hateful, cruel, criminal, incriminating, criminalized by Adorno and by the logic that he announces and that I am developing here. In the principle and ends of that morality there would be death, putting to death, and murder. (Moreover, much remains to be said here regarding animality in general and the animality of the human, concerning the problem of capital punishment, whose necessity in princi-ple Kant firmly upheld in the very name of the concept and of the possi-bility of laws and rights, whereas not only Beccaria but Sade contested it.) This criminalization of practical reason can be interpreted in a number of different ways. One could say, first, that in the end such a bellicose hatred in the name of human rights, far from rescuing man from the animality that he claims to rise above, confirms the waging of a kind of species war and confirms that the man of practical reason remains bestial in his defen-sive and repressive aggressivity, in his exploiting the animal to death. One could also say, second, that bad will, even a perverse malice, inhabits and animates so-called good moral will; and that this "evil," the malady and malignity of this evil [*mal*], is borne not *in* and *on* the animal, but *against* the animal, to which it is a question of doing and wishing harm. For reasons that remain to be analyzed—this is one essential dimension that I shall have to leave aside for today—Kantian thinking regarding "evil" should be reinterpreted from this point of view. The whole sentiment of suspicion about a profound perversity within Kantian morality (which Adorno did not introduce), is no doubt what guided Nietzsche in his genealogy of morals. One could say, in the third place, that this perversity is precisely the other or the unconscious of the "I think" (interpreted along Nietzschean but also Freudian lines); it is the other that thinks me and the other that follows me where I am (following), that other which haunts in advance the "I think that accompanies all my representations." We will therefore be required, once we come to Levinas and to Lacan, to ask whether it is then enough to speak of the other or the unconscious, whether a logic of the wholly other and of the unconscious, a primordial reference to the other as is found in Levinas and in Lacan, is sufficient, by itself, to remove the anthropocentric prejudice that comes down from Descartes, that is to say, along the whole Epipromethean-Islamic-Judeo-Christian descendancy. (My response will be "no," as you will have already understood, both for Levinas and for Lacan.) One can say, finally, that this unthought in the "I think," where the animal that I am (following) follows me from the place of the other or of the unconscious, is indeed a function of *machinality*, which haunts automatically, like an evil conjuring genius, the Cartesian concept of animal-machine as much as the Kantian concept of providence, of a providential machine, a *Maschinenwesen der Vorsehung*, so as to teleologize in advance, by means of prescription and prediction, the history of war machines that are presumed to have a civilizing effect. But then the state of culture and regular sociality that human wars supposedly lead to, according to the providential design of the *Maschinenwesen der Vorsehung*, would still be the prosecution of a war without mercy against the animal in the form of a *pax humana*, just one moment in this war to the death, which should in effect end in a world without animals, without any animal worthy of the name and living for something other than to become a means for man: livestock, tool, meat, body, or experimental life form.

ॐ

Let us return for a moment to Adorno, having stretched his remark a little far from the literal context of the fragment but, I hope, without betraying it. One would almost be tempted to say that this aggravation of Kantian or idealist hatred of the animal, this zoophobia, is not—in the spirit and even the letter of Adorno's text—foreign to a Germanization or at least a fascization of the subject. Adorno states that Kant leaves no place for compassion (*Mitleid*), no commiseration between human and animal (as one who "can suffer," as Bentham said). Nothing, Adorno says, is more abhorrent, more hateful, more odious (*verhasster*) to Kantian man than the memory of a resemblance or affinity between human and animality (*die Erinnerung an die Tierähnlichkeit des Menschen*). The Kantian has nothing but hate for the animality of the human. It is even his "taboo," in all the senses of the term, and it begins as a sacred injunction against impurity. It is the taboo of this animality that is both forbidden and held in respect, with the ambivalence of religious panic that precisely brands [*frappe*] the animal as *totem* and *taboo*. Adorno's remark thus comes into relation with the whole Freudian problematic of the religions of father and son. He speaks of "tabooization [*Tabuirung*]." An operation of conjuration is what in general characterizes all the insults with which the idealist berates the materialist. And this conjuration tends at the same time to consecrate and to forbid a taboo. The taboo is at once religiously excluded, kept in silence, reduced to silence, consecrated, and sacrificed, branded as forbidden or just plain branded. Hatred of the "taboo" animal would be a general trait of idealism and transcendentalism. Earlier, Adorno had noted the affinity between the pretension to transcendentalism and this project of human mastery over nature and over animality. The Kantian determination of the human subject (the single example of the rational and finite being, single example of *intuitus derivativus*) would be a prominent form of this transcendental idealism. Then, all of a sudden, Adorno takes things much further: for an idealist system, he says, animals virtually play the same role as Jews did for a fascist system. Animals would be the Jews of idealists, who would thus be nothing but virtual fascists. And such a fascism begins whenever one insults an animal, even the animal in man. Authentic idealism (*das echter Idealismus*) consists in *insulting* the animal in the human or in treating the human as animal. Adorno twice makes reference to the idea of insult (*schimpfen*). It doesn't just imply verbal aggression, but an aggression that consists in degrading, reviling, devaluing someone, contesting his or her dignity. One doesn't insult some thing but someone. Adorno doesn't go so far as to say that the idealist insults the animal, but that he insults the materialist or insults man by calling him an animal, which implies that "animal" is an insult. "The animal that therefore I am" can also be heard as a sort of self-accusation (whenever I have just committed a *bêtise* and I blame myself openly, denouncing myself, pointing to myself: what an ass I am [*bête que je suis*]). The moment of self-denigration, insult of the self by the self.

How far can one take this reference to Judaism, to idealist hatred of the animal as hatred of the Jew, which one could easily extend, according to the now-familiar outlines of the same logic, to a certain hatred of femininity, even childhood? (Evil intended, harm done to the animal, insulting the animal would therefore be a fact of the male, of the human as *homo*, but also as *vir*. The animal's problem [*mal*] is the male. Evil comes to the animal through the male.) It would be relatively simple to show that this violence done to the animal is, if not in essence, then at least predominantly male, and, like the very dominance of that predominance, warlike, strategic, stalking, *viriloid*. There may be huntswomen like Diana and Amazon horsewomen, but no one will contest that in its most overwhelming phenomenal form, from hunt to bullfight, from mythologies to abattoirs, except for rare exceptions it is the male that goes after the animal, just as it was Adam whom God charged with establishing his dominion over the beasts. (It was in order to name that sacrificial scene that I spoke elsewhere, as though of a single phenomenon and a single law, of *carnophallogocentrism*.[51] Let me note very quickly in passing, concerning intellectual autobiography, that whereas the deconstruction of "logocentrism" had, for necessary reasons, to be developed over the years as deconstruction of "phallogocentrism," then of "carnophallogocentrism," its very first substitution of the concept of trace or mark for those of speech, sign, or signifier was destined in advance, and quite deliberately, to cross the frontiers of anthropocentrism, the limits of a language confined to human words and discourse. Mark, gramma, trace, and différance refer differentially to all living things, all the relations between living and nonliving.)

How far, then, can one take this reference to Judaism, and why would Kant—who is generally praised for a sort of profound Judaism, in contrast to Hegel, who nevertheless has more complicated, less typically Cartesian, views on animality (one would have to find the means to examine closely this question in Hegel, as well as in Marx and Husserl)—instead be anti-Judaic if not anti-Semitic? In her beautiful and rich preface to Amyot's translation of Plutarch's animal-related treatises, Élisabeth de Fontenay is not content to recall, as did Hannah Arendt, that Kant was "Eichmann's favorite author." Writing against those who denounce the calling into question of humanist axiomatics on the subject of the animal as an "irresponsible deconstructionist drift," she offers this reminder:

> Those who evoke the *summa injuria* [an allusion to Nazi zoophilia and Hitler's vegetarianism] only in order to better make fun of pity for anonymous and mute suffering are out of luck, for it happens

that some great Jewish writers and thinkers of this century were ob-
sessed by the question of the animal: Kafka, Singer, Canetti, Hork-
heimer, Adorno. By insisting on inscribing that in their work, they
will have contributed to an interrogation of rationalist humanism
and of the solid ground of its decisions. Victims of historic catastro-
phes have in fact felt animals to be victims also, comparable up to a
certain point to themselves and their kind.[52]

I quote this passage (others around it should also be cited) in order to
subscribe to it, no doubt. But also in order to raise two questions. The
first, which I'll pass over very quickly, concerns the allusion to "deconstruction." In order not to be too "irresponsible" (to refer to the accusation *against* which Élisabeth de Fontenay precisely protests), it seems to
me that, among other precautions and concerns for complexities, a "deconstruction" should not take to task the "rationalist humanism" (Élisabeth de Fontenay's term) of such cruel discourse directed against animals,
whose repercussions, agonistics, and polemology we are in the process of
analyzing. Those discourses do in fact cite rationalist humanism and
probably present themselves as such. But this so-called "rationalist humanism" is in a hurry to enclose and circumscribe the concept of the
human as much as that of reason. The deconstruction that matters to me
here should also promote itself in the name of another history, another
concept of history, and of the history *of* the human as well as that of reason. An immense history, a macro- and microhistory. The simplisticness,
misunderstanding, and violent disavowal that we are analyzing at present
also seem to me to be betrayals of repressed human possibilities, of other
powers of reason, of a more comprehensive logic of argument, of a more
demanding responsibility concerning the power of questioning and response, concerning science as well, and, for example—but this is only an
example—as regards the most open and critical forms of zoological or
ethological knowledge.

∽

The second question will serve as a transition. Élisabeth de Fontenay
brings to our attention how so many Jewish thinkers of the century in fact
inscribed the question of the animal within their corpus. It therefore appears all the more urgent to raise the question of the fact that the Jewish
thinker who, no doubt with justification, passes in this century for the
most concerned with ethics and sanctity, Emmanuel Levinas, did not
make the animal anything like a focus of interrogation within his work.
This silence seems to me here, at least from the point of view that counts

for us, more significant than all the differences that might separate Levinas from Descartes and from Kant on the question of the subject, of ethics, and of the person. I would be the last to want to misrepresent, and especially to erase, those differences, indeed, oppositions or ruptures. But they do not displace in the least the axis of a thinking of the human subject that, by situating the possibility and necessity of sacrifice at the heart of its ethics, fails to feel concerned or looked at, if I may say so, by the *animot* and fails to recognize in it any of the traits attributed to the human face. Such an invariant is all the more remarkable inasmuch as it persists throughout differences, oppositions, ruptures, or displacements. If I say "thinking of the subject," that is first of all to justify Levinas's inclusion in the tradition of the subject that we are analyzing. For this question of the animal is not just interesting and serious in its own right. It also provides us with an indispensable intertwining thread for reading philosophers and for gaining access to a sort of secret "architectonics" in the construction—and therefore in the deconstruction—of a discursive apparatus, a coherence, if not a system. One understands a philosopher only by heeding closely what he means to demonstrate, and in reality fails to demonstrate, concerning the limit between human and animal.

Now, even if Levinas inflects what he inherits, even if he inverts what could be described as the traditional and ontological tendency concerning the subject, even if he does that in a strong, original, and, let's say, subversive manner (for there would also be on his part a "subversion of the subject," to borrow Lacan's expression from a text that we will deal with later), even if he submits the subject to a radical heteronomy, even if he makes of the subject a subject that is subjected to the law of substitution, even if he says about the subject that it is above all a "host" (host of the infinite, moreover, according to a Cartesian tradition of the idea of the infinite to which he lays claim and which will have him say, in the end, "I am [following] after the infinite"), even if he reminds us that the subject is a "hostage" ("the subject is a host," the "subject is hostage,"[53] he writes, obsessed, pursued, persecuted), this subject of ethics, the face, remains first of all a fraternal and human face. I have insisted, moreover, on the stakes of this value given to fraternity, a central and determinant value for Levinas's interpretation of a face that is first of all that of my brother and my neighbor (however distant or foreign he be). It is more clear here than ever. It is a matter of putting the animal outside of the ethical circuit. One could illustrate that interpretation with thousands of quotations. If, in his new heteronomous and ethical definition, the human subject is a face, according the animal or the *animot* any of the traits, rights, duties, affections, or possibilities recognized in the face of the other is out of the question. That can be a surprise, coming from a thinking that is so "ob-sessed" (I am purposely using Levinas's word), so preoccupied by an ob-session with the other and with his infinite alterity. If I am responsible for the other, and before the other, and in the place of the other, on behalf of the other, isn't the animal more other still, more radically other, if I might put it that way, than the other in whom I recognize my brother, than the other in whom I identify my fellow or my neighbor? If I have a duty [*devoir*]—something owed before any debt, before any right—toward the other, wouldn't it then also be toward the animal, which is still more other than the other human, my brother or my neighbor? In fact, no. It seems precisely that for Levinas the *animot* is not an other. Except (what appears to be an exception) for a famous passage about which I'll say a word shortly, but which doesn't, however, seem to me to be as audacious as is often maintained (it is the famous story of Bobby, the Kantian dog), never to my knowledge does Levinas evoke the gaze of the *animot* as the gaze of that naked and vulnerable face to which he has dedicated so many beautiful and gripping analyses. The animal has no face, he does not have the naked face that looks at me to the extent of my forgetting the color of its eyes. The word *nudity*, which is used so fre-quently, which is so indispensable for Levinas in describing the face, skin, and vulnerability of the other or of my relation to the other, of my respon-sibility for the other when I say "here I am," never concerns nudity in its sexual difference and never appears within the field of my relation to the animal. The animal has neither face nor even skin in the sense Levinas has taught us to give to those words. There is, to my knowledge, no atten-tion ever seriously given to the animal gaze, no more than to the differ-ence among animals, as though I could no more be looked at by a cat, dog, monkey, or horse, than by a snake or some blind protozoon.

My dear friend John Llewelyn, who was with us here in 1992, has dedi-cated fundamental, lucid, and courageous analyses to these themes, nota-bly in *The Middle Voice of Ecological Conscience*. I wish to pay homage to him and allow myself to recommend that you read his book, especially since, sharing his concern and appealing to him, I shall perhaps proceed a little differently. In the very rich chapter that he dedicates to Levinas ("*Who* is my neighbour?"), Llewelyn reports that one day, here, in fact, at Cerisy in 1986, he asked Levinas a number of questions. For example: Does the fact of having a face imply an aptitude for language? Does the animal have a face? Can one read "Thou shalt not kill" in the eyes of the animal? Here is Levinas's response as transcribed by Llewelyn: "I cannot say at what moment you have the right to be called 'face.' The human face is completely different and only afterwards do we discover the face of an animal. I don't know if a snake has a face. I can't answer that question. A more specific analysis is needed."[54] A brief remark, first of all on the statement "The human face is completely different and only afterwards do we discover the face of an animal." It indeed seems to suggest that this discovery after the fact operates on the basis of an analogical transposition or anthropomorphism, which is a way of rendering it secondary if not of finding it suspect, and in any case amounts to confirming, for better or for worse, that the thinking and experience of the face are originarily human, that is to say, fraternal. Such a reading appears to be reinforced by another response during a later interview (1988), also quoted by Llewelyn. While recognizing that ethics extends to all living beings and that we are not to make an animal suffer "needlessly" (which is the position of the Universal Declaration of Animal Rights), Levinas insists on the originary, paradigmatic, "prototypical" character of ethics as human, the space of a relation between humans, only humans; it is for this that they are human. It is only afterward, by means of an analogical transposition, that we become sensitive to animal suffering. It is only by means of a transference, indeed, through metaphor or allegory, that such suffering obligates us. Certainly, the human face is and says "I am," in the end, only in front of the other and after the other, but that is always the other human, and the latter comes before an animal, which never looks at him to say "Thou shalt not kill," even if it be as if to say "Help, I am suffering," with the implication "like you":

> It is clear that, without considering animals as human beings, the ethical extends to all living beings. We do not want to make an animal suffer needlessly and so on. But the *prototype of this is human ethics*. Vegetarianism, for example, arises from the *transference* to animals of the idea of suffering. The animal suffers. It is because we, as human, know what suffering is that we can have this obligation.[55]

Listen again to the other response, the response that declares "I don't know if a snake has a face. I can't answer that question. A more specific analysis is needed." This response seems at the same time fine, dizzyingly risky, exposed, but also quite cautious. It presents itself in the first instance as a nonresponse. Better yet, an admission of nonresponse; a declaration of nonresponse: "I can't answer that question," he says. Declining responsibility, if one can say that, Levinas thus replies that he can't answer. He replies that he would very much like to respond, that no doubt he should, but he can't. He is incapable of it. Not incapable in general of responding in general, as Descartes' animal would be incapable of responding, but incapable here of responding *to* this very question and of answering *for* this question on the animal, concerning the face of the animal: "I can't answer that question" is what he says, according to John Llewelyn's translation. But this response in the form of a nonresponse is human. Quite human, all too human. No animal at all, Levinas implies, would admit in the same way to the incapacity to answer what is in sum the question of responding: for to have a face is to be able to respond or answer, by means of the "Here I am," before the other and for the other, for one's self for the other. And in responding that he can't respond, Levinas says, "Here I am"; he responds, but by admitting that he can't respond to the question of knowing what a face is, namely, of knowing what responding is, and he can thus no longer answer for his whole discourse on the face. For declaring that he doesn't know where the right to be called "face" begins means confessing that one doesn't know at bottom what a face is, what the word means, what governs its usage, and that means confessing that one didn't say what responding means. Doesn't that amount, as a result, to calling into question the whole legitimacy of the discourse and ethics of the "face" of the other, the legitimacy and even the sense of every proposition concerning the alterity of the other, the other as my neighbor or my brother, etc.?

It is difficult to assess, or in fact to ascribe any limit at all to the gravity and consequences of these declarations in the form of a modest avowal ("I cannot say at what moment you have [or one has] the right to be called 'face,'" or "I can't answer that question," that of knowing whether the animal, in this case a snake, has a face). But at the same time the expectation, indeed, the promise, or in any case the simple reference to the necessity of a more specific analysis (to come, therefore, to be refined in the future), and of an analysis that—this is my hypothesis at least— would risk calling into question the whole order and configuration [*ordonnancement*] of Levinas's discourse, is at the same time a responsible, courageous, and humble way to leave every chance to what is to come. And it is clearly in the breach opened by "more specific analyses" that we are now, and have for a long time been, engaged.

Nevertheless, something in Levinas seems to remain closed off, saying "no" with one hand to the future that he barely opens with the other. For such a future is threatening to him and to the whole tradition that he so eminently represents. As I see it, this *no(t)* said [*ce* non *dit*], this saying *no*, is found throughout his work concerning the hypothesis of whether the animal has a face, or conversely, whether or not man really has one that is one, in the rigorous purity of the demands to which Levinas submits this concept. And this "no," which echoes everywhere, can be heard in this response in the form of a nonresponse as soon as Levinas chooses *an example* of an animal in order to support his declaration of nonknowledge. The example is not chosen by chance; it is the snake ("I don't know if a snake has a face"). For the immense allegorical or mythical weight, and to begin with, the biblical and poetic weight, which we spoke of earlier ("Beast I am, but a sharp one / Whose venom however vile / Can far out-vie the hemlock's wisdom"), makes attributing a face to this figure of temptation or evil highly improbable. That is no doubt what Levinas's rhetoric wants to convince us of, although one could be tempted, on the contrary, to see in a figure of bestial evil a still more inevitable idea of the face. Where there is evil there is face. What remains faceless is pure indifference to good and evil. In particular, in choosing the serpent Levinas can avoid lighting on more disturbing examples. He avoids still more having to answer the question concerning so many other animals—for example, the cat, the dog, the horse, the monkey, the orangutan, the chimpanzee—whom it would be difficult to refuse a face and a gaze. And hence to refuse the "Thou shalt not kill" that Levinas reserves for the face, for the face of the human for the human, or for God's commandment in instituting the nakedness of the human face.

Levinas promotes "Thou shalt not kill" from sixth to first place in the Decalogue, and he recalls so often that it is the first commandment to come from the face of the other, being confused, in fact, with the very epiphany of the face. Yet one should clearly understand what is forbidden by "Thou shalt not kill," which is often translated by Levinas as "You shall commit no murder." It forbids murder, namely, homicide, but doesn't forbid putting to death in general, no more than it responds to a respect for life, a respect in principle for life in general (*torat haïm*). It is a "Thou shalt not kill" that doesn't forbid one to kill an animal; it forbids only the murder of the face. Moreover, there is no murder other than of the face, that is to say, of the face of the other, my neighbor, my brother, the human, or another human. Putting to death or sacrificing the animal, exploiting it to death—none of those, within this logic, in fact constitutes murder. They are not forbidden by "Thou shalt not kill." That is because the animal, at bottom, inasmuch as it is incapable of being the victim of a murder, doesn't die. And from that point of view, Levinas also remains profoundly Heideggerian. Like Descartes and Kant, and like Heidegger, he gives secondary importance, in his definition of the self or the "Here I am," to existence as life, as livingness [*vivance*], as is the case with Descartes' "I think therefore I am," but also with Heidegger's Dasein, which, however much it may first appear as (possible-impossible) being-toward-death, does not in the first instance declare itself to be a living thing. Paradoxically, it is a mortal, indeed, one who is dying without essentially having anything to do, in its being-there, in its "I am," with life. And if Heidegger in *Being and Time* starts by calling subjectivity into question and by explaining why he must avoid applying the nouns *man* and *life* to Dasein, the analytic still begins with "I am," picking up the ontological examination of it where Descartes left off, yet an "I am" that, for Heidegger as for Descartes, does not say first and foremost "I am living" or "I breathe." At the heart of all these difficulties, there is always the unthought side of a thinking of life (and it is by means of that, through the question of life and of the "living present," of the autobiography of the ego in its living present, that my deconstructive reading of Husserl began, as well, in fact, as everything that followed from that).

If the animal doesn't die, that is, if one can put it to death without "killing" it or murdering it, without committing murder, without "Thou shalt not kill" concerning it or regarding me in the context of it [*sans que . . . le regarde ou me regarde à son sujet*], it is because the animal remains foreign to everything that defines sanctity, the separation and thus the ethics of the person as face (substitution, *illeity*, being-host or being-hostage, visitation, peace, goodness, paternity, and, above all, that which coordinates the relation between ethics or metaphysics and the command "Thou shalt not kill" or "You will not commit murder," namely, responsibility). If I am insisting in particular on the responsibility of one who responds "Here I am" and who presents himself as responsible for the other by means of substitution, it is because Levinas comes back to that all the time as first inspiration for his "first philosophy." But it is also for two other reasons: first, *because* "Here I am" as responsibility implies this self-presentation, this *autotelic*, autodeictic, autobiographical movement, exposing oneself before the law; and second, *because* "Here I am" as responsibility implies the possibility of "responding," of answering for oneself in the response to the appeal or command of the other. Now, in the tradition that we are tracking here, the animal, according to Levinas, seems deprived of all possibility, in fact, of all power of saying "Here I am" and of responding, hence of all responsibility. It is nobody, certainly not a "person," a word that Levinas always kept intact. That is why the animal doesn't die. That is why its nonresponse cannot be compared to the nonresponse (another very important concept for him) by means of which he nevertheless defines death, understood as the death of the face of the other human. Death is not for him, in the first instance, a passage from being to nothingness, an annihilation, but, as he often says, the moment when the other no longer responds. Well, this nonresponse of the face, of the corpse as facial corpse, would have no affinity with animal nonresponse and nonresponsibility. Everything seems to hinge here on these two understandings of nonresponse, at the heart of the disturbing analogy between them. (What never even crosses the mind of any of the thinkers we are listening to or will listen to here on the subject of the response, from Descartes to Lacan, is the question of how an iterability that is essential to every response, and to the ideality of every response, can and cannot fail to introduce nonresponse, automatic reaction, mechanical reaction into the most alive, most "authentic," and most responsible response.) The corpse of the face doesn't return to being animal the moment when, like the animal, it doesn't respond. The nonresponse of this "he doesn't respond" of the dead face means "he is no longer responding" there where "he will have responded," whereas the animal's "it doesn't respond" means "it has never responded," "it never will respond," "it would never have responded," "it will never have been able to respond." Thus, at one and the same time the animal is deprived of the power and the right to respond, of course, and therefore of responsibility (and hence of the law, etc.), yet it is also deprived of nonresponse, of the right of nonresponse that is accorded the human face by means of secrecy or in death. Similarly, and still within the same logic of a temptation that is rapidly discounted, one might imagine that the animal, the animal-other, the other as animal, occupies the place of the third person and thus of the first appeal to justice, in between humans and the faces of those who look upon each other as brothers or neighbors. But no. When Levinas reflects on the other of the other who is not simply a fellow [*semblable*] and who brings the question of justice to the fore, that nonfellow remains human, a brother and not another other, not an other other than the human, other than "the other human," who is still called "human" and responds only to that name.[56]

Why does this disavowal, this foreclosing or sidelining of the *animot* surprise us more coming from Levinas than from the other thinkers of the "I think," from Descartes or Kant, for example? Because the principle of life (*torat haïm*) remains a great intangible Judaic principle (even though it has never prevented animal sacrifice within Judaism—an enormous problem that I'll leave aside here).

Levinas manifests a type of ironic incredulity when, in his text on Bobby, which we are about to encounter, he evokes the "vegetarian principle" and then exclaims (with an exclamation mark!) that "If we are to believe Genesis, Adam, the father of us all, was one!" In fact, the two accounts from Genesis are extremely clear on this matter: before the fall and the institution of nakedness, God clearly commanded Adam to feed himself as a gatherer and not as a hunter. He has to eat what grows on the surface of the earth and on trees. It is later, after the fall, that Abel will have himself preferred by God by offering up to him the sacrifices of a husbandman, whereas poor Cain remains a sedentary cultivator. Finally, Cain had been more faithful to God's arch-primary commandment, and the whole history, that is to say, the fault and criminality that install historicity, is linked to God's preference for Abel's animal offering and, perhaps, to the remorse that follows as expressed through the protection that is promised to the wandering descendants of Cain. But everything in Levinas that echoes like a protest against putting down sedentary roots and making place sacred would situate him on the side of those who raise livestock, on the good side of Abel, who is also he who dominates and raises animals, then makes a sacrifice of them to God.

One might be surprised, from another point of view, by what remains, in its very originality, a profound anthropocentrism and humanism. For a thinking of the other, of the infinitely other who looks at me, should, on the contrary, privilege the question and the request of the animal. Not in order to put it in front of that of man, but in order to think that of man, of the brother and the neighbor from the perspective of an animal question and request, of an audible or silent appeal that calls within us outside of us, from the most far away, before us after us, preceding and pursuing us in an unavoidable way, so unavoidable that it leaves the trace of so many symptoms and wounds, of stigmata of disavowal within the discourse of whomever seeks to remain deaf to that appeal. In a certain way, whether they wish to or not, or whether they know it or not, Descartes, Kant, and Levinas do nothing but speak and hear tell of the *animot*, clearly. But they always do so by means of disavowal and foreclosure. The *animot* finds itself disavowed, foreclosed, sacrificed, and humiliated by them, and in the first instance with respect to what is closest to them, within themselves, on the edge of the infinite vertigo of the "I am" and of "I am who I am (following) and by whom I am followed as much as preceded." Their "I am" is always "I am after the animal even when I don't know it." And this disavowal of foreclosure is just as powerful when they don't speak of it or when they speak of it in order to deny to the *animot* everything they attribute to the human.

In order to identify certain reference points or examples of this disavowal, let us sketch out a reading of the famous text on Bobby, which has attracted the attention of so many readers, in particular, the fitting attention of my friends John Llewelyn and Alain David.[57] Under the title "The Name of a Dog, or Natural Rights," this brief, rich, playful, moving text appeared in 1975 in a collection dedicated to Bram Van Velde and entitled *Celui qui ne peut se servir de mots* (*He Who Cannot Use Words*; in homage, I suppose, to the figure of the painter, therefore, to *zōgraphia*, to another sort of animal and dog whose language lacks words).[58] These pages appear all the more fascinating because they seem to jar with the rest of Levinas's work and form a sort of hapax, for it is there a question, he says, of a "Kantian" dog, and indeed "the last Kantian in Nazi Germany." This autobiographical text reveals what was, for Levinas, a time of war and captivity. In a prisoner-of-war camp, Camp 1492 (what a number, what a date! he notes),[59] this "cherished dog" alone looked upon the men as men: "For him—there was no doubt—we were men" (153).

In order to be serious, and responsible, at the risk of bringing back down to earth all the enchanted readers who, dreaming of reconciling Levinas's ethics with the animals, set about idolizing this dog, it is necessary to limit straightaway the scope of this hymn to Bobby. In at least three ways. First, this touching sentence "For him—there was no doubt [c'était incontestable]—we were men" says nothing about this testimonial right to what is undeniable, so calmly laid claim to at the very point where it calls for examination. Second, it says nothing, in particular, about what is to be included under the rubric "man" at the point where it is said that "For him . . . we were men." For hunted, beaten, or slaughtered animals we are also men, alas, whom they identify only too quickly, regrettably, as men. Since Levinas means something else, namely, that for the dog Bobby we were human persons, faces worthy of respect and of the "Thou shalt not kill," it is all the more extraordinary that the principle merit recognized in this Kantian dog is that of recognizing us, as men and as moral persons. Third, another limit, more serious still, derives from Levinas's hastening to add, in the same sentence, in order to take back from this Kantian dog everything that he has just so generously given him, moreover, with an explicit consciousness of that generosity: "The last Kantian in Nazi Germany, without the brain needed to universalize the maxims for drives, this dog was a descendant of the dogs of Egypt" (ibid., translation modified). There would be much to say concerning this allusion to Egypt, which Levinas contrasts with Greece, the *Odyssey*, and Ithaca, where the dog that recognized Ulysses did so in a place of return and nostalgia, in the embrace [*regard*] of a fatherland, whereas the Kantian dog let loose his friendly growl in the desert: "Here, we were nowhere" (ibid.). But how can one ignore that a Kantian who doesn't have "the brain needed" to universalize maxims would not be Kantian, especially if the maxims in question are the maxims of "drives" that would have made Kant bark. Bobby is thus anything but Kantian. This allegorical or fabulous Kantian is at the very best an infirm neo-Kantian, a Kantian deprived of reason, a Kantian without universalizable maxims.

Reckoning only by the measure of what we glimpsed in a certain unconscious of pure practical reason, namely, the cruel and merciless war that a virtual "fascist" (in Adorno's terms) Kantian idealism declares on animal life, calling Bobby a Kantian is no compliment. One risks making of him at best a guardian of the peace, at worst an example of dog eat dog.[60] I don't intend to tear into [m'acharner sur] this marvelous paean to Bobby, which, moreover, opens by turning away from flesh [le désacharnement]. It is true that the verse from Exodus (22:31) that inspires from its beginning this whole meditation is anything but a charter for vegetarianism. In saying "And ye shall be holy men unto me: neither shall ye eat any flesh that is torn of beasts in the field; ye shall cast it to the dogs," the verse doesn't prescribe meatless food but, as with all the preceding verses, it commands that the treatment, raising, sacrifice, and exchange of animals be submitted to rituals and regulations. The verses that immediately precede the epigraph to "Name of a Dog," verses that Levinas doesn't quote, command thus: "the firstborn of thy sons shalt thou give unto me. / Likewise shalt thou do with thine oxen, and with thy sheep: Seven days it shall be with his dam; on the eighth day thou shalt give it me" (22:29–30).

This "Name of a Dog" calls for infinite commentary, and with all the requisite patience. Unable to do that here, I shall be content simply to punctuate a punctuation. In Adieu to Emmanuel Levinas, I took the liberty of evoking the need to one day take a systematic look at the rhetoric of exclamation marks in Levinas.[61] In this instance I noted at least eleven of them within eight small pages.[62] All of them seem to me to connote a disavowal. Moreover, two of them follow the utterance "But no! But no!" which in truth attests to the truth of a "But yes! But yes!" when it comes to a dog that recognizes the other and thus responds to the other by responding to his name, answering, therefore, for his name: "Perhaps the dog that recognized Ulysses beneath his disguise on his return from the Odyssey was a forbear of our own. But no! But no! There, they were in Ithaca and the Fatherland. Here, we were nowhere. The last Kantian in Nazi Germany, without the brain needed to universalize the maxims for drives, this dog was a descendant of the dogs of Egypt."[63]

Two other exclamation marks—and I'll call them, therefore, two disavowal marks or, as Rousseau might have said, marks of irony, that is to say, of allegorical incredulity—signal to my mind that the text is doing something else, even the exact contrary of what Levinas says or means to say. Unless it be that God is contradicting his Dictum [son Dit] and that the whole question of the animal plays within that contradiction.[64] Levinas intends to speak, and in the verse from the Bible, of a particular dog, the one that responds to the proper name *Bobby*: this one, Bobby, without allegory, fable, or theology. Yet the opposite occurs, both in the Bible and in the story of Bobby, where this dog is but the figure for a Kantian dog, since he is lacking the essential thing that would be demanded by a Kantian morality that took into account the dignity (*Würde*) of a rational being capable of universalizing the maxims of his actions. Like the biblical text, and despite what he says about it, Levinas's text is at once metaphorical, allegorical, and theological, anthropotheological, hence anthropomorphic, and it remains that "without respite [*sans trêve*]" at the very moment when Levinas proclaims, claims, *prétend*, by exclaiming, the opposite. Two pages earlier, following three more exclamation marks that scan allusions to the sublimation of "hunting games!" to the principle of vegetarianism, which, "if we are to believe Genesis," was adopted by Adam, "the father of us all!" and to the interdictions that should "limit . . . the butchery that every day claims our 'consecrated mouths' [*notre bouche de 'saints hommes'*]!" Levinas indeed exclaims: "But enough of [*trêve de*] this theology! It is the dog mentioned at the end of the verse that I am especially interested in. I am thinking of Bobby" (151). And this is how he takes up again, much later, without respite, the same disavowal under the sign of the indefatigable expression *trêve de*:

> But enough of allegories! We have read too many fables and we are still taking the name of a dog in the figurative sense. So, in the terms of a venerable hermeneutics, more ancient than La Fontaine, orally transmitted from early antiquity—the hermeneutics of the talmudic Doctors—this biblical text, troubled by parables, here challenges the metaphor: in Exodus 22:31 the dog is a dog. Literally a dog! (152)

An eleventh exclamation mark is found right in the middle of the text, at the eleventh hour, giving a tone of incredulity in the face of what in fact remains incredible, and hence purely allegorical or figurative, namely, a transcendence in Levinas's sense, hence a veritable opening to ethics, on the part of an animal, which would thus see recognized in it what elsewhere Levinas even denies to woman as such—precisely, transcendence.[65] After admitting, in a way, that this biblical dog is only a "figure of humanity!" Levinas uses the Kantian expression "friend of man" in order to designate the dog that is capable of transcendence. It is a question of the dogs of Egypt, which are thunderstruck at the moment of the "death of the firstborn," when "Israel is about to be released from the house of bondage." You will hear how the dog, which is still in lack and *privation*, as Heidegger will decidedly say, "without," still lacking the *logos* and ethics, "with neither ethics nor *logos*," in Levinas's words, sees itself convoked, in its very silence, as a witness, simply as witness to the humanity of man. This mute witness is there merely to attest to the dignity (*Würde*) of man:

> Slaves who served the slaves of the State will henceforth follow the most high Voice, the most free path. It is a figure of humanity! Man's freedom is that of an emancipated man remembering his servitude and feeling solidarity for all enslaved people. A rabble of slaves will celebrate this high mystery of man, and "not a dog shall growl." At the supreme hour of its institution, with neither ethics nor *logos*, the dog will attest to the dignity of its person. This is what the friend of man means. There is a transcendence in the animal! And the clear verse with which we began is given a new meaning. It reminds us of the debt that is always open.
>
> But perhaps the subtle exegesis we are quoting gets lost in rhetoric? Indeed.
>
> There were seventy of us in a forestry commando unit for Jewish prisoners of war in Nazi Germany. . . . We were subhuman [*nous n'étions qu'une quasi-humanité*], a gang of apes. (152–53, translation modified)

Let's not hide the fact, this allegorical dog that becomes witness to the dignity of man is an other without alterity, without *logos*, without ethics, without the power to universalize maxims. It can witness to us only for us, being too other to be our brother or neighbor, not enough other to be the wholly other, the nakedness of whose face dictates to us "Thou shalt not kill." In other words, what we are reading through the unconscious of these exclamatory disavowals is the fact that it is not sufficient to subvert the traditional subject by making it a subject-host or hostage of the other in order to recognize in what continues to be called "the animal," in the singular ("a transcendence in the animal!" "animal faith," etc.), something other than a deprivation of humanity. The animal remains for Levinas what it will have been for the whole Cartesian-type tradition: a machine that doesn't speak, that doesn't have access to sense, that can at best imitate "signifiers without a signified" (as you are about to hear), a sort of monkey with "monkey talk," precisely what the Nazis sought to reduce their Jewish prisoners to. For, after emphasizing the fact that racism is not a biological concept and that anti-Semitism "is the archetype of all internment," Levinas says about "social oppression" that it "merely imitates this model." And he writes the following, which doesn't appear to break with the traditional reference to the ape:

It [social oppression] shuts people away in a class, deprives them of expression and condemns them to being "signifiers without a signi-fied" and from there to violence and fighting. How can we deliver a message about our humanity which, from behind the bars of quota-tion marks, will come across [*s'étende*: *s'entende*, rather; no doubt there is a typo (*coquille*) there] as anything other than monkey talk [*parler simiesque*]? (153)

It is, therefore, not sufficient for an ethics to recall the subject to its being-subject, host or hostage, subjected to the other, to the wholly other or to every other. More than that is required to break with the Cartesian tradition of an animal without language and without response. It takes more than that, we'll come to that, even within a logic and ethics of the unconscious, which, without renouncing the concept of the subject, would lay claim to some "subversion" of it.

3

And Say the Animal Responded?

to Jacques Lacan

Would an ethics like that Levinas attempts be sufficient to recall the subject to its being-subject, its being-host or -hostage, that is to say, its being-subjected-to-the-other, to the Wholly Other or to every single other?

I don't think so. More than that is required to break with the Cartesian tradition of the animal-machine without language and without response.[1] It takes more than that, even within a logic or an ethics of the unconscious that, without renouncing the concept of the subject, would lay claim to some "subversion" of it.

By evoking this Lacanian title, "The Subversion of the Subject," we therefore move from one ethical disavowal to another. I have chosen, in this context, to trace that movement by following the paths that have just been opened, those of the other, of witnessing, and of the "signifiers without a signified" that Levinas associates with the *simiesque*. In Lacan's 1960 text "The Subversion of the Subject and the Dialectic of Desire in the Freudian Unconscious," a certain passage names "the animal" or "an animal," in the singular and without any further details. It perhaps marks what is at once a step beyond and a step this side of Freud regarding relations among the human, the unconscious, and the *animot*. This remarkable page at first gives the impression, and raises the hope that things are going to change, notably, concerning the concept of communication or information that is assigned to what is called the "animal," the animal in general. It is thought that the latter is capable only of a coded message or of a meaning that is narrowly indicative [*signalisante*], strictly constrained;

one that is fixed in its programming. Lacan begins by taking to task the platitude of "modern information theory." It is true that at that point he is talking about the human subject and not the animal, but he writes the following, which seems to announce, or allow one to hope for, a further note:

> The Other as previous site of the pure subject of the signifier holds the master position, even before coming into existence, to use Hegel's term against him, as absolute Master. For what is omitted in the platitude of modern information theory is the fact that one can speak of a code only if it is already the code of the Other, and that is something quite different from what is in question in the message, since it is from this code that the subject is constituted, which means that it is from the Other that the subject receives even the message that he emits.[2]

We'll come back, after a digression, to this page of "The Subversion of the Subject and the Dialectic of Desire in the Freudian Unconscious." It *poses* (and I emphasize the word *poses*, since it puts forward in the form of a thesis, or presupposes without providing any proof) the idea of an animal characterized by an incapacity to *pretend to pretend* [feindre de feindre] or to *erase its traces*, an incapacity that makes it unable to be a "subject," that is to say, "subject of the signifier."

The digression I shall now outline will allow us to go back over earlier texts by Lacan, places that, it seems to me, announce *at the same time* a theoretical mutation and a stagnant confirmation of inherited thinking, its presuppositions, and its dogma.

What still held out hope for a decisive displacement of the traditional problematic was, for example, the taking into account of a specular function in the sexualization of the animal, as early as 1936, in "The Mirror Stage." Such an idea was quite rare at the time. And that was the case even if—this amounts to a massive limitation—the passage through the mirror forever immobilized the animal, according to Lacan, within the snare of the imaginary, thus depriving it of any access to the symbolic, that is to say, to the law and to whatever is held to be proper to the human. The animal will never be, as man is, "prey to language." Later, in "The Direction of the Treatment," we read: "It must be posited that, produced as it is by any animal at the mercy of language [*en proie au langage*], man's desire is the desire of the Other" (264). This figure of the prey symptomatically and recurrently characterizes the "animal" obsession in Lacan at the very moment when he insists on dissociating the anthropological from the zoological: man is an animal but a speaking one, and he is less a beast of prey than a beast that is prey to language. There is no desire, and thus no unconscious, except for the human; it in no way exists for the animal, unless that be as an effect of the human unconscious, as if the domestic or tamed animal translated within itself the unconscious of man by some contagious transference or mute interiorization (the terms of which would, moreover, still need to be taken into account). Being careful to distinguish the unconscious drive from instinct or the "genetic," to which he relegates the animal, Lacan holds in "Position de l'inconscient" ("Position of the Unconscious") that the animal could not itself have an unconscious, an unconscious of its own, if such a thing could be said and if the logic of the expression didn't seem ridiculous. But, to begin with, it perhaps seems ridiculous to Lacan himself, since he writes that "in the propaedeutic experience one can illustrate the effect of enunciation by asking the child if he can imagine the unconscious in the animal, short of some effect of language, and of human language."[3]

Each word of this sentence deserves critical examination. Its thesis is clear: the animal has neither unconscious nor language, nor the other, except as an effect of the human order, that is by contagion, appropriation, domestication.

No doubt taking account of sexualizing specularity in the animal is a remarkable advance, even if it captures the *animot* in the mirror, and even if it keeps the hen-pigeon or migrating locust in captivity within the imaginary. Referring to the effects of a Gestalt proven by a "biological experimentation" that would find repugnant the language of "psychic causality," Lacan credits that theory with recognizing nevertheless that "the maturation of the gonad in the hen-pigeon" relies on the "sight of a fellow creature [*congénère*]," that is to say, another pigeon of either sex. And that is true even to the extent that a simple mirror reflection will suffice. It is also sufficient for a migrating locust to perceive a similar visual image in order to mature from solitude to gregariousness. In a way that is for me significant, Lacan speaks of movement from the "solitary" to the "gregarious" form, and not to the social form, as though the difference between *gregarious* and *social* were the difference between animal and human. This motif, and the words *gregarious* and even *gregariousness* [*grégarisme*], reappear forcefully in the context of animality some ten years later, in "Propos sur la causalité psychique" ("Remarks on Psychic Causality," 1946).[4] Moreover, at the end of this text Lacan declares Descartes to be unsurpassable. The analysis of the specular effect in the pigeon is developed further here, but it still works in the same direction: according to then-recent research by Harrisson (1939), the ovulation of the hen-pigeon is produced by the simple *sight* of a form evoking another member of the species, of a visual reflection, in short, even in the absence of an actual male.⁵ It is indeed a matter of a specular gaze, of an image and a visual image, rather than identification by means of odor or sound. Even if the mating game is physically preempted by a sheet of glass, and even if the couple consists of two females, ovulation still takes place. It happens after twelve days when the couple is heterosexual, if we can use the term, and after a period of up to two months for two females. A mirror is all it takes.⁶

One of the interesting things about this interpretation is that, after all, as with Descartes, and according to the tried and true biblical and Promethean tradition to which I keep returning, it relates the fixity of animal determinism within the context of information and communication to a type of originary perfection of that animal. Conversely, if "human knowledge has greater autonomy than animal knowledge in relation to the field of force of desire,"⁷ and if "the human order is distinguished from nature,"⁸ it is, paradoxically, because of an imperfection, because of an originary lack or defect [*défaut*] in man, who has, in sum, received speech and technics only inasmuch as he lacks something. Here I am speaking of what Lacan situates at the center of his "mirror stage," namely the "fact of a real *specific prematurity of birth* in man" (4, Lacan's italics). The defect tied to this prematurity would correspond to the "objective notion of anatomical incompleteness of the pyramidal system," to what embryologists call "*foetalization*," which, Lacan recalls, is linked to a certain "intraorganic mirror" (ibid.). An *autotelic* specularity of the inside is thus linked to a defect, to a prematurity, to an incompleteness of the little man.

What I have just referred to, rather quickly, here on the threshold of "The Subversion of the Subject," as a limited but incontestable advance, has to be registered with the greatest caution. For not only is the animal held within the imaginary and unable to accede to the symbolic, to the unconscious and to language (and hence, so as not to lose our general thread, to autobiographical auto-deixis), but the description of its semiotic power remains determined, in the *Discours de Rome* ("The Function and Field of Speech and Language in Psychoanalysis," 1953), in the most dogmatically traditional manner, fixed within Cartesian fixity, within the presupposition of a code that permits only *reactions* to stimuli and not *responses* to questions. I say "semiotic" system and not "language," for Lacan also refuses the animal language, recognizing in its case only what he calls a "code," the "fixity of coding" or a "system of signalling." These are different ways of naming what, within a cognitivist problematic of the animal that often repeats the most worn-out truisms of metaphysics even as it appears to resist them, is called "prewired response [*réponse pré-câblée*]" or "prewired behavior."[9]

Lacan is so precise and firm when it comes to accrediting the old yet modernized topos of the bee that he seems, if I might say so, not to have a clear conscience. I detect an unavowed anxiety behind the authority of this new, yet so old, old discourse concerning the bee. Lacan claims to be relying on what he blithely calls the "animal kingdom" in order to critique the current notion of "language as a sign" as opposed to "human languages." When bees appear to "respond" to a "message," they do not *respond* but *react*; they merely obey a fixed program, whereas the human subject responds to the other, to the question from or of the other. This discourse is quite literally Cartesian. Later, as we shall see, Lacan expressly contrasts *reaction* with *response* as an opposition between human and animal kingdoms, in the same way that he opposes nature and convention:

> I shall show the inadequacy of the conception of "language as a sign" by the very manifestation that best illustrates it in the animal kingdom, a manifestation which, if it had not recently been the object of an authentic discovery, it seems it would have been necessary to invent for this purpose.
>
> It is now generally admitted that when the bee returns to the hive from its honey-gathering it indicates to its companions by two sorts of dance the existence of nectar and its relative distance, near or far, from the hive. The second type of dance is the most remarkable, for the plane in which the bee traces the figure-of-eight curve—which is why it has been called the "wagging dance,"—and the frequency of the figures executed within a given time, designate, on the one hand, exactly the direction to be followed, determined in relation to the inclination of the sun (on which bees are able to orient themselves in all weathers, thanks to their sensitivity to polarized light), and, on the other hand, the distance, up to several miles, at which the nectar is to be found. And the other bees respond to this message by setting off immediately for the place thus designated.
>
> It took some ten years of patient observation for Karl von Frisch to decode this kind of message, for it is certainly a code, or system of signalling, whose generic character alone forbids us to qualify it as conventional.
>
> But is it necessarily a language? We can say that it is distinguished from language precisely by the *fixed* [my italics] correlation of its signs to the reality that they signify. For in a language signs take on their value from their relations to each other in the lexical distribution of semantemes as much as in the positional, or even flectional,

use of morphemes, in sharp contrast to the *fixity* [my italics again] of the coding used by bees. And the diversity of human languages [*langues*] takes on its full value from this enlightening discovery.

Furthermore, while the message of the kind described here determines the action of the *socius*, it is never retransmitted by it. This means that the message remains *fixed* [my italics still] in its function as a relay of the action, from which no subject detaches it as a symbol of communication itself. (84–85)

Even if one were to subscribe provisionally to this logic (to which I do not in fact object in the slightest, wanting simply to reinscribe it quite differently, and beyond any simple opposition between animal and human), it is difficult, as Lacan does explicitly, to reserve the differentiality of signs for human language only, as opposed to animal coding. What he attributes to signs that, "in a language" understood as belonging to the human order, "take on their value from their relations to each other" and so on, and not just from the "fixed correlation" between signs and reality, can and must be accorded to any code, animal or human.

As for the absence of a response in the animal-machine, as for the trenchant distinction between *reaction* and *response*, there is nothing fortuitous in the fact that the most Cartesian passage of all is found following the discourse on the bee, on its system of information, which would keep it excluded from the "field of speech and language." It is indeed a matter of the constitution of the subject as human subject once the latter crosses the frontier of information to gain access to speech:

> For the function of language is not to inform but to evoke.
>
> What I seek in speech is the response of the other. What constitutes me as subject is my question. In order to be recognized by the other, I utter what was only in view of what will be. In order to find him, I call him by a name that he must assume or refuse in order to reply to me.
>
> . . .
>
> If I now place myself in front of the other to question him, there is no cybernetic computer imaginable that can make a *reaction out of what the response is*. The definition of response as the second term in the "stimulus response" circuit is simply a metaphor sustained by the subjectivity imputed to the animal, a subjectivity that is then ignored in the physical schema to which the metaphor reduces it. This is what I have called putting the rabbit into the hat so as to be able to pull it out again later. *But a reaction is not a response.*

If I press an electric button and a light goes on, there is no response except for *my* desire. (86, translation modified, my italics, except for Lacan's "*my* desire")

Once again, we are not concerned with erasing every difference between what we are calling *reaction* and what we commonly name *response*. It is not a matter of confusing what happens when one presses a computer key and what happens when one asks a question of an interlocutor. We are even less concerned with attributing to what Lacan calls "the animal" what he also calls a "subjectivity" or an "unconscious," which would, for example, allow us to put the animal in an analytical situation (even if such analogous scenarios cannot be completely excluded for *certain* animals, in *certain* contexts—and if time permitted we could imagine some hypotheses that would refine that analogy). My hesitation concerns only the purity, the rigor, and the indivisibility of the frontier that separates—already with respect to "us humans"—reaction from response and in consequence, especially, the purity, rigor, and indivisibility of the concept of responsibility that is derived from it. The general concern that I am thus formulating becomes more serious, in at least three ways:

1. when one is required really to take into account a logic of the unconscious that should proscribe all immediate and conscious assurance of the freedom presupposed by every responsibility;

2. especially when—and this is singularly so for Lacan—the logic of the unconscious is founded on a logic of repetition, which, in my opinion, will always inscribe a destiny of iterability, hence some automaticity of the reaction in every response, however originary, free, critical [*décisoire*], and a-reactional it might seem;

3. when, and this is true of Lacan in particular, one gives credence to the materiality of speech and to the corporality of language.

Lacan reminds us of this last on the following page: "Speech is in fact a gift of language, and language is not immaterial. It is a subtle body, but body it is" (87). Yet in the interval he will have founded all "responsibility," and to begin with all psychoanalytic responsibility, thus all psychoanalytic ethics, on the distinction, which I find so problematic, between *reaction* and *response*. He will even have founded there, and this is precisely what I wish to demonstrate, his concept of the *subject*: "Henceforth the decisive function of my own response appears, and this function is not, as has been said, simply to be received by the subject as acceptance or rejection of his discourse, but really to recognize him or to abolish him as subject. Such is the nature of the analyst's *responsibility* whenever he intervenes by means of speech" (87, translation modified).

Why do the stakes here seem to be so much more serious? In problematizing, as I am doing, the purity and indivisibility of a line between reaction and response, and especially the possibility of tracing such a line, between the human *in general* and the animal *in general*, one risks—something that won't fail to cause them anxiety as they reproach me for it—casting doubt on all responsibility, all ethics, every decision, etc. To that I would respond—for it is indeed a matter of responding—with what follows, schematically, by means of principles, with three points.

1. *On the one hand*, casting doubt on responsibility, on decision, on one's own being-ethical, seems to me to be—and is perhaps what should forever remain—the unrescindable essence of ethics, decision, and responsibility. All firm knowledge, certainty, and assurance on this subject would suffice, precisely, to confirm the very thing one wishes to disavow, namely, the reactionality in the response. I indeed said "to disavow," and it is for that reason that I situate disavowal at the heart of all these discourses on the animal.

2. *On the other hand*, far from erasing the difference—a nonoppositional and infinitely differentiated, qualitative, and intensive difference between reaction and response—it is a matter, on the contrary, of taking that difference into account within the whole differentiated field of experience and of a world of life forms, and of doing that without reducing this differentiated and multiple difference, in a conversely massive and homogenizing manner, to one between the human subject, on the one hand, and the nonsubject that is the animal in general, on the other, where the latter comes to be, in another sense, the nonsubject that is subjected to the human subject.

3. *Finally*, it would be a matter of developing another "logic" of decision, of the response and of the event, as I have also attempted to deploy elsewhere, and which seems to me less incompatible than one might think with what Lacan himself, in "The Subversion of the Subject," maintains concerning the code as "code of the Other." He refers to that Other as the one from whom "the subject receives even the message that he emits" (305). This axiom should complicate the simple distinction between *responsibility* and *reaction*, and all that follows from it. It would therefore be a matter of reinscribing this *différance* between reaction and response, and hence this historicity of ethical, juridical, or political responsibility, within another thinking of life, of the living, within another relation of the living to their ipseity, to their *autos*, to their own autokinesis and reactional automaticity, to death, to technics, or to the mechanical [*machinique*].

Following that digression, if we are now to come to the later text entitled "The Subversion of the Subject and the Dialectic of Desire in the

Freudian Unconscious," we will indeed find the same logic, and the same oppositions—notably, those between the imaginary and the symbolic, and between the specular capture of which the animal is capable and the symbolic order of the signifier to which it has no access. At the juncture between imaginary and symbolic is played out the whole question of autobiography, of autobiography in general, no doubt, but also that of the theoretician or of the institution within whose history the theoretician articulates and signs his discourse on the juncture in question, that is to say, Lacan's discourse as autobiographical analysis. (Although we cannot undertake this within the limits constraining us here, it would be necessary to give back a more accurate perspective, that of the years following the war, with the ideological stakes involved, to the whole essentially anthropological design of the period with respect to its claim to go beyond every *positive* anthropology and every metaphysical and humanist anthropocentrism. And especially, in a most legitimate way, to go beyond biologism, behaviorist physicalism, geneticism, and so on. For Heidegger, as for Lacan and many others, it was above all a matter of validating a new *fundamental* anthropology and of rigorously responding *to* the question and answering *for* the question "What is the human?")

In "The Subversion of the Subject," a more refined analysis is brought to bear on other conceptual distinctions. They seem to me as problematic as those we have just analyzed; moreover, they remain indissociable from them. There occurs what is apparently a parenthesis ("Observe, in parentheses . . ."), but a parenthesis that is, to my mind, capital. It relates precisely to the testimonial dimension in general, that is to say, to what subtends the problematic that matters to us here. Who witnesses [*témoigne*] to what and for whom? Who proves, who looks, who observes whom and what? What is there of knowledge, of certainty, and of truth?

> Observe, in parentheses, that this Other, which is distinguished as the locus of Speech, imposes itself no less as witness to the Truth. Without the dimension that it constitutes, the deception practised by Speech would be indistinguishable from the very different pretence to be found in physical combat or sexual display [*parade*]. (305)

The figure of the animal suddenly surfaces in this difference between pretense [*feinte*] and deception [*tromperie*]. There is, according to Lacan, a clear distinction between what the animal is quite capable of, namely, strategic pretense (warrior, predatory, or seductive suit, pursuit, or persecution) and what it is incapable of and incapable of witnessing to, namely, the deception of speech [*la tromperie de la parole*] within the order of the signifier and of Truth. The deception of speech of course means, as we shall see, lying (and the animal would not properly know how to lie according to common sense, according to Lacan and to many others, even if, as one knows, it understands how to pretend); but more precisely deception involves lying as what, in promising what is true, includes the supplementary possibility of telling the truth in order to lead the other astray, in order to have him believe something other than what is true. (We know the Jewish story recounted by Freud and so often quoted by Lacan: "Why do you tell me that you are going to X in order to have me believe you are going to Y, whereas you are indeed going to X?") According to Lacan it is that type of lie, that deceit, and that pretense in the second degree of which the animal would be incapable, whereas the "subject of the signifier," within the human order, would possess such a power and, better still, would emerge as subject, instituting itself and coming to itself as subject *by virtue of this power*, a second-degree reflexive power, a power that is *conscious* of deceiving by pretending to pretend. One of the interests of this analysis derives no doubt from the fact that in this case Lacan gives much importance, in any case more than anyone else in philosophy and more than he himself does in earlier writings, to the capacity to pretend, which he attributes to what he still calls "the animal," "an animal," to what he here nicknames its "*dancity*" [dansité] with an *a*. *Dancity* refers to the capacity to pretend by means of a dance or lure, by means of the choreography of the hunt or seduction, the parade that is practiced before lovemaking or as a movement of self-protection when making war, hence all the forms of the "I am (following)" or "I am followed" that we are tracking here. But in spite of what Lacan thus acknowledges in or accords to the animal, he maintains the latter within the imaginary or presymbolic (as we noted, in the "mirror stage," following the examples of the hen-pigeon or migrating locust). He keeps "the animal" prisoner within the specularity of the imaginary; he holds, rather, that the animal keeps itself in such captivity, speaking about it in terms of "imaginary capture." Above all, he maintains "the animal" within the first degree of pretense (pretense without pretense of pretense) or, which here amounts to the same thing, within the first degree of the trace: the capacity to trace, to leave a track and to track, but not to distract the tracking or lead the tracker astray by *erasing* its trace or covering its tracks.[10]

An important "But" will in effect fold this paragraph in two ("But an animal does not pretend to pretend"; 305). A balance sheet separates the accounting of what has to be accorded the animal (pretense and the trace, inscription of the trace) and what has to be denied it (deception, lying, pretense of pretense, and erasing of traces). But—what the articulation of this "But" perhaps leaves undetected, discreetly in the shadows, among all the traits that are listed, is a reference to life, to the "vital." Everything accorded the animal is conceded on the grounds of "vital situations," even though one would be tempted to conclude that the animal, whether hunter or game, is held to be incapable of an authentic relation to death or of testifying to an equally essential mortality in the heart of Truth or Speech. The animal is a living creature that is only living, as it were an "immortal" living thing. As Heidegger states—Lacan is here closer to him than ever, in particular, as we shall see, in terms of what binds the *logos* to the possibility of "deceiving" or "being deceived"—the animal doesn't die.[11] For the same reason, moreover, it would also be ignorant of mourning, the tomb, and the cadaver, which for Lacan constitutes a "signifier":

> Observe, in parentheses, that this Other, which is distinguished as the locus of Speech, imposes itself no less as witness to the Truth. Without the dimension that it constitutes, the *deception* practised by Speech would be indistinguishable from the very different *pretence* to be found in physical combat or sexual display [*parade*]. Pretense of this kind is deployed in imaginary capture, and is integrated into the play of approach and rejection that constituted the original dance, in which these two *vital* situations find their rhythm, and in accordance with which the partners ordered their movements— what I will dare to call their "dancity" [*dansité*]. Indeed, animals, too, show that they are capable of such behaviour when they are being hunted; they manage to put their pursuers off the scent [*dépister*][12] by making a false start. This can go so far as to suggest on the part of the game animal the nobility of honoring the element of display to be found in the hunt [Of course, that is only a figurative and anthropomorphic suggestion, like a "rabbit in the hat," for it will immediately be made clear by the ensuing "But" that honor and nobility, tied to vouching for one's word or the gift of speech (*la Parole donnée*) and to the symbolic, is precisely what the animal is incapable of. An animal does not give its word, and one does not give one's word to the animal, except by means of a projection or anthropomorphic transference. One can't lie to an animal, either, especially by pretending to hide from it something that one shows it. Isn't that patently obvious? True enough, though it remains to be seen (*Voire*). In any case it is the whole organization of this discourse that we are calling into question here.] *But an animal does not pretend to pretend.* He does not make tracks whose deception lies in the

fact that they will be taken as false, while being in fact true ones, ones, that is, that indicate his true trail. *Nor does an animal cover up its tracks, which would be tantamount to making itself the subject of the signifier.*[13]

What does it mean to be the subject of, or subject to the signifier, that of which the animal is here reputed to be incapable? What does it signify? Let us first note in passing that this confirms the old (Adamic and Promethean) theme of the animal's profound innocence, its being incapable of the "signifier," of lying and deceit, and of pretended pretense, which gets linked here, in a most traditional way, to the theme of a cruelty that doesn't recognize itself as such—the cruel innocence, therefore, of a living creature to whom evil is foreign, living anterior to the difference between good and evil.[14]

But to be subject of the signifier also means, still yet, two indissociable things that are coupled within the subjecthood of the subject. The subject of the signifier is subject(ed) to the signifier. Lacan never stops insisting on the "dominance" of "the signifier over the subject" and over "the symbolic order which is constitutive for the subject."[15] The "subject" does not have mastery over it. Entry into the human order of the law presupposes this passive finitude, this infirmity, this lack from which the animal does not suffer. The animal does not know evil, lying, deceit. What it lacks is precisely the lack by virtue of which the human becomes subject of the signifier, subject subjected to the signifier. But to be subject of the signifier is also to be a subjecting subject, a subject as *master*, an active and deciding subject of the signifier, having in any case sufficient mastery to be capable of pretending to pretend and hence of being able to put into effect one's power to destroy the trace. This mastery is the superiority of man over the *animot*, even if it gains its assurance from the privilege constituted by a defect [*défaut*], a lack [*manque*], or a fault [*faute*], a failing [*défaillance*] that derives as much from the generic prematurity of birth as from the castration complex, which Lacan designates, in a text I shall cite in a moment, as the Freudian and scientific (or at least nonmythological) version of original sin or the Adamic fall.

It is there that the passage from imaginary to symbolic is determined as a passage from animal to human order. It is there that subjecthood, as order of the signifier from the place of the Other, appears as something missed by the traditional philosophy of the subject and of relations between human and animal. That is, at least, what Lacan alleges at the moment he subtly reintroduces an anthropocentrist logic and strongly reinforces the *fixism* of the Cartesian cogito as a thesis on the animal-machine in general:

All this has been articulated only in a confused way even by professional philosophers. But it is clear that Speech begins only with the passage from "pretence" to the order of the signifier, and that the signifier requires another locus—the locus of the Other, the Other witness, the witness Other than any of the partners—for the speech that it supports to be capable of lying, that is to say, of presenting itself as Truth.

Thus it is from somewhere other than the Reality that it concerns that Truth derives its guarantee: it is from Speech. Just as it is from Speech that Truth receives the mark that establishes it in a fictional structure. (305–6)

This allusion to a "structure of fiction" would refer us back to the debate concerning "The Purloined Letter."[16] Without reopening it to that extent, let us note here the reflective sharpness of the word *fiction*. The concept toward which it leads is no longer merely that of the *figure* or simple *feint* but the reflexive and abyssal concept of a *feigned feint* or *pretended pretense*. It is by means of the power to pretend a pretense that one accedes to Speech, to the order of Truth, to the symbolic order, in short, to the order of the human.

(Even before detailing once more the principle behind the reading being attempted here, I would like at least to advance a hypothesis. Although Lacan often repeats that there is no Other of the Other [e.g., 316], although for Levinas, by contrast, and from another point of view, the question of justice is born from this request of the third and from an other of the other who would not be "simply [one's] fellow,"[17] one wonders whether the common if disavowed crossover between these two discourses on the other and the third is not at least the context for an instance of the animal, of the animal-*other*, of the other *as animal*, of the living-mortal-*other*, of the nonfellow, in any case, the nonbrother [of the divine or of the animal, here inseparable], in short, of the ahuman combining god and animal according to all the theo-zoomorphic possibilities that properly constitute the myths, religions, idolatries, and even sacrificial practices within the monotheisms that claim to break with idolatry. Moreover, the word *ahuman* does not scare Lacan, since, in a postscript to "The Subversion of the Subject," he notes that he was in no way insulted by the epithet "ahuman," which one of the participants in the conference attributed to his talk [324].)

What is Lacan doing when he holds that "the signifier requires another locus—the locus of the Other, the Other witness, the witness Other than any of the partners?" In order to break with the image and with the likeness of a fellow, must not this beyond of partnership—thus beyond the specular or imaginary duel—be at least situated in a place of alterity that is radical enough to break with every identification of an image of self, with every fellow living creature, and so with every fraternity[18] or human proximity, with all humanity? Must not this place of the Other be ahuman? If this is indeed the case, then the ahuman or at least the figure of some—in a word—*divinanimality*, even if it were to be felt through the human, would be the quasi-transcendental referent, the excluded, foreclosed, disavowed, tamed, and sacrificed foundation of what it founds, namely, the symbolic order, the human order, law and justice. Does not this necessity function secretly in Levinas and in Lacan, who, moreover, cross paths so often in spite of all the differences in the world? That is one of the reasons why it is so difficult to utter a discourse of mastery or of transcendence with regard to the animal and simultaneously to claim to do it in the name of God, in the name of the name of the Father, or in the name of the Law. Must not one recognize Father, Law, Animal, etc. as being at bottom the same thing? Or rather, indissociable figures of the same Thing? One could conjoin the Mother within that juncture, and it would probably not change anything. Nietzsche and Kafka perhaps understood that better than the philosophers or theoreticians, at least those who belong to the tradition that we are trying to analyze here.

Once more, of course, my prime concern is not to mount a frontal attack on the logic of this discourse and what it implies for the Lacan of the period of the *Écrits* (1966). For the moment, I shall have to leave in suspense the question of whether, in later texts or in certain seminars (published or unpublished, accessible or inaccessible), the armature of this logic came to be explicitly reexamined. Especially since Lacan seems progressively to abandon, if not to repudiate, the oppositional distinction between imaginary and symbolic that forms the very axiomatics of this discourse on the animal. As always, I am trying to take into account the strongest systematic organization of a discourse in the form in which it comes together at a relatively determinable moment of that process. The texts distributed over a thirty-year period and collected within a single volume, solidly bound in their integrity [*reliés à soi*], namely, the *Écrits*, provide us in this regard with a reliable purchase on that process and allow us to follow its tracks. Among the published and accessible texts that follow the *Écrits*, I think that one would have, in particular, to try to follow the path that leads, in an interesting but continuous way, to the analyses of animal mimetism, for example, still from the perspective of the gaze, precisely, of the image and the "seeing oneself looking," being seen looking even by a can of sardines that doesn't see me. ("To begin with, if what

Petit-Jean said to me, namely, that the can did not see me, had any meaning, it was because in a sense, it was looking at me, all the same. It was looking at me at the level of the point of light, the point at which everything that looks at me is situated—and I am not speaking metaphorically."[19])

Instead of objecting to this argument, therefore, I would be tempted to emphasize that the logical and thus rational fragility of certain of its articulations should induce us to recast in a general way the whole conceptual framework.

It seems difficult, in the first place, to identify or determine a limit, that is to say, an indivisible threshold between pretense and pretense of pretense. Moreover, even supposing that that limit were conceptually accessible, something I don't think is so, we would still have to know in the name of what knowledge or what testimony (knowledge is not the same as testimony) one could calmly declare that the *animal in general* is incapable of pretending pretense. Lacan does not invoke here any ethological knowledge (whose increasing and spectacular refinement is proportional to the refinement of the *animot*) or any experience, observation, or personal attestation that would be worthy of credence. The status of the affirmation that refuses the pretense of pretense to the animal is that of a simple dogma. But there is no doubt a dissimulated motivation to this humanist or anthropocentric dogmatism, and that is the probably obscure but indisputable feeling that it is indeed difficult, even impossible, to discern between pretense and a pretense of pretense, between an aptitude for pretense and an aptitude for the pretense of pretense. How could one distinguish, for example, in the most elementary sexual mating game, between a feint and a feint of a feint? If it here provides the criterion for such a distinction, one can conclude that every pretense of pretense remains a simple pretense (animal or imaginary, in Lacan's terms) or else, on the contrary, and just as likely, that every pretense, however simple it may be, gets repeated and reposited undecidably, in its possibility, as pretense of pretense (human or symbolic in Lacan's terms). As I shall make clear in a moment, a symptomatology (and, of course, a psychoanalysis) can and must conclude with the possibility, for every pretense, of being pretense of pretense, and for every pretense of pretense of being a simple pretense. As a result, the distinction between lie and pretense becomes precarious, likewise that between Speech and Truth (in Lacan's sense), and everything from which he claims to distinguish them. Pretense presupposes taking the other into account; it therefore supposes, simultaneously, the pretense of pretense—a simple supplementary move by the other within the strategy of the game. That supplementarity is at work from the moment of the first pretense. Moreover, Lacan cannot deny that the animal takes the other into account. His article "On a Question Preliminary to Any Possible Treatment of Psychosis" (1957–58) contains a remark headed in that direction, which I would have liked to insert into this network in a careful and patient manner: putting it at the same time in tension, if not in contradiction, with Lacan's discourse on the imaginary capture of the animal (thereby deprived of the other, in sum), and in harmony with the discourse on pathology, evil, lack, or defect that marks the relation to the other as such in the human, but which is already announced in the animal:

> To take up Charcot's formula, which so delighted Freud, "this does not prevent [the Other] from existing" in his place O.
> For if he is taken away, man can no longer even sustain himself in the position of Narcissus. As if by elastic, the *anima* springs back on to the *animus* and the *animus* on to the animal, which between S and *o* sustains with its *Umwelt* "external relations" noticeably closer than ours, without, moreover, one being able to say that its relation with the Other is negligible, but only that it does not appear otherwise than in the sporadic sketches of neurosis. (*Écrits*, 195, translation modified)

In other words, the animal resembles the human and enters into relation with the Other (in a more feeble manner, and by reason of a more "restricted" adaptation to the milieu, hence, as we were saying earlier, more "fixed," better "wired") only to the extent of its sickness, of a neurotic defect that brings it closer to man, to man as failure [*défaut*] of the premature and still insufficiently determined animal. If there were a continuity between animal and human orders, as between animal psychology and human psychology, it would follow this line of evil, of fault and defect. Lacan, moreover, has claimed, in his own defense, not to hold to a discontinuity between the two psychologies (animal and human), *at least as psychologies*: "May this digression at least counteract the misunderstanding that we could have provided the occasion for in the eyes of some, those who impute to us the doctrine of a discontinuity between animal psychology and human psychology that is far from being what we think."[20]

What does that mean? That the radical discontinuity between animal and human, the absolute and indivisible discontinuity that he, however, confirms and compounds, no longer derives from the psychological as such, from *anima* and *psychē*, but instead from the appearance of a different order.

Yet an analogous (I don't say "identical") conceptual undecidability comes to trouble the opposition, which is so decisive for Lacan, between leaving tracks [*tracer*] and covering one's tracks [*effacer ses traces*]. The animal can trace, inscribe, or leave a track or trace, but, Lacan adds, it does not "cover up its tracks, which would be tantamount to making itself the subject of the signifier." But there again, supposing one can trust the distinction, Lacan doesn't justify, either by means of testimony or by some ethological knowledge, this affirmation that "the animal," as he calls it, the animal *in general* does not cover its tracks. Apart from the fact that, as I have tried to show elsewhere (and this is why so long ago I substituted the concept of trace for that of signifier), the structure of the trace presupposes that *to trace* amounts to *erasing a trace* (always present-absent) as much as to imprinting it, all sorts of sometimes ritual animal practices—for example, in burial and mourning—associate the experience of the trace with that of the erasure of the trace. A pretense, moreover, even a simple pretense, consists in rendering a sensible trace illegible or imperceptible. How can it be denied that the simple substitution of one trace for another, the marking of their diacritical difference in the most elementary inscription, which Lacan concedes to the animal, involves erasure as much as the imprint? It is as difficult to assign a frontier between pretense and pretense of pretense, to have an indivisible line pass through the middle of a feigned feint, as it is to situate one between inscription and erasure of the trace.

But let us take this further and pose a type of question that I would have wished, had I the time, to pose generally. It is *not just* a matter of asking whether one has the right to refuse the animal such and such a power (speech, reason, experience of death, mourning, culture, institutions, technics, clothing, lying, pretense of pretense, covering of tracks, gift, laughter, crying, respect, etc.—the list is necessarily without limit, and the most powerful philosophical tradition in which we live has refused the "animal" *all of that*). It *also* means asking whether what calls itself human has the right rigorously to attribute to man, which means therefore to attribute to himself, what he refuses the animal, and whether he can ever possess the *pure, rigorous, indivisible* concept, as such, of that attribution. Thus, were we even to suppose—something I am not ready to concede—that the "animal" was incapable of covering its tracks, by what right could one concede that power to the human, to the "subject of the signifier"? Especially from a psychoanalytic point of view? Granted, every human can, within the space of doxic phenomenality, have the *consciousness* of covering its tracks. But who could ever judge the effectivity of such a gesture? Is it necessary to recall that every erased trace, in consciousness, can leave a trace of its erasure whose symptom (individual or social, historical, political, etc.) will always be capable of ensuring its return? And is it necessary, above all, to remind a psychoanalyst of that? And to recall that every reference to the capacity to erase the trace still speaks the language of the conscious, even imaginary ego? (One can sense all the virtual consequences crowding in here on behalf of the question that is our subject, namely, autobiography.)

All this will not amount to saying (something I have developed at length elsewhere) that the trace cannot be erased. On the contrary. It is inherent to a trace that it is always being erased and always capable of being erased [*Il appartient à une trace de toujours s'effacer et de toujours pouvoir s'effacer*]. But the fact that it *is* erased [*qu'elle s'efface*], that it can always *be* erased or erase *itself*, and this from the first instant of its inscription, through and beyond any repression, does not mean that someone, God, human, or animal, can be its master subject and possess the power to erase *it*. On the contrary. In this regard the human no more has the *power* to cover its tracks than does the so-called "animal." *Radically* to erase its traces, that is to say, by the same token *radically* to destroy, deny, put to death, even put itself to death.

But let us especially not conclude, therefore, that the traces of the one and of the others are ineffaceable, or that death and destruction are impossible. Traces erase (themselves), like everything else, but the structure of the trace is such that it cannot be in anyone's *power* to erase *it* and especially not to "judge" its erasure, even less so by means of a constitutive power assured of being able to erase, performatively, what erases itself. The distinction might appear subtle and fragile, but its subtle fragility affects all the solid oppositions that we are in the process of tracking down [*dé-pister*], beginning with that between symbolic and imaginary, which underwrites, finally, this whole anthropocentric reinstitution of the superiority of the human order over the animal order, of the law over the living, etc., wherever such a subtle form of phallogocentrism seems, in its way, to testify to the panic Freud spoke of: the wounded reaction not to humanity's *first* trauma, the Copernican (the earth revolves around the sun), nor its *third* trauma, the Freudian (the decentering of consciousness under the gaze of the unconscious), but rather to its *second* trauma, the Darwinian.

Before we leave, provisionally, Lacan's text, I would like to define a task and proffer a reminder. The task is one that would involve us, from the vantage of everything that we have here inscribed under the sign of the Cartesian *cogito*, in closely analyzing Lacan's references to Descartes.

As is the case with references to Hegel, with which it is often associated, the appeal to Descartes, to the Cartesian "I think," is constant, determinate, complex, and differentiated. Within that rich network and that wide-reaching process, our problematic sets a first signpost. It can be found in the pages immediately following the paragraph on the difference between the nonpretending pretense of the animal and the pretending pretense of the human capable of erasing its own traces. Lacan metes out both praise and criticism.

On the one hand, the "Cartesian cogito did not fail to recognize" what is essential, namely, that the consciousness of existence, the *sum*, is not immanent to it but transcendent, and thus beyond specular or imaginary capture. That amounts to confirming that an animal *cogito* would remain a captive of the identificatory image, a situation that could be formalized by saying that the animal accedes to the ego [*moi*] only by lacking the I [*Je*], but an I that itself accedes to the signifier only from the perspective of a lack: the (animal) self lacks the lack. Lacan writes, for example:

> From this point on, the ego is a function of mastery, a play of presence, of bearing [*prestance*], and of constituted rivalry [none of these traits is refused the animal]. In the capture to which it is subjected by its imaginary nature, the ego masks its duplicity, that is to say, the consciousness in which it assures itself of an incontestable existence (a naivety to be found in the meditation of Fénelon) is in no way immanent in it, but, on the contrary, is transcendent, since it is supported by the unbroken line of the ego ideal (which the Cartesian *cogito* did not fail to recognize). As a result, the transcendental ego itself is relativized, implicated as it is in the *méconnaissance* in which the ego's identifications take root. (307)

But *on the other hand*, therefore, the *ego cogito* gets dislodged from its position as central subject. It loses its mastery, its central power; it becomes subject subjected to the signifier.

The imaginary process extends thus from the specular image all the way to "the constitution of the ego by way of subjectification by the signifier" (ibid.). That seems to confirm that the becoming-subject of the ego passes by way of the signifier, Speech, Truth, etc., that is to say, by losing its immediate transparency, consciousness as consciousness of the self identical to itself. Which ends only in an apparent paradox: the subject is confirmed in the eminence of its power by being subverted and brought back to its own lack, meaning that animality is on the side of the conscious *ego*, whereas the humanity of the human subject is on the side of the unconscious, the law of the signifier, Speech, the pretended pretense, etc.:

> The promotion of consciousness as being essential to the subject in the historical after-effects of the Cartesian *cogito* is for me the deceptive accentuation of the transparency of the I in action at the expense of the opacity of the signifier that determines the I; and the sliding movement [*glissement*] by which the *Bewusstsein* serves to cover up the confusion of the *Selbst* eventually reveals, with all Hegel's own rigour, the reason for his error in *The Phenomenology of Mind.* (Ibid.)

The accent on transparency is thus said to be "deceptive [*trompeuse*]." That not only means a case of "making a mistake" about the error, but of "being deceived" by the deceit, or lie, the lying-to-oneself as belief, the "making believe" in the transparency of the ego or of self to itself. Such would be the risk of the traditional interpretation of the Cartesian *cogito*, perhaps that of the self-interpretation of Descartes himself, of his intellectual auto-biography, one never knows. Whence Lacan's promotion of the *cogito* and his diagnosis of the lie, of deceit, and of a deceptive transparency in the very heart of the *cogito*.

"Hegel's own rigour," he says. One would then have to follow the interpretation proposed by Lacan of the struggle between Master and Slave, at the point where it amounts to a "decomposition of the equilibrium of counterpart [*semblable*] to counterpart" (308). The same motif of the "alienating dialectic of Master and Slave" appears in "Variantes de la cure-type" ("Variations on the Cure-Type"; 1955). Animal specularity, with its lures and aberrations, comes to "durably structure the human subject" by reason of the prematurity of birth, said to be a "fact in which one apprehends this dehiscence in the natural harmony, demanded by Hegel as the fecund illness, the happy fault of life, where man, by being distinguished in his essence, discovers his existence."[21] We could situate the reinscription of the question of the animal, in our reinterpretation of Lacan's reinterpretation of Hegel, at the point where Lacan reintroduces this reminder regarding the imaginary, regarding "specular capture" and the "generic prematuration of birth," the "danger . . . which Hegel was unaware of" (308). There again, as Lacan makes clear, it is life that is at stake, and the passage to the human order of the subject, beyond the animal imaginary, is indeed a question of life and death: "The struggle that establishes this initial enslavement is rightly called a struggle of pure prestige [which means according to Lacan that it is no longer animal], and the stake, life itself, is well suited to echo that danger of the generic prematuration of birth, which Hegel was unaware of, and in which I see the dynamic motivation of specular capture" (308, translation modified).

How should we understand this word *generic*, since it qualifies so forcefully the insistent and determinate concept of "prematuration," namely, the absolute event without which the whole discourse would lose its "motivation [*ressort*]," as Lacan himself says, beginning with the relevance of the distinction between imaginary and symbolic? Is the "generic" a trait of "humankind [*du genre humain*]" as a kind of animal, or a trait of the human inasmuch as it escapes classification [*genre*], precisely, escaping the generic or the genetic—precisely by means of the defect of a certain de-generation [*dé-génération*] rather than de-generacy [*dé-générescence*], by means of a de-generation whose very defect engenders symbolic "generation," the relation between generations, the law of the Name of the Father, Speech, Truth, Deceit, the pretended pretense, the power to erase one's traces, etc.?

On the basis of this question, which we shall leave in suspense, as a task, at the point where it proceeds, nevertheless, from this traditional logic of the originary defect, I come back to what I announced as a final reminder, namely, what brings together this whole perspectival configuration of the defect within the history of original fault, of an original sin that finds its mythical relay in the story of Oedipus, then its nonmythic relay, its scientific relay, in the "castration complex," as formulated by Freud. In the passage that follows, I shall italicize *lack* and *defect*, and we shall find there again all the stages of our trajectory: Genesis, the serpent, the question of the I and "What am I (following)?" or "Who am I (following)?" (both *être* and *suivre*), a quotation from Valéry's "Silhouette of a Serpent" ("the universe is a *defect* in the purity of Non-Being"), etc.:

> This is what the subject lacks in order to think himself exhausted by his *cogito*, namely, that which is unthinkable for him. But where does this being, who appears in some way *defective* [*en défaut*] in the sea of proper nouns, originate?
>
> We cannot ask this question of the subject as "I." He *lacks* everything needed to know the answer, since if this subject "I" was dead, he would not, as I said earlier, know it. He does not know, therefore, that I am alive. How, therefore, will "I" prove to myself that I am?
>
> For I can only just prove to the Other that he exists, not, of course, with the proofs for the existence of God, with which over the centuries he has been killed off, but by loving him, a solution

introduced by the Christian *kerygma*. Indeed, it is too precarious a solution for me even to think of using it as a means of circumventing our problem, namely: "What am 'I'?"

"I" am in the place from which a voice is heard clamouring "the universe is a *defect* in the purity of Non-Being."

And not without reason, for by protecting itself this place makes Being itself languish. This place is called *Jouissance*, and it is the *absence* of this that makes the universe vain.

Am I responsible for it, then? Yes, probably. Is this *jouissance*, the *lack* of which makes the Other insubstantial, mine, then? Experience proves that it is usually forbidden me, not only, as certain fools believe, because of a bad arrangement of society, but rather because of the *fault* [*faute*] of the Other if he existed: and since the Other does not exist, all that remains to me is to assume the *fault* upon "I," that is to say, to believe in that to which experience leads us all, Freud in the vanguard, namely, to *original sin*. For even if we did not have Freud's express, and sorrowful avowal, the fact would remain that the myth Freud gave us—the latest-born myth in history—is no more use than that of the forbidden apple, except for the fact, and this has nothing to do with its power as myth, that, though more succinct, it is distinctly less stultifying [*crétinisant*].

But what is not a myth, and which Freud nevertheless formulated soon after the Oedipus complex, is the castration complex. (317–18, translation modified)

4

"I don't know why we are doing this"

I don't know why we are doing this . . . or where you are getting your stamina from [laughter] . . . to be able to continue to listen to me! Don't think for a moment that I am insisting on having the last word, or on being not only "the last of the Jews," or "the last of the eschatologists," but really "the last to speak," the last of the last, speaking. By no means, but since the other day I cut myself off at the moment that was perhaps the most important moment for me, I thought that in all honesty I had to say a little more to you concerning what, at bottom, I would have liked to say, concerning the place I wanted to get to. But doing that work honestly would have required, on the one hand, my being able to write a very long text, which is what I hope to do one day, and on the other hand, keeping you here far too long. So I gave up on it. I have just a few notes, and I'll propose simply an outline of what I would have tried to do if I had time and if we had the time together.

I would probably have picked things up, at the point where we were interested in the question of the pretense of the pretense in Lacan, of deception, the difference among pretense, deception, and lying when it comes to language and speech [*parole*], connecting that with a certain passage in Heidegger, toward the very end of the book I'll speak of, a seminar that Heidegger gave after *Being and Time*, in 1929–30, translated as *The Fundamental Concepts of Metaphysics: World, Finitude, Solitude*. Toward the end of a long elaboration concerning the animal (which I'll come back to in a moment), he broaches what is to his mind the essential thing: what

141

the animal lacks is the "as such [*die 'als'-Struktur*]," an essential trait for our whole problematic that, in the end, will have already lined the route of our previous trajectories through Levinas and Lacan, when one and the other ask themselves the question of the other. What the animal lacks is therefore the "as such [*en tant que tel*]," the other as such.

The animal thus has a relation to the being [*l'étant*] but not to the being as such, something that Heidegger, to his credit, localizes, complicates, precisely treats "as such" thematically, with a breadth and rigor of analysis that I find incomparable. The question of deception comes up at the moment when, having posited that the animal, in its opening to the world, doesn't have access to the world as such, to the "as such," Heidegger is intent on noting that this "as such" doesn't depend on language, on the *logos*. When one says, therefore, that the animal doesn't have the *logos*, that means, above all, that it doesn't possess the "as such" that *founds* the *logos*. He thus analyzes the relation between what he calls the apophantic, "apophantic structure," and the apophantic *logos*, that is to say, the becoming-language of the "as such." And it is at that moment, in paragraph 72b—the point at which I would have picked it up if I had picked it up—that he broaches the question of the *logos* and of deception:

> That *logos* to whose essence there belongs (among other things) the ability to be deceptive is a pointing out. To deceive means: to pretend something, to present something as something it is not, or to present something that is not such and such as indeed such and such. This deception, this being deceptive that belongs to the essence of the *logos*—this proffering of something as something it is not—this pretending, with respect to whatever the deception is about, is a *concealing*. That *logos* which has the possibility of being able to conceal is an exhibiting.[1]

He then posits, in the form of a question, the relation of the *logos* to the "as such" as its condition of possibility: "Is the 'as'-structure merely a property of the *logos*, or ultimately something originary: the condition of the possibility of any *logos* in general being what it is?" (311). And further along—naturally I am going to skip a lot, I am going to walk by skipping, we don't have time to follow things in a continuous way—he posits that this structure of the "as such" is refused to the animal:

> In all its behaviourally driven activity, the animal is *taken* by whatever it is relating to in this behaviour. That *to which* it stands in relation is thus never given to it in its what-being as such [a proposition that will return in page after page of this long treatise]: it is not

given as what it is and how it is, *not as a being*. The animal's behaviour is never an apprehending of something as something. Insofar as we address this possibility of taking *something as something* as characteristic of the phenomenon of world, the "as"-structure is an essential determination of the structure of world. The "*as*" is thereby given as a *possible approach to the problem of world*. (Ibid.)

The structure of the "as," refused the animal, is thus reserved for the human: "We formally traced the 'as'-structure back to the propositional statement. The propositional statement is a normal form of human discourse" (ibid.). That is where I would have continued my discussion in order to begin a reading of this seminar, and I would have done it precisely because we had come to a certain point in our problematic while reading Lacan. But that wouldn't have allowed me to avoid a large step back, which I'll attempt now.

ॐ

Of course, as you know, what matters to me in the seminar of 1929–30, in these nuclear propositions concerning stone, animal, and man, and notably the "poor in world [*weltarm*]" animal, has in one way or another already been interesting me for a long time. What I would like to say here, at bottom, has already been said in "The Ends of Man," in "Geschlecht," in "Heidegger's Hand," in *Of Spirit*, where I explicitly spoke about this text and these propositions, in "Heidegger's Ear," in *Aporias* (in this very place), some of you were here, when we broached the question of the animal that "doesn't die," but "croaks [*crève*]," that has an end but doesn't die, not properly—and that is a determinate difference between animal and human for Heidegger, who leaves in suspense the question of knowing whether it is inasmuch as it doesn't speak, that it doesn't die, or not. Thus, in a certain way, I have already raised all those questions and I don't wish to return to them.

Given that, if I was wanting to propose a different reading of this seminar, it is because, in our current context, it has certain merits as regards previous discourses on the animal, which we need to emphasize. On the one hand, to its credit it takes into account a certain ethological knowledge—the way in which it takes it into account is another story (if I had time I would try to show how, in taking it into account, it doesn't take it into account), but all the same—with copious references to von Uexküll, Driesch, Buytendijk: a serious piece of work! On the other hand, Heidegger tries there to go beyond the mechanicist/finalist alternative; he says so explicitly and resolutely situates himself outside, or prior to, all the doctrinal oppositions that until now have characterized philosophical discourses on the animal, whether humanist or not. Next—and here I would like to insist again, and a little more deliberately than I have up to this point—this seminar is from 1929–30, and it belongs, with all the accompanying ambiguities, to a constant gesture of Heidegger's, whose political implications are to be taken seriously, namely, the need to distance oneself from every form of biologism. That is also a gesture common to Levinas and Lacan: even when their insistence, their humanism is elaborated against metaphysical humanism, it also represents the gesture of taking an ethico-political position vis-à-vis all discourses or forms of biologism that risk threatening the culture within which they speak. Finally, another interesting thing concerning this text is the fact that it is a "seminar," which retains all the marks of a long seminar (and one mustn't forget what a seminar is, with its share of contingency, improvisation, and labor, and a relatively unjustifiable fixation on certain statements), a seminar that comes after *Being and Time*. For *Being and Time* is a book within which (I think I pointed that out in *Aporias*) the question of the animal is practically never raised. Except in two places: one that concerns death, precisely, the whole discourse on the "being-toward-death" from which the animal is excluded—the animal doesn't "die," the animal isn't a *Dasein* "toward-death"—and the other is the very brief remark that I quoted here a few days ago, where Heidegger says that the question of knowing whether the animal has a time (the question of the temporalization of the animal) "remains a problem," remains therefore in suspense (and in a certain manner that is the problem that he courageously opens up in this seminar).

But the main reason why I didn't want to go too fast with this seminar was that all the propositions concerning the "poor in world" animal are advanced within a far more vast problematic that is not that of the animal. One would thus have to reconstitute the space in which this question of the animal comes to the fore. That space is the space of much more general questions that must not be lost from sight, even if they apparently get lost along the way: the questions, as the title indicates, of world, finitude, and solitude. So, before coming to certain parts (for we won't have time to go very far) that concern the animal directly, I would like to mark out some points of reference in the general constitution of this problematic of world in which the "thesis" comes to be inscribed, since, in Heidegger's very terms, it is a "thesis." As I have already said, Heidegger only rarely advances "theses"; still, he is going to put forward the proposition that the animal is *weltarm* as a "thesis." He will even present three "theses":

"the stone is without world [*weltlos*]," "the animal is poor in world [*welt-arm*]," "man is world-forming [*weltbilden*; the term is difficult to translate]."

Some points of reference, therefore, from what precedes the chapter dedicated to the animal.

From the very beginning, it is a case of nothing less than determining philosophy on its own basis, something that Heidegger does, as he puts it, by following a thread picked up from Novalis. What interests him at bottom in all that is the *Grundstimmung*, the fundamental attunement [*tonalité*], *Heimweh*, homesickness [*nostalgie*]. And it is from within a reflection on fundamental attunement that the question of the animal will come up, which is not without importance.

"*Das Heimweh als die Grundstimmung des Philosophierens und die Fragen nach Welt, Endlichkeit, Vereinzelung.*" That is the title of the paragraph: "Homesickness as the fundamental attunement of philosophizing, and the questions concerning world, finitude, individuation [*esseule-ment*]" (5). (Is *esseulement* the best translation for *Vereinzelung*? Singularization? Singleness [*esseulement*]? Solitude? It's very complicated.) Once more, it is clearly a matter of replying to the question "What is man?" And to reply to the question "What is man?" one has to reply to the question "What is world?" From the beginning of the paragraph, therefore, Heidegger asks: "Yet what is man, that he philosophizes in the ground of his essence, and what is this philosophizing? What are we in this? Where do we want to go? Did we once stumble into the universe by chance? Novalis on one occasion says in a fragment: 'Philosophy is really homesickness [*ist eigentlich Heimweh*], an urge [*ein Trieb*, a drive] to be at home everywhere'" (ibid.). We will see the question of the "at home" come back, notably—if we have the time to get there—at the moment where this question is specified as what it means to be at home with "the animal." What is "living with the animal"? What is "cohabiting" with the animal? That is the question of *mitgehen* and *mitexistieren*. The animal can *mitgehen* with us in the house; a cat, for example, which is often said to be a narcissistic animal, can inhabit the same place as us, it can "go with us," "walk with us," it can be "with us" in the house, live "with us," but "it doesn't exist with us" in the house.

The fact that this story of the *Heimweh*, homesickness [*mal de pays*], opens this seminar is not without importance. Nor is the fact that soon after the quote from Novalis comes lying. He has just quoted a poet, Novalis, and he adds: "Does not Aristotle say in his Metaphysics: *polla pseudontai aoidoi*: Poets tell many a lie?" (ibid.).[2] But in the middle of the same paragraph, which I have excerpted in a somewhat artificial way, what do we see appear, pass by? An animal:

> Novalis on one occasion says in a fragment: "Philosophy is really homesickness, an urge to be at home everywhere." A strange definition [*Eine merkwürdige Definition*], romantic of course [*romantisch natürlich*]. Homesickness [*Heimweh*]—does such a thing still exist today at all [*gibt es dergleichen heute überhaupt noch*]? Has it not become an incomprehensible word, even in everyday life [*ein unverständliches Wort geworden, selbst im alltäglichen Leben*]? Has not contemporary city man, the ape of civilization, long since eradicated homesickness [*Denn hat nicht der heutige städtische Mensch und Affe der Zivilisation das Heimweh längst abgeschafft*]? (Ibid.)

In other words—and the ape, like the *simiesque* in Levinas, is an insult—the city-dweller who has lost all sense of the country, who has shaken off homesickness, who has lost feelings of nostalgia ("nostalgia isn't what it used to be," as it were), the modern city-dweller is an ape of civilization. He laughs when one speaks to him of homesickness.

The whole beginning of the seminar, therefore, concerns homesickness and melancholy, philosophy, and metaphysics as forms of nostalgia. In this long preface, if one may call it that, which precedes the point where he approaches the animal, I would have chosen, for reasons that you know, certain passages on Descartes, because what matters to me would be to show, in a provocative way, of course, that Heidegger's discourse is still Cartesian, whereas the prime target, in *Being and Time* but also here, is, of course, Descartes. Not only Descartes' mechanism, but also Descartes' *cogito*. To give you an idea of that, I'll refer you to a paragraph entitled "The ambiguity of the critical stance in Descartes and in modern philosophy," where Descartes is essentially reproached for trusting appearances, within his very critical gesture:

> It is no accident that with the advent of the increased and explicit tendency to raise philosophy to the rank of an absolute science in Descartes, a peculiar ambiguity of philosophy simultaneously works itself out in a special way. Descartes' fundamental tendency was to make philosophy into absolute knowledge. Precisely with him we see something remarkable. Here philosophizing begins with *doubt*, and it seems as though everything is put into question. Yet it only seems so [*Aber es sieht nur so aus*]. Dasein, the I (the ego), is not put into question at all [*Das Dasein, das Ich (das Ego) wird gar nicht in Frage gestellt*]. This illusion and this ambiguity of a critical stance

runs right through the whole of modern philosophy up to the most recent present. (20)

He had already maintained this in *Being and Time* by showing how, at bottom, Descartes failed to pose the ontological question of what *being* meant in the *ego sum*: the latter doesn't pose the ontological question, and in the end his *ego sum* remains dogmatic.[3]

This point of reference, simply as point of reference, must not, therefore, be forgotten if one is to show, as I would have wanted to do, that at this very moment, when Heidegger's gesture is to move forward in the direction of a new question, a new questioning concerning the world and the animal, when he claims to deconstruct the whole metaphysical tradition, notably that of subjectivity, Cartesian subjectivity, etc., insofar as the animal is concerned he remains, in spite of everything, profoundly Cartesian.

With that in place, I'll jump ahead from these preliminary paragraphs toward chapter 1 of part 1, where Heidegger raises the question of the "awakening" of consciousness, a question that will be indispensable for marking the reach that the criterion of the apophantic, the "as such," gives itself. For Heidegger it will not in fact be a matter of simply linking the "as such ['*als*'-*Struktur*]" to a structure of conscience or representation. It will involve a more radical reach: "Awakening [*Weckung*]: not ascertaining something at hand [*kein Feststellen eines Vorhandenen*; you will remember the distinction in *Being and Time* among the three modalities of being: what is *Vorhanden*—present-at-hand, like a thing; what is *Zuhanden*, equipment, the ready-to-hand represented by the tool; and finally *Dasein*], but letting what is asleep become wakeful [*sondern ein Wachwerdenlassen des Schlafenden*]" (59, paragraph heading).

The question of awakening includes the question of sleep, which cannot be separated from that of the animal. Awakening is thus "letting what is asleep become wakeful," and Heidegger naturally takes to task those who would reduce the distinction between waking and sleeping to a distinction between consciousness and unconsciousness. What he calls waking is not consciousness; what he calls sleeping is not the unconscious. Here is the passage:

> whenever we awaken an attunement [*Stimmung*], this entails that it was already there, and yet not there. On the negative side, we have seen that the distinction between being there [*Dasein*] and not being there [*Nichtdasein*] is not equivalent to that between consciousness and unconsciousness. From this, however, we may conclude something further: If attunement is something that belongs to man, is

"in him," as we say, or if man has an attunement, and if this cannot be clarified with the aid of consciousness and unconsciousness, then we will not come close to this matter at all so long as we take man as something distinguished from material things by the fact that he has consciousness, that he is an animal endowed with reason, a rational animal, or an ego with pure life-experiences that has been tacked on to a body. (62)

Heidegger's intention is thus to define the essence of the human otherwise than through consciousness, otherwise than through the reason that might be attributed to a certain animal (one finds these statements again in the *Letter on Humanism*), and even less through the "I," "an ego with pure life-experiences that has been tacked on to a body." "This conception of man as a living being, a living being that in addition has reason, has led to a complete failure to recognize the essence of attunement," he adds (ibid.). For what he wants to define is the *Grundstimmung*. What is an attunement? What is a homesickness, a melancholy, an affective tonality? We won't understand what an affective tonality is so long as we define man as a consciousness, an unconscious, an animal endowed with reason, etc. Hence: "the awakening of attunement, and the attempt to broach this strange task, in the end coincide with the demand for a complete transformation of our conception of man [*mit der Forderung einer völligen Umstellung unserer Auffassung vom Menschen*]." (ibid.).

And, of course, he can no more avoid the question of what happens when an animal sleeps than could Freud, or all the others we have referred to up until now. A little further along he writes (one should spend a long time on this):

We do not say that the stone is asleep or awake. Yet what about the plant? Here already we are uncertain. It is highly questionable whether the plant sleeps, precisely because it is questionable whether it is awake. We know the animal sleeps. Yet the question remains as to whether its sleep is the same as that of man [*ob dieser Schlaf der selbe ist wie der Schlaf des Menschen*], and indeed the question as to what sleep in general is [*und was denn der Schlaf überhaupt ist*]. (Ibid.)

He wants to pose the question of sleeping or waking independently of the whole metaphysics of consciousness, unconsciousness; he wants to start from an opposition waking-sleep that doesn't depend on a logic of consciousness, etc.: "This problem [here he is announcing what he will take up much later in the seminar, and we are going to jump over hundreds of pages] is intimately bound up with the question concerning the structure of being pertaining to these various kinds of beings: stone, plant, animal, man [*Stein, Pflanze, Tier, Mensch*]" (ibid.).

So from the beginning of the seminar it is on the basis of the question of sleep and waking that he announces this typology of beings that we are now going to come to. I would have liked—but I won't have time to do it—given the problematic of subjection and the link that I tried to put in place last time, to look closely at what Aristotle says about sleep (and Aristotle is a fundamental reference for this seminar, from one end of it to the other):

> Aristotle, who has written a treatise specifically on waking and sleeping (*Peri upnou kai egrēgorseōs*), a treatise which has a peculiar character of its own, has noticed something remarkable in saying that sleep is an *akinēsia*. He does not connect sleep with consciousness, or unconsciousness. Rather, he says that sleep is a *desmos*, a being bound, a peculiar way in which *aisthēsis* is bound [the question of binding is going to come back regularly, the stricture also, and subjection by means of the animal's narrowing (*resserrement*)—I am anticipating enormously in saying this—the animal is finally, in comparison to man, simply caught in tighter networks of constraint, "a ring," Heidegger will say, tighter rings; it is a problematic of binding]. It is not only a way in which perception is bound, but also our essence, in that it cannot take in other beings which it itself is not [hence the animal is too well bound]. This characterization of sleep is more than an image, and opens up a broad perspective which has by no means been grasped in its metaphysical intent. For fundamental metaphysical reasons we must forego entering into the problem of sleep, and must attempt to clarify on *another path* what it means to awaken an attunement. (62–63)

And evidently it is on that track, this "other path," that he sets out: the question of attunement, of boredom, etc.

ᘐ

From there, I'll leap ahead to part 2 of the seminar, where Heidegger will approach the question of the animal as such. As I have already said, this question of the animal will—by means of a very strange process, for, although it is the guiding thread, it will finally invade the whole space—come to specify the question of world. And the question of world itself belongs to a set of three questions (everything is in threes in this seminar): "the questions concerning world, individuation, and finitude, as what is given to questioning through the fundamental attunement of profound boredom in our contemporary Dasein. The essence of time as the root of the three questions" (169, §39 title).

In other words, the three questions, world, individuation, and finitude, are linked as if by a common root, namely, the question of time. From the architectonic point of view, this is very important, because in *Being and Time* it was in relation to time that Heidegger asked himself how things stood regarding the animal. Does the animal have time, have a time: "It remains a problem in itself to define . . . how and where the Being of animals, for instance, is constituted by some kind of 'time.'"[4] One must pay attention to this gesture, an apparently pedagogical gesture in Heidegger, but one that is more than pedagogical, and that each time consists in positing things in threes, and saying he is going to uncover their common root or else the median thesis. Here, the question or common root of the three questions is the essence of time and for that reason the question "What is world, etc.?" begins with the question "What is the instant?" "The moment of vision [*Augenblick*] which properly makes Dasein possible is simultaneously announced in this telling refusal of beings as a whole" (169). The "blink of an eye," the instant of the blink of an eye. What is the instant? The questions "What is world? What is finitude? What is individuation?" are developed on the basis of the question "What is the instant?" I'll give one more example of these three in one, this one in three: "Our three questions were posed in the following order: [1.] What is world? [2.] What is finitude? [3.] What is individuation? We have developed them in such a way, however, that finitude has emerged as the third and pressing question. Yet third in what sense? *As the unifying and original root of the other two*" (170). Once more! Just before, time was the root common to the three questions, now it is finitude; finitude comes in third, after being in the middle, in second place, as the "unifying and original root of the other two." And hence not only the question of temporalization but that of finitude is going to organize the whole seminar. Exactly as in *Being and Time*: time as the transcendental horizon of the question of being. He therefore repeats things, in a certain way, by proceeding along a path he had already opened up in *Being and Time*. But, of course, if it is finitude that is to be insisted upon, this question of finitude as origin of the three questions that support that question "What is man?" it is because what man and the animal have in common, let us remember, is finitude, a certain finitude. They are both mortal. The stone isn't "finite": it is finite but there is no "finitude" to the stone. One would never speak of the finitude of the stone, whereas one can speak of a finitude of the animal, like that of man. But the distinction that Heidegger is going to draw, in the gesture that we are going to repeat after him, is the limit between animal and human, such that only the human is "finite" in the sense of finitude that is in question here. The animal isn't finite in this sense. Although, wouldn't you say, this statement is difficult to accept! It doesn't have finitude just as it doesn't have speech, just as it doesn't die "properly," properly speaking, etc. This question of finitude will traverse the entire seminar.

Still, before entering into the texts that matter most to us concerning the animal, there is one more stage concerning world, where we get closest to the emergence of the "three theses" that will structure the discourse on the animal. (One can see how it advances in the final analysis: it is a seminar; one sees its different stages; one sees Heidegger coming back each week, writing his seminar, I suppose, from week to week—which means that I find this text at the same time very strong, obeying an unusual and somewhat baroque necessity, somewhat strange in its composition, and if I had time, I would have liked to do justice as much to the status, to the method, and to the most particular procedure employed by this text, which should be followed, as a result, stage by stage.) Thus, in §42, part 2, chapter 2, right in the middle of the book, the question is the question of world itself, "The Beginning of Metaphysical Questioning with the Question of World." That is the chapter heading, immediately followed by the title of §42: "The path of a comparative examination ["Der Weg der vergleichenden Betrachtung," and this is the only time, to my knowledge, that Heidegger uses the word *comparative*, that he announces that he is going to proceed by means of a comparative move] of three guiding theses: the stone is worldless [*weltlos*], the animal is poor in world [*weltarm*], man is world-forming [*weltbildend*]" (176). These three theses are theses on world. They are not theses on the stone, on the animal, or on man, but theses on the world; it is a matter of knowing what world is that will enable me to say these things. And the moments that I find the most interesting, and at the same time the most discreet, along this path are the moments when Heidegger more or less says: We don't finally know what world is! At bottom it is a very obscure concept! At the point where he advances like an army, armed with theses, solid, positive theses, it buckles, and he says in the end: decidedly, this concept of world is obscure. At bottom he doesn't know what "world" means. And a reading that really sought, as it were, to ascribe to Heidegger the most problematic or the most aporetic thinking would say: at bottom, all that, all these theses, apparently so positive and sure of themselves, on man, on the animal, and on the stone, merely aim, in a way, by means of this theatrical strategy, this grand pedagogical theatrical strategy, to circumscribe a moment where Heidegger says: at bottom, we don't know what world is, it's a very obscure notion, one that is becoming more and more obscure. But in order to remain sensitive to how serious such an utterance is, coming from someone like Heidegger, one must remember that earlier, in "On the Essence of Ground," but also and especially in *Being and Time*, which is a book on the world, on being-in-the-world, he had proposed a radically new approach to the question of world. Once more, therefore, in this seminar he poses the question of world: "We begin with the first of our three questions: *What is world?* [*Wir beginnen mit der ersten der drei fragen: Was ist Welt?*]" (ibid.). And he distinguishes three possibilities (three again), three "paths" for dealing with the question: two of them he has already followed through, in his previous works, and he is going to follow up on a new one. The "*first path* toward an initial clarification" is that of historiography, "the *history of the word* 'world,'" first of all. But "the history of the word provides only the exterior": one has therefore to go further, into the "historical development of the concept it contains." That is the path he attempted to pursue, he says, in "On the Essence of Ground."[5] On that path, which begins with the Greek *cosmos*, the Christian conception of world is particularly important:

> The most familiar aspect of the problem reveals itself in the distinction between God and world. The world is the totality of beings outside of and other than God [hence *creature*, the totality of the created]. Expressed in Christian terms, such beings thus also represent the realm of created being as distinct from uncreated being. And man in turn is also a part of the world understood in this sense. Yet man is not simply regarded as part of the world within which he appears and which he makes up in part. Man also stands over against the world. This standing-over-against is a "*having*" of world [and he italicizes "*having*": *Dieses Gegenüberstehen ist ein* Haben *der Welt*; man, therefore, has the world, whereas of the animal it will be said that it doesn't have it, rather, that it has it without having it or that it doesn't have while at the same time having it; it's going to be very complicated] as that in which man moves, with which he engages, which he both masters and serves, and to which he is exposed. Thus man is, first, a part of the world, and second, as this part he is at once both master and servant of the world [*zugleich Herr und Knecht der Welt*]. (176–77)

But he abandons this first path like a first sketch. The second way, leaving behind the "*historical path*" followed in *Being and Time*, is that of the "characterization of the *phenomenon of world*":

In contrast to this *historical path* [*Im Unterschied zu diesem* histori-schen Weg] toward an understanding of the concept of world, I at-tempted in *Being and Time* to provide a preliminary characterization of the *phenomenon of world* by interpreting the *way in which we at first and for the most part move about in our everyday world*. . . . That which is so close and intelligible to us in our everyday dealings is actually and fundamentally remote and unintelligible to us. (177)

He recalls thereby what he had done two or three years earlier. He says nothing against the treatment of world in *Being and Time*, against the analysis of "being-in-the-world [*In-der-Welt sein*]," but what interests him here is a "*third* path." If one therefore wants to take seriously the theses on the animal, it is necessary to know that Heidegger develops them within a new problematic of world, which is neither that attempted in "The Es-sence of Ground" nor that of *Being and Time*; he wants a third path (three again, it's three every time): "Instead we have chosen to follow a *third* path at this point—the path of a *comparative examination* [vergleichenden Betrachtung]" (ibid.).

I am going to read this passage a little more closely, because the animals are coming:

As we have said, man is not merely a *part of the world* but is also master and servant of the world in the sense of "*having*" world. Man has world. But what then about the other beings which, like man, are also part of the world: the animals and plants, the material things like the stone, for example [this is the single example of material things]? Are they merely parts [*Stücke*] of the world, as distinct from man who in addition *has* world? Or does the animal too have world, and if so, in what way? In the same way as man, or in some other way? [*In derselben Weise wie der Mensch, oder anders?* And everything will turn around this "other way."] And how would we grasp this otherness? [*Wie ist diese Andersheit zu fassen?* There resides the ques-tion . . . the question of "alterity."] And what about the stone? However crudely, certain distinctions manifest themselves here. We can formulate these distinctions in the following three theses: [1.] the stone (material object) is *worldless*; [2.] the animal is *poor in world*; [3.] man is *world-forming*. (Ibid.)

One could continue to read closely, but what matters to me here is Heidegger's strategy, and it is very unusual: once he has posed his three theses, in a comparative examination, within these triads of questions, terms, etc., he says that the best way to enter into this triple comparative question is by going to the middle. He will therefore choose "the intermediate thesis [*der mittleren These*]" (185, chapter 3 heading).

The difficulty derives from the fact that it is a matter of gaining access to the essence of animality—that is indeed what he calls the thing—which is determinable only to the extent that one has first made clear the living nature of the living thing: "the *essence of the animality* of the animal [*das* Wesen der Tierheit *des Tieres*]. . . . we can only determine the animality of the animal if we are clear about what constitutes the *living character of a living being* [*die* Lebendigkeit des Lebenden]" (179). Yet the "*living character of a living being*" is what the animal has in common with man. Therefore, one will not be able to speak of the essence of animality in general unless—and although as his discussion progresses Heidegger cites many examples of animals—the categorization of all animals within a "general essence of animality," in spite of their differences (differences between lizard and chimpanzee, for example), remains beyond question. His question is that of "the *essence of the animality* of the animal [*das* Wesen der Tierheit *des Tieres*]," in contrast to that of "the *essence of the humanity* of man [*das* Wesen der Menschheit *des Menschen*]." Why? Because "the *living character of a living being*, as distinct from the non-living being" is "the possibility of dying" (ibid.). It is apparently because the animal can die that it is distinguished from the stone, which cannot die: "A stone cannot be dead because it is never alive" (ibid.). Hence one should—we don't have the time to do so—put this passage into relation with what he says elsewhere, in the texts that I cited in this very place in *Aporias*, where Heidegger literally says "the animal doesn't die," it stops living, it croaks. Here he says that it dies:

> Then again, we can only determine the animality of the animal if we are clear about what constitutes the *living character of a living being*, as distinct from the non-living being [*im Unterschied zum Leblosen*] which does not even have the possibility of dying [*das nicht einmal die Möglichkeit hat zu sterben*]. A stone cannot be dead because it is never alive [*Ein Stein kann nicht tot sein, weil er nicht lebt*]. (Ibid.)

In other words, what he implies here is that the "animal dies." On the basis of that he poses the question of the essence of animality on the basis of the essence of the living. But how can one reconcile this sentence with what he says elsewhere, with so much insistence, namely, that what is proper to the animal is the fact that "it doesn't die." That it finishes living (*verenden*) without dying, without *sterben*, for it is the verb *sterben*, used here, that the animal lacks in the other texts that I cited on that earlier occasion. Here the animal "dies," in contrast to the stone. As a result there is posed anew, like an enigma, like those Heidegger regularly produces, the question of what "life" is, "in its essence," what the "living character of a living being" is. And naturally, all that emerges against the background that I have already insisted greatly on, and even here again this week, namely, that *Dasein* is explicitly defined by Heidegger as a "being [*existant*]" that is not, essentially, a "living" being. The determination regarding life, reference to it, is not essential in order to determine *Dasein*. Hence, with this question of the animal, besides the whole enormous problematic field that is opened up, there is raised the question of life not only in animals but also in *Dasein*. That is to say that, in reading the texts that we are now entering into, one must not stop being interested at the same time in the question of what are called "animals," with the examples he gives, but also in the question of the animality of *Dasein*, which Heidegger, naturally, leaves aside or in suspense—I would say from one end to the other of his life and his thinking.

I would like to read—but what time is it? Six o'clock already! OK . . . —I would have liked to insist on the moments of vertigo and circularity in this text. That's what would take time: taking an interest in the difficult moments, admitted to and made explicit by Heidegger, regarding what he calls the circularity of his manner of proceeding, the vertigo—and he insists a lot on that word (*Schwindel*): turning round and round. He notices that these comparative considerations are caught in a circle, and that that circle makes one dizzy. He insists a lot on this dizziness, which, he says, is *unheimlich*: "Schwindel ist unheimlich." And there are many moments in the text, which I would have liked to point out, where one's head spins and where Heidegger confesses that the vertigo is *unheimlich* but that it is necessary.[6] This vertigo is that of an interrogation into the animal, and, finally, it's the concept of world itself that becomes problematic and fragile.

But since we have just ten minutes, it would be better for me to step back from the text. One of the most difficult places is where Heidegger, having to defend the thesis that the animal is *weltarm*, is keen to mark that that impoverishment is not caught in a hierarchy, that it is not simply a "less." This is very difficult to defend: why "poor" when poor means less rich, all the same? So, he says, there is no hierarchy there, no "evaluative ranking" (194). Yet this impoverishment is to be determined on the basis of "deprivation," and he develops there a whole analysis of *privation*. The animal is "deprived," and deprivation is not simply a negative sentiment. He first said that the stone is not deprived; it doesn't have world but it isn't deprived; and since the stone doesn't have world but isn't deprived, it can't be said that it is "poor" in world. In other words, to say that the animal is poor in world is to demonstrate that it has world. And Heidegger consistently says deliberately contradictory things, namely, that the animal has a world in the mode of "not having." The animal is "deprived," and this privation implies that "it is in a mood": feeling poor "in mood," *Ar-mut* ("nämlich wie ihm dabei *zu Mute* ist—*Ar-mut*"; 195), is a manner of feeling that one is, an attunement, a sentiment; the animal experiences the privation of this world. Thus, no hierarchy, no teleology, neither finalism nor mechanicism, and the grand tradition of the Aristotelian *steresis*, of privation. In the end the animal is said to be "circumscribed" in this privation—and Heidegger speaks of its being "immured" (198), of "encirclement" (253), of being "absorbed," of "captivation [*Benommenheit*]" (238ff.); it is enclosed in a captivation but with the sentiment of deprivation. Naturally these are texts that need to be looked at very closely, so that if one accuses Heidegger of putting the animal below man one doesn't forget that he claims to do something else, namely, by saying that this impoverishment doesn't constitute a less, that it even in a certain way signifies a plus: a sentiment of privation that shows that the animal can feel something, whereas the stone cannot. And one should analyze this *Benommenheit*, this numbness that is translated by "captivation [*accaparement*]." It is in an essential relation to the question of the apophantic, to the "as such": the lizard, for example (and one needs to come back to all the lizards in this text), has a relation to the stone that appears to it, to the sun that appears to it, but they don't appear to it *as* stone, *as* sun.

Of course, to go very fast, as I have already suggested on past occasions, the deconstructive strategy that I would have tried to put in place, had I the time, would involve not contesting what Heidegger says about the "as such" but marking that perhaps—precisely in order to analyze, formalize, take account of these contradictory statements of the type "the animal *has and doesn't have* world," thus *has and doesn't have* the "as such"—in the end, one has to get out of this opposition, which is an absolutely structuring operation throughout philosophy, including in Heidegger, between the "as such" and the "not as such," as if one could choose only between the "as such ['*als'-Struktur*]" and its opposite. And I think that a differential analysis of the *animot*, of animals, should complicate this problematic of the "as such." One of the elements I would have liked to insist on, one of the points of purchase on this problematic, is the moment when

Heidegger, analyzing the question of the lie and the apophantic *logos*, alludes to the fact (this is something that I have myself very much and regularly insisted on, because it seems to me to represent very important strategic stakes) that Aristotle himself takes into account a nonapophantic moment in the *logos*, a moment that isn't declarative, enunciative, and the example he gives is that of requesting:[7] "Requesting, *euchē*, for example, is a non-apophantic *logos*" (quoted at 309).[8] He is here distinguishing between a *logos apophantikos*, "exhibiting discourse"—and when I say "I" it is an exhibiting discourse [*parole monstrative*], "I," that is to say, "Me, I am speaking to you," I show myself—and a nonapophantic marking (I wouldn't say *logos* here), for example, prayer, which doesn't show anything, which in a certain way "doesn't say anything." And the possibility of a nonapophantic *logos* here would, in my opinion, open a breach in the whole apparatus, but I don't have time to show that.

In order to finish, very quickly, I am going to read you the passage concerning domestic animals, because it is what we were talking about earlier, with the cat, which is a domestic animal, but according to me not a tamed one, not trained, not "domesticated." It comes in paragraph 50, whose title is "Having and not having world as the potentiality for granting transposedness." The question that Heidegger is elaborating at that moment is: Can we transpose (*versetzen*) what we say about man to *Dasein*? What does *versetzen*, to transpose, mean, first of all from man to man, between humans? What does one do when one transposes, an essential question for this comparative analysis? What is "transposing," and can we transpose in the animal? That is the whole question of anthropomorphism, etc. Well, within this grand question, which is developed at great length, of the being-transposed-into-others, which he characterizes as an essence of the human *Dasein*, being capable of transposing as proper to *Dasein*, he writes:

> Being transposed into others belongs to the essence of human Dasein. [*Das Versetztsein in Andere gehört zum Wesen des menschlichen Daseins.*] As long as we keep this insight in view then we already possess an essential point of orientation with respect to the particular problem concerning the possibility of human self-transposition into the animal. But how does this really help us? Have we thereby dispelled the difficulty which besets us when we attempt to transpose ourselves into an animal in any given case? (209)

And, in the matter of transposition, he then comes to this passage, which I wanted to read to you, and after that I'll stop:

Let us consider the case of domestic animals [*die Haustiere*] as a striking example. We do not describe them as such simply because they turn up in the house [*weil sie im Haus vorkommen*] but because they belong to the house [*weil sie zum Haus gehören*; ants are not domestic animals; domestic animals are not simply *in* the house, they are *part of* the house], i.e., they serve the house in a certain sense [*d.h. für das Haus in gewisser Weise dienen*]. Yet they do not belong to the house in the way in which the roof belongs to the house as protection against storms. [They aren't part of the house like just anything at all, they are not useful the way tools are useful—the roof, for example—which are useful otherwise.] We keep domestic pets in the house with us, they *"live" with us*. [He italicizes "they *'live' with us*" and puts it in quotation marks.] But we do not live with them if living means: *being* in an animal kind of way. [*Aber wir leben nicht mit ihnen, wenn Leben besagt:* Sein *in der Weise des Tieres*. In other words, the animal lives with us but we don't live with it if living means what an animal does: hence *living* changes its sense here.] Yet we *are with* [italics] them nonetheless. [*Gleichwohl* sind *wir* mit *ihnen.*] But this being-with is not an *existing-with* [*Dieses Mitsein ist aber auch kein* Mitexistieren], because a dog does not exist but merely lives [*ein Hund nicht existiert, sondern nur lebt*; and the word *existence* here naturally has the whole reach that is guaranteed it by the analytic of *Dasein*: the dog doesn't have a Dasein, it doesn't exist, it merely lives, and the difference between "exist" and "live" is the difference in the *Mit*, in *Mitgehen* or this *Mitsein*, the dissymmetrical difference between the animal and us]. Through this being with animals we enable them to move within our world. We say that the dog is lying underneath the table or is running up the stairs and so on. Yet when we consider the dog itself—does it comport itself toward the table as table, toward the stairs as stairs? (210)

And there you have it! That is why, at a given moment, he will say concerning the "as such": he climbs the stairs, sometimes better than us, faster than us, but he doesn't have a relation to the stairs "as such." And that is why, in another passage, he says that one has to cross out [*raturer*] all the words when one speaks of what appears to the animal. In sum, a generalized *Durchstreichung!*[9] Strike out all the words if these words are determined semantically by *existence*. If the words are determined based on the existence of *Dasein*, none of these words is suitable for the animal. They therefore have to be crossed out. They have to be withdrawn. For that reason I took the liberty of pointing out, in this very place, this allusion to the crossing out of the animal. But can the animal itself cross out?

Not only in the sense of the feint of a feint, following Lacan, but in the sense, which I brought up, of the possibility of an animal-machine that would put into effect all the necessary *ratures* in the texts of Heidegger? The text continues:

> All the same, it does go up the stairs with us. It feeds with us—and yet, we really do not "feed" [*nein, wir fressen nicht*]. It eats with us—and yet, it does not really "eat." Nevertheless, it is with us [it does it with us; *Und doch mit uns*]! A going along with [*ein Mit-gehen*] . . . , a transposedness [*eine Versetztheit*], and yet not [*und doch nicht*]. (Ibid.)

That is the moment of negation-disavowal, and that is where it takes place. But it doesn't mean that he is wrong. Of course, the animal doesn't eat like us, but neither does any one person eat in the same way; there are structural differences, even when one eats from the same plate! . . . But what I wanted to suggest—and of course this is something that I am proposing in a few words and whose ambition exceeds me—is that these differences are not those between "as such" and "not as such."

"Nevertheless, it is with us! A . . . , a . . . , and yet not"! That exclamation mark is something I would have liked to follow throughout this enormous discourse, I'll do it, I hope, if I have the time and the strength: I'd like to do justice to this text because it is so rich, it should be followed through step by step, with a somewhat more elaborate commentary than what I am improvising here.

Further along, he again speaks of death, of human death, as in *Being and Time*; he speaks also of the animal drive, of the sexual drive, of nesting, etc. But, be that as it may, it remains that: "If it is the case that the animal does not comport itself toward beings as such, then behaviour involves *no letting-be* of beings as such—none at all and in no way whatsoever [*Wenn dem so ist, daß das Tier sich nicht zu Seiendem als solchem verhält, dann liegt im Benehmen überhaupt* kein Seinlassen *das Seienden als solchen—überhaupt keines, in keinem Modus*]" (253).

The animal doesn't know how to "let be," let the thing be such as it is. It always has a relation of utility, of putting-in-perspective; it doesn't let the thing be what it is, appear as such without a project guided by a narrow "sphere" of drives, of desires.[10] One of the questions to be raised, therefore, would be to know whether man does that. In other words, in order to indicate the governing principle of the strategy I would like to follow, it would not simply consist in unfolding, multiplying, leafing through the structure of the "as such," or the opposition between "as such" and "not as such," no more than it would consist in giving back to the animal what Heidegger says it is deprived of; it would obey the necessity of asking oneself whether man, the human itself, has the "as such." Precisely when it comes to beings or to very determining experiences, those that mark us in particular—death is, of course, the prime example (I approached the question from that point of view in this very place), but everywhere else—can one free the relation of *Dasein* (not to say "man") to beings from every living, utilitarian, perspective-making project, from every vital design, such that man himself could "let the being be"? For that is the relation to the being as such, that is to say, the relation to what is inasmuch as one lets it be what it is, that is to say, that one doesn't approach it or apprehend it from our own perspective, from our own design. In order to have a relation to the sun as it is, it is necessary that, in a certain way, I relate to the sun such as it is in my absence, and it is in effect like that that objectivity is constituted, starting from death. To relate to the thing such as it is in itself—supposing that it were possible—means apprehending it such as it is, such as it would be even if I weren't there. I can die, or simply leave the room; I know that it will be what it is and will remain what it is. That is why death is also such an important demarcation line; it is starting from mortality and from the possibility of being dead that one can let things be such as they are, in my absence, in a way, and my presence is there only to reveal what the thing would be in my absence. So can the human do that, purely? Is there a relation of apprehension to the being "as such"—the "ontological difference," therefore—to the being [*être*] of the being [*l'étant*], such that it lets the being of the being be, such as it is, in the absence of every kind of design, living? It is evident that the difference between Nietzsche and Heidegger is that Nietzsche would have said no: everything is in a perspective; the relation to a being, even the "truest," the most "objective," that which respects most the essence of what is such as it is, is caught in a movement that we'll call here that of the living, of life, and from this point of view, whatever the difference between animals, it remains an "animal" relation. Hence the strategy in question would consist in pluralizing and varying the "as such," and, instead of simply giving speech back to the animal, or giving to the animal what the human deprives it of, as it were, in marking that the human is, in a way, similarly "deprived," by means of a privation that is not a privation, and that there is no pure and simple "as such." There you have it. That would presume a radical reinterpretation of what is living, naturally, but not in terms of the "essence of the living," of the "essence of the animal." That is the question . . . Naturally, I am not hiding this; the stakes are so radical that they concern "ontological difference," the "question of being," the whole framework of Heideggerian discourse.

Notes

Foreword

1. Jacques Derrida, "L'animal que donc je suis (à suivre)," in *L'animal autobiographique*, ed. Marie-Louise Mallet (Paris: Galilée, 1999); "The Animal That Therefore I Am (More to Follow)," trans. David Wills, *Critical Inquiry* 28, 2 (2002): 369–418. The parenthesis also reminds us that we would have to hear the *je suis* of the title in at least two registers, those of being [*être*] and following [*suivre*].

2. Jacques Derrida, "Et si l'animal répondait?" in *Cahier de L'Herne*, no. 83, *Jacques Derrida*, ed. Marie-Louis Mallet and Ginette Michaud (Paris: L'Herne, 2004); "And Say the Animal Responded," trans. David Wills, in *Zoontologies: the Question of the Animal*, ed. Cary Wolfe (Minneapolis: University of Minnesota Press, 2003). Earlier translations have been revised for this volume.

3. See below, Chapter 3, p. 135.

4. See below, Chapter 1, p. 27.

5. See below, Chapter 3, p. 135.

6. Jacques Derrida, "The Ends of Man," *Philosophy and Phenomenological Research* 30, 1 (1969): 31–57; " 'Geschlecht': Sexual Difference, Ontological Difference," trans. Ruben Berezdivin, in *A Derrida Reader: Between the Blinds*, ed. Peggy Kamuf (New York: Columbia University Press, 1991), 380–402; "Heidegger's Hand (*Geschlecht* II)," trans. John P. Leavey, Jr., in *Deconstruction and Philosophy: The Texts of Jacques Derrida*, ed. John Sallis (Chicago: University of Chicago Press, 1987), 161–96; *Of Spirit: Heidegger and the Question*, trans. Geoffrey Bennington and Rachel Bowlby (Chicago: University of Chicago Press, 1989); "Heidegger's Ear: Philopolemology (*Geschlecht* IV)," trans. John P.

Leavey, Jr., in *Reading Heidegger*, ed. John Sallis (Bloomington: Indiana University Press, 1993), 163–218; *Aporias*, trans. Thomas Dutoit (Stanford, Calif.: Stanford University Press, 1994).

The Animal That Therefore I Am (More to Follow)

NOTE: As suggested in Marie-Louise Mallet's Foreword, the *je suis* of Derrida's French title—"L'animal que donc je suis (à suivre)"—plays on the shared first person singular present form of *être* ("to be") and *suivre* ("to follow"). My translation attempts to condense such possibilities as: "the animal that therefore I am (to be continued)," "the animal that therefore I become by following," and "the animal that therefore I follow, whose logic is to be tracked in what follows." What is obviously in play is Descartes' formulation of consciousness and of the thinking animal as human ("je pense donc je suis"), a priority that is rewritten to read "the animal that therefore I follow after." Throughout the book, especially its first two chapters, "I am" has, very often, to be read also as "I follow," and vice versa. I have used the formula "I am (following)," except where the context, or demands of fluency, dictate a choice of one or the other possibility.—Trans.

1. Jean-Luc Nancy was ill and unable to attend the 1997 conference. But he sent the text of his lecture, which was read and included in the proceedings.—Ed.

2. The adverbial fragment *depuis le temps*, which is not usually used as such in French, is repeated throughout the text. The relative form, *depuis le temps que*, has the sense of "for so long now." I have used either that formulation or "since so long ago," except where Derrida's repetitions allow for the contrived phrase "since time." In all cases the reader should bear in mind Derrida's reference to the mythological and philosophical "prehistory" of conceptualizations of the animal that he is calling into question.—Trans.

3. *que l'animal nous regarde*: also, "that the animal has been our concern." Derrida plays on this double sense of *regarder* ("to look at" and "to concern") in various cases below.—Trans.

4. *j'ai du mal*: the expression also evokes the sense of evil or a curse. Here and below Derrida implies a recasting of the Genesis myth such that it is an animal that brings man to consciousness of his nakedness and of good and evil, rather than being the cause (via woman) of his fall.—Trans.

5. *à poil*: a common expression for "naked," literally meaning "down to one's (animal) hairs."—Trans.

6. *bête*: French *bête* (L. *bestia*) has the somewhat archaic sense of the English "beast," but is also used as a slightly familiar word for "animal." As an adjective it means "stupid," which I have often translated below as "asinine" in order to retain some connotation of animality (however partial in contrast to the generality of *bête*). *Une bêtise* (the word exists in literary English) is an "idiocy," or simply "stupid thing," "mistake," as in *faire / dire une bêtise*, "make a stupid mistake / say something stupid." I have taken the liberty, in translating it below,

of coining the portmanteau "asinanity" (in order, once again, to retain the pejorative reference to animality).—Trans.

7. Sarah Kofman, *Autobiogriffures: Du chat Murr d'Hoffmann* (Paris: Galilée, 1984).

8. Michel de Montaigne, "Apology for Raymond Sebond," in *The Complete Works of Montaigne*, trans. Donald M. Frame (Stanford, Calif.: Stanford University Press, 1957), bk. 2, chap. 12, 331. The "Apology" needs to be examined very closely, especially to the extent that Montaigne doesn't just revive, in its luxuriant richness, a tradition that attributes much to the animal, beginning with a type of language. We would situate as most pertinent in this respect, marking in advance a difference from the modern (Cartesian or post-Cartesian) form of a hegemonic tradition that we shall analyze later, the moment where Montaigne recognizes in the animal more than a right to communication, to the sign, to language as sign (something Descartes will not deny): namely, *a capacity to respond.* For example: "it is not credible that Nature has denied us this resource that she has given to many other animals: for what is it but speech, this faculty we see in them of complaining, rejoicing, calling to each other for help, inviting each other to love, as they do by the use of their voice? How could they not speak to one another? They certainly speak to us, and we to them. In how many ways do we not speak to our dogs? *And they answer us.* We talk to them in another language, with other names, than to birds, hogs, oxen, horses; and we change the idiom according to the species." And following a quotation from Dante concerning the ant: "It seems that Lactantius attributes to beasts not only speech but also laughter" (335, my italics). Further page numbers will be given in the text.

9. "The Cat" is, as we well know, the title of two poems. Only the first of those directly addresses its subject in the singular, familiar form ("Viens, mon beau chat . . ."), before recognizing in it the figure of "the woman I love" [*ma femme*]. Baudelaire even names the cat's gaze ("the image of the woman I love rises before me: her gaze, like yours, dear creature [*Je vois ma femme en esprit. Son regard / Comme le tien, aimable bête]*" and "When my eyes are drawn . . . towards my beloved cat . . . and find I am looking into myself [*Quand mes yeux, vers ce chat que j'aime . . . Et que je regarde en moi-même]*") and its voice ("To utter the longest of sentences it has no need of words [*Pour dire les plus longues phrases, Elle n'a pas besoin de mots]*"). (Charles Baudelaire, "Le Chat" and "Le Chat," *Les Fleurs du mal*, in *The Complete Verse of Baudelaire*, trans. and ed. Francis Scarfe, 2 vols. [London: Anvil Press Poetry, 1986], 1:98, 121–22.)

10. Rainer Maria Rilke, "Schwarze Katze," in *Neue Gedichte / New Poems*, trans. Stephen Cohn (Manchester: Carcanet Press, 1992), 202–3 (on another, later occasion, I'll have to try to read this poem that I have rediscovered thanks to Werner Hamacher). The poem is dedicated, if that is the word, to "your gaze" (*dein Blick*) and to a specter (*Ein Gespenst*)—those are its first words; one could set it into play with the poem he signs concerning "The Panther" (60–61; which again begins by naming the gaze [his gaze this time: *Sein Blick* are the first

words]), rediscovered thanks to Richard Macksey, who has also translated it into English. Since the conference at Cerisy, cat lovers and friends the world over have been giving me cats like this. This would also be the moment to salute Jean-Claude Lebensztejn's forthcoming masterpiece entitled *Miaulique (Fantaisie Chromatique)* [Paris: Le Passage, 2002—Ed.].

A propos, why does one say in French "has the cat got your tongue" [*donner sa langue au chat*] to mean that one has thrown in the towel?

11. "An animal's eyes have the power to speak a great language. . . . Sometimes I look into a cat's eyes" (Martin Buber, *I and Thou*, trans. Ronald Gregor Smith [New York: Charles Scribner's Sons, 1958], 96–97). Buber also speaks of "the capacity to turn its glance to us." "The beginning of this cat's glance, lighting up under the touch of my glance, indisputably questioned me: 'Is it possible that you think of me? . . . Do I really exist?' . . . ('I' here is a transcription for a word, that we do not have, denoting self without the ego)" (97).

12. Lewis Carroll, *Through the Looking Glass*, in *The Complete Works of Lewis Carroll* (New York: Modern Library, 1936), 268. Derrida's French reference is *Alice au pays des merveilles: De l'autre côté du miroir*, trans. Jacques Papy, ed. Jean Gattegno (Paris: Gallimard, 1994).

13. First published under the title "Che cos'è la poesia?" in the Italian revue *Poesia* 1, 11 (1988); reprinted in *Poësie* 50 (1989), and finally in *Points de suspension—Entretiens* (Paris: Galilée, 1992); "*Che cos'è la poesia?*" trans. Peggy Kamuf, in Jacques Derrida, *Points . . . : Interviews 1974–1994*, ed. Elisabeth Weber (Stanford, Calif.: Stanford University Press, 1995).

14. Lewis Carroll, *Alice's Adventures in Wonderland*, in *Complete Works*, 89, 90.

15. Carroll, *Looking Glass*, 269.

16. Carroll, *Alice*, 72.

17. *chasser*: also "to hunt."—Trans.

18. Emmanuel Levinas, *Ethics and Infinity*, trans. Richard A. Cohen (Pittsburgh: Duquesne University Press, 1985), 85.

19. This introduction was followed, on the same day and the next day, by two sessions during which I proposed readings of Descartes, Kant, Heidegger, Levinas, and Lacan. Carried out as patiently and micrologically as possible, those interpretations were meant to put to the test the working hypotheses that I am sketching out here on the threshold of a work in progress. [Those sessions constitute the following two chapters.—Ed.]

20. In this section Derrida consistently compares two authoritative French translations of Genesis (Bereshit), those by Chouraqui (Desclée de Brouwer) and Dhormes (Pléiade). My translations lose some of the subtleties. For comparison, readers can consult the King James Version, The Jerusalem Bible, or *The JPS Torah Commentary (Genesis)* (Philadelphia: Jewish Publication Society, 1989).—Trans.

21. "Elohim dit : 'Faisons l'homme à notre image, à notre ressemblance! Qu'ils aient autorité sur les poissons de la mer et sur les oiseaux des cieux, sur les

bestiaux, sur toutes les bêtes sauvages et sur tous les reptiles qui rampent sur la terre!' Elohim créa donc l'homme à son image, à l'image d'Elohim il le créa. Il les créa homme et femelle. Elohim les bénit et Elohim leur dit : 'Fructifiez et multipliez-vous, remplissez la terre et soumettez-la, ayez autorité sur les poissons de la mer et sur les oiseaux des cieux, sur tout vivant qui remue sur la terre!'"—Trans.

22. "Elohim dit : 'Nous ferons Adâm-le Glébeux— / A notre replique, selon notre ressemblance. / Ils assujettiront le poisson de la mer, le volatile des ciels, / la bête, toute la terre, tout reptile qui rampe sur la terre.' / Elohim créa le glébeux à sa réplique, / A la réplique d'Elohim, il les crée, / mâle et femelle, il les crée. / Elohim les bénit. Elohim leur dit: / Fructifiez, multipliez, emplissez la terre, con-quérez-la. / Assujettisez le poisson de la mer, le volatile des ciels, / tout vivant qui rampe sur la terre."—Trans.

23. "Les deux sont nus, le glébeux et sa femme: ils n'en blêmissent pas."—Trans.

24. "Il les fait venir vers le glébeux pour voir ce qu'il leur criera."—Trans.

25. "Ils les amena vers l'homme pour voir comment il les appellerait." —Trans.

26. Walter Benjamin, "On Language as Such and on the Language of Man," *Selected Writings*, vol. 1, *1913–1926*, ed. Marcus Bullock and Michael W. Jen-nings (Cambridge: Harvard University Press, 1996).

27. "Captivation" in the English translation. See the discussion in Chapter 4 below.—Trans.

28. Martin Heidegger, *Being and Time*, trans. John Macquarie and Edward Robinson (New York: Harper and Row, 1962), 396.

29. *vous entraîner à ma suite*: also "to train you to follow me."—Trans.

30. *s'effacer*: more literally, "erasing" or "effacing itself," "to erase itself" or "oneself."—Trans.

31. *Les animaux me regardent. Avec ou sans figure, justement*: also, "Animals look at me. With or without a face, precisely."—Trans.

32. Jacques Derrida, "Un ver à soie," *Contretemps* 2/3 (1997), rpt. in Hélène Cixous and Jacques Derrida, *Voiles* (Paris: Galilée, 1998), 23–85; "A Silkworm of One's Own," trans. Geoffrey Bennington, in Hélène Cixous and Jacques Der-rida, *Veils* (Stanford, Calif.: Stanford University Press, 2001), 17–92; "Envois," in *The Post Card*, trans. Alan Bass (Chicago: University of Chicago Press, 1987), 1–256; "Che cos'è la poesia," trans. Peggy Kamuf, in *A Derrida Reader: Between the Blinds*, ed. Peggy Kamuf (New York: Columbia University Press, 1991), 221–37; "Fourmis," in *Lectures de la différence sexuelle*, ed. Anne Berger (Paris: Des Femmes, 1994), 69–102.

33. *nu comme un vers*: cf. Chaucer, "naked as a worm," modern, "naked as a jaybird."—Trans.

34. Derrida, "A Silkworm of One's Own," 88–89, 90.

35. This portmanteau neologism, combining "animal" and "word," is pro-nounced, in the singular or the plural, the same way as the plural of "animal."

With its singular article and plural-sounding ending, it jars in oral French. See Derrida's discussion below.—Trans.

36. Jacques Derrida, *Of Spirit: Heidegger and the Question*, trans. Geoff Bennington and Rachel Bowlby (Chicago: University of Chicago Press, 1989), 134. Would the language Heidegger speaks of, a language "without" question, without question mark, this language "before" the question, this language of the *Zusage* (acquiescence, affirmation, agreement, etc.), therefore be a language without a response? A "moment" of language that is in its essence released from all relation to an expected response? But if one links the concept of the animal, as they all do from Descartes to Heidegger, from Kant to Levinas and Lacan, to the double im-possibility, the double incapacity of question and response, is it because the "moment," the instance and possibility of the *Zusage* belong to an "experience" of language about which one could say, even if it is not in itself "animal," that it is not something that the "animal" could be deprived of? That would be enough to destabilize a whole tradition, to deprive it of its fundamental argument.

37. Jacques Derrida, *Dissemination*, trans. Barbara Johnson (Chicago: University of Chicago Press, 1981), 119.

38. *chimérique sera mon adresse*: cf. above, "*Limitrophy* is therefore my subject," and below, "the truth of modesty will, in the end, be our subject." Derrida is no doubt alluding to two previous Cerisy lectures, that on Ponge in 1975, where he asserted "Francis Ponge will be my thing," and that on Nietzsche in 1972, where he stated "Woman will be my subject." See Jacques Derrida, *Signsponge*, trans. Richard Rand (New York: Columbia University Press, 1984), 10, and *Spurs: Nietzsche's Styles / Éperons: Les Styles de Nietzsche*, trans. Barbara Harlow (Chicago: University of Chicago Press, 1979), 36/37.—Trans.

39. *Dansité*: a neologism coined by Lacan, pronounced the same as *densité* ("density"). See Chapter 3 in this volume.—Trans.

40. "Caïn dit à Iahvé : 'Ma faute est trop grande pour que je la porte!' 'Mon tort est trop grand pour être porté.'"—Trans.

41. "Je me cacherai de devant toi. Je serai fugitif et fuyard sur la terre et il arrivera que quiconque me rencontrera me tuera" (Dhormes). "Je me voilerai face à toi. Je serai mouvant, errant sur terre: / et c'est qui me trouvera me tuera" (Chouraqui).—Trans.

42. "Alors Iahvé dit à Caïn: 'Pourquoi éprouves-tu de la colère et pourquoi ton visage est abattu? Si tu agis bien, ne te relèveras-tu? Que si tu n'agis pas bien le Péché est tapi à ta porte: son élan est vers toi, mais toi, domine-le!"—Trans.

43. "à l'ouverture la faute est tapie; à toi sa passion. Toi, gouverne-la."—Trans.

44. Genesis 6:6: "Jehovah repented for having put man on the earth . . . 'I repent for having made them.'" "Iahvé se repentit d'avoir fait l'homme sur la terre . . . je me repens de les avoir faits'" (Dhormes). Chouraqui uses the verb *regretter* ("to regret, be sorry"). The King James Version says "It repenteth the Lord . . . it repenteth me." I insist on what is almost remorse, for it immediately

precedes Noah's ark and the new covenant: this time with *all the living* that will accompany Noah. I shall return to this elsewhere.

45. René Descartes, *Discourse on the Method*, in *The Philosophical Writings of Descartes*, vol. 1, trans. John Cottingham, Robert Stoothoff, and Dugald Murdoch (Cambridge: Cambridge University Press, 1985), 131.

46. *Ça*: also "Id."—Trans.

"But as for me, who am I (following)?"

NOTE: Titles for Chapters 2 and 4 are not given in the French publication. For convenience I have followed the convention of adopting the first words of those chapters. The quote is from Descartes' *Second Meditation*, as discussed and referenced below. The English translation, which generally follows the original Latin text, here drops a French emphasis and changes "who" to "what": "As to myself, what can I now say that I am [cf. *Mais moi, qui suis-je*]?"—Trans.

1. Plato, "Phaedrus," trans. R. Hackforth, in *The Collected Dialogues*, ed. Edith Hamilton and Huntington Cairns (Princeton: Princeton University Press, 1989), 521 (§275d).

2. *le fait qu'il est privé, et qu'il prive l'homme de réponse*: the comma and repeated formulation isolate *privé*, hence my translation. But the syntax also reads: "the fact that it is deprived of the response and deprives the human of the same."—Trans.

3. Plato, "Phaedrus," 478 (§230a).

4. See Jacques Derrida, *Speech and Phenomena*, trans. David B. Allison (Evanston, Ill.: Northwestern University Press, 1973).

5. See Chapter 1, n. 5, in this volume. *A nu, à cru*, and *à poil* are all more or less synonymous. *Un animal monté comme un cheval* ("a mounted animal, like a horse") can also mean "an animal hung like a horse."—Trans.

6. *pièce*: also "play/drama" and "piece (of the discussion)."—Trans.

7. *rossignol*: also "nightingale."—Trans.

8. *portée*: also "litter (of animals)," as well as "reach," "extent," "gamut."—Trans.

9. *Je rêve, donc, au fond d'un terrier introuvable et à venir*: also "I am dreaming therefore, at bottom, of a undiscoverable burrow to come."—Trans.

10. *sur lequel, littéralement, il s'acharne*: the verb *acharner* means "to hound" or "go at relentlessly," with an archaic sense of "whetting a hunting animal's appetite with flesh (cf. L. *caro*)."—Trans.

11. Michel Haar, "Du symbolisme animal en général, et notamment du serpent," *Alter* 3 (1995), special issue on the animal.

12. "Bête je suis, mais bête aiguë / De qui le venin quoique vil / Laisse loin la sage ciguë!": Paul Valéry, "Ébauche d'un serpent / Silhouette of a Serpent," in *Charms*, in *The Collected Works of Paul Valéry*, vol. 1, *Poems*, trans. David Paul, ed. Jackson Mathews (Princeton, N.J.: Princeton University Press, 1971), 184/185.

13. "La splendeur de l'azur aiguise / Cette guivre qui me déguise / D'animale simplicité" (ibid.).

14. "Cieux, son erreur! Temps, sa ruine! / Et l'abîme animal, béant! . . . / Quelle chute dans l'origine / Étincelle au lieu de néant!" (ibid., 188/189).

15. "Et de mes pièges le plus haut, / Tu gardes les cœurs de connaître / Que l'univers n'est qu'un défaut / Dans la pureté du Non-être!" (ibid., 186/187).

16. "Étincelle au lieu de néant! . . . / Mais, le premier mot de son Verbe, / MOI! . . . Des astres le plus superbe / Qu'ait parlés le fou créateur, / Je suis! . . . Je serai! . . . J'illumine / La diminution divine / De tous les feux du Séducteur!" (ibid., 188/189).

17. "Je suis Celui qui modifie / . . . / Je suis au fond de sa faveur / Cette inimitable saveur / Que tu ne trouves qu'à toi-même!" (ibid., 190–92/191–93).

18. "Vous êtes des hommes tout nus, / Ô bêtes blanches et béates!" (ibid., 190/191).

19. "Et toi qui me suis en rampant / Dieu de mes dieux morts en automne / Tu mesures combien d'empans / J'ai droit que la terre me donne / Ô mon ombre, ô mon vieux serpent"; my translation (cf. Guillaume Apollinaire, "La Chanson du mal-aimé," in *Alcools*, trans. Anne Hyde Greet [Berkeley: University of California Press, 1965], 28/29).

20. Quoted in Alexandre Leupin, *Barbarolexis: Medieval Writing and Sexuality* (Cambridge: Harvard University Press, 1989), 149.

21. René Descartes, *Meditations on First Philosophy*, trans. John Cottingham, in *The Philosophical Writings of Descartes*, vol. 2 (Cambridge: Cambridge University Press, 1984), 18. Further references will be given in the text, preceded by *M*. As explained above, the English translation follows the Latin, whereas Derrida's analysis often refers to the French. I have therefore modified the English translation here and in subsequent instances, in order to follow Derrida's emphases. Cf. René Descartes, *Meditationes de prima philosophia: Méditations métaphysiques*, trans. Duc de Luynes (Paris: Vrin, 1966): "Mais moi, qui suis-je, maintenant que je suppose qu'il y a quelqu'un qui est extrêmement puissant et, si je l'ose dire, malicieux et rusé, qui emploie toutes ses forces et toute son industrie à me tromper?" (27).—Trans.

22. Adrien Baillet, *Vie de M. Descartes* (Paris, 1691), quoted in Geneviève Rodis-Lewis, "Introduction historique," in *Meditationes de prima philosophia*, xi (my translation—Trans.).

23. Martin Heidegger, "Letter on 'Humanism,'" trans. Frank A. Capuzzi, in *Pathmarks*, ed. William McNeill (Cambridge: Cambridge University Press, 1998), 245–46.

24. Stéphane Mallarmé, *Igitur*, trans. Mary Ann Caws, in *Selected Poetry and Prose*, ed. Mary Ann Caws (New York: New Directions, 1982). Page references will be given in the text.

25. Derrida is referring to the *donc* in *l'animal que donc je suis*.—Trans.

26. René Descartes, *Discourse on the Method*, trans. Robert Stoothoff, in *The Philosophical Writings of Descartes*, vol. 1 (Cambridge: Cambridge University Press, 1985), 140–41. Further references will be given in the text, preceded by *D*. The French word translated by "witness" is consistently a form of the verb

témoigner, "to witness," "testify." The English translation, based on the Latin, has again been modified (cf. *Discours de la méthode*, in René Descartes, *Oeuvres et lettres* [Paris: Gallimard, Éditions de la Pléiade, 1953], 165–66).—Trans.

27. Letter to R. P. Vatier, 22 February 1638, in René Descartes, *The Correspondence*, trans. John Cottingham, Robert Stoothoff, Dugald Murdoch, and Anthony Kenny, in *The Philosophical Writings of Descartes*, vol. 3 (Cambridge: Cambridge University Press, 1985), 86.

28. À ***, in Descartes, *Oeuvres et lettres*, 1004. All translations from this letter are mine. (Despite "sifting through the whole of Descartes' extant correspondence with the purpose of extracting all the material of significant philosophical interest. . . . we have construed 'philosophical' in the broad sense in which Descartes himself understood it," the editors of *The Philosophical Writings of Descartes* do not include this letter [cf. *The Philosophical Writings of Descartes*, vol. 3, vii–viii].)—Trans.

29. In fact, *moyens*, "means," but there is explicit reference to *Discourse on Method*. See excerpted quote below.—Trans.

30. À ***, in Descartes, *Oeuvres et lettres*, 1004–5.

31. Ibid., 1005.

32. *au coeur duquel il faut . . . se rendre*: also "the matter that one must get to the heart of."—Trans.

33. Porphyry, *On Abstinence from Killing Animals*, trans. Gillian Clark (Ithaca, N.Y.: Cornell University Press, 2000), 82–83.

34. À ***, in Descartes, *Oeuvres et lettres*, 1000.

35. *répondeur automatique*: also "answering machine."—Trans.

36. À ***, in Descartes, *Oeuvres et lettres*, 1003.

37. In Florence Burgat, *Animal, mon prochain* (Paris: Odile Jacob, 1997), 56–59.

UNIVERSAL DECLARATION OF ANIMAL RIGHTS

Preamble:
—Considering that Life is one, all living beings having a common origin and having diversified in the course of the evolution of the species,
—Considering that all living beings possess natural rights, and that any animal with a nervous system has specific rights,
—Considering that the contempt for, and even the simple ignorance of, these natural rights, cause serious damage to Nature and lead men to commit crimes against animals,
—Considering that the coexistence of species implies a recognition by the human species of the right of other animal species to live,
—Considering that the respect of animals by humans is inseparable from the respect of men for each other,
It is hereby proclaimed that:
Article 1
All animals have equal rights to exist within the context of biological equilibrium. This equality of rights does not overshadow the diversity of species and of individuals.
Article 2

All animal life has the right to be respected.

Article 3

1. Animals must not be subjected to bad treatment or to cruel acts.

2. If it is necessary to kill an animal, it must be instantaneous, painless, and cause no apprehension.

3. A dead animal must be treated with decency.

Article 4

1. Wild animals have the right to live and to reproduce in freedom in their own natural environment.

2. The prolonged deprivation of the freedom of wild animals, hunting and fishing practiced as a pastime, as well as any use of wild animals for reasons that are not vital, are contrary to this fundamental right.

Article 5

1. Any animal which is dependent on man has the right to proper sustenance and care.

2. It must under no circumstances be abandoned or killed unjustifiably.

3. All forms of breeding and uses of the animal must respect the physiology and behavior specific to the species.

4. Exhibitions, shows, and films involving animals must also respect their dignity and must not include any violence whatsoever.

Article 6

1. Experiments on animals entailing physical or psychological suffering violate the rights of animals.

2. Replacement methods must be developed and systematically implemented.

Article 7

Any act unnecessarily involving the death of an animal, and any decision leading to such an act, constitute a crime against life.

Article 8

1. Any act compromising the survival of a wild species and any decision leading to such an act are tantamount to genocide, that is to say, a crime against the species.

2. The massacre of wild animals and the pollution and destruction of biotopes are acts of genocide.

Article 9

1. The specific legal status of animals and their rights must be recognized by law.

2. The protection and safety of animals must be represented at the level of governmental organizations.

Article 10

Educational and schooling authorities must ensure that citizens learn from childhood to observe, understand, and respect animals.

The Universal Declaration of Animal Rights was solemnly proclaimed in Paris on 15 October 1978 at UNESCO headquarters. The text, revised by the International League of Animal Rights in 1989, was submitted to the UNESCO Director General in 1990 and made public that same year.

38. *des voyants*: also "seers" or "seeing things."—Trans.

39. *faire signe*: also "get in touch," or "say hello."—Trans.

40. I don't have time to demonstrate this here with the appropriate textual support, but I ask you to take me at my word, at least for the moment.

41. Saint Augustine, *Confessions*, trans. Henry Chadwick (Oxford: Oxford University Press, 1991), 66 (bk. 4.14).

42. *encre*: homonym of *ancre*, "anchor."—Trans.

43. Immanuel Kant, *Anthropology from a Pragmatic Point of View*, ed. and trans. Robert B. Louden (Cambridge: Cambridge University Press, 2006), 15.

44. Ibid.

45. Ibid., 235.

46. Ibid.

47. Ibid., 232–33n.

48. Cf. Burgat, *Animal, mon prochain*, 61.

49. Immanuel Kant, *Groundwork of the Metaphysics of Morals*, trans. and ed. Mary Gregor (Cambridge: Cambridge University Press, 1997), 42–43.

50. Theodor W. Adorno, *Beethoven: The Philosophy of Music*, ed. Rolf Tiedemann, trans. Edmund Jephcott (Stanford, Calif.: Stanford University Press, 1998), 80 (fragment 202).

51. Jacques Derrida, "'Eating Well' or the Calculation of the Subject," trans. Peter Connor and Avital Ronell, in Derrida, *Points . . . : Interviews, 1974–1994*, ed. Elisabeth Weber (Stanford, Calif.: Stanford University Press, 1995).

52. Élisabeth de Fontenay, "La raison du plus fort," in Plutarch, *Trois traités pour les animaux* (Paris: POL, 1992), 71, my translation.

53. A theme that I treat at length (notably chaps. 2 and 3 of "A Word of Welcome") in Jacques Derrida, *Adieu to Emmanuel Levinas*, trans. Michael Naas and Pascale-Anne Brault (Stanford, Calif.: Stanford University Press, 1999), esp. 45–70.

54. Emmanuel Levinas, "The Paradox of Morality: An Interview with Emmanuel Levinas," in *The Provocation of Levinas: Rethinking the Other*, ed. Robert Bernasconi and David Wood (London: Routledge, 1988), 171–72. Quoted in John Llewelyn, *The Middle Voice of Ecological Conscience: A Chiasmatic Reading of Responsibility in the Neighborhood of Levinas, Heidegger and Others* (New York: St. Martin's Press, 1991), 65.

55. Levinas, "The Paradox of Morality," 172. Cf. Llewelyn, 64; my italics.

56. Emmanuel Levinas, "Peace and Proximity," in Levinas, *Basic Philosophical Writings*, ed. Adriaan T. Peperzak, Simon Critchley, and Robert Bernasconi (Bloomington: Indiana University Press, 1996), 168; quoted and discussed in Derrida, *Adieu to Emmanuel Levinas*, 32ff.

57. Cf. Alain David, "Cynesthèse: Auto-portrait du chien," in *L'animal autobiographique*, ed. Marie-Louise Mallet (Paris: Galilée, 1999).

58. Emmanuel Levinas, "Nom d'un chien ou le droit naturel," in *Celui qui ne peut se servir de mots* (Montpellier: Fata Morgana, 1975); "The Name of a Dog, or Natural Rights," in Levinas, *Difficult Freedom*, trans. Sean Hand (Baltimore: The Johns Hopkins University Press, 1990).

59. "An extraordinary coincidence . . . the number 1492, the year of the expulsion of the Jews from Spain under the Catholic Ferdinand V" ("Name of a Dog," 152). Further references are given in the text.

60. *Un loup pour l'animal*: a play on the expression *l'homme est un loup pour l'homme*, "men are pitiless, they turn on one another."—Trans.

61. Cf. Derrida, *Adieu to Emmanuel Levinas*, 68.

62. Three pages in English translation.—Trans.

63. Translation modified, cf. Levinas, "Nom d'un chien," 108.—Trans.

64. Cf. *Adieu to Emmanuel Levinas*, 30: "the terrible contradiction of the Saying by the Saying, Contra-diction itself." See also 118.

65. Cf. ibid., 39ff.

And Say the Animal Responded?

1. Earlier in the lecture, in the course of rereading Descartes, I elaborated at length upon what I shall here call the *question of the reply* or *response* and defined the hegemonic permanence of the "Cartesianism" that dominates the discourse and practice of human or humanist modernity with respect to the animal. A programmed machine like the animal is said to be incapable not of emitting signs but rather, according to the fifth part of the *Discourse on Method*, of "responding." Like animals, machines with "the organs and outward shape [*figure*, face] of a monkey . . . could never use words, or put together other signs, as we do in order to declare our thoughts to others. For we can certainly conceive of a machine so constructed that it utters words, and even utters words which correspond to bodily actions causing a change in its organs (e.g., if you touch it in one spot it asks what you want of it, if you touch it in another it cries out that you are hurting it, and so on). But it is not conceivable that such a machine should produce different arrangements of words so as to give an appropriately meaningful answer [*répondre*] to whatever is said in its presence, as the dullest of men can do." Descartes, *Discourse on the Method*, 139–40.

2. Jacques Lacan, "The Subversion of the Subject and the Dialectic of Desire in the Freudian Unconscious," in *Écrits: A Selection*, trans. Alan Sheridan (New York: Norton, 1977), 305. Further references to the Sheridan translation of *Écrits* will be given in the text. Other translations from *Écrits* are my own.—Trans.

3. Jacques Lacan, "Position de l'inconscient," *Écrits* (Paris: Seuil, 1966), 834. [The original French version of *Écrits* will henceforth be identified as "*Écrits* (French).")]

4. See esp. *Écrits* (French), 190–91.

5. Cf. *Proceedings of the Royal Society*, Series B (Biological Sciences), no. 845, February 3, 1939, vol. 126.—Trans.

6. See *Écrits* (French), 189–91, and also 342, 345–46, 452.

7. "The Mirror Stage as Formative of the Function of the I as Revealed in the Psychoanalytic Experience," *Écrits*, 3.

8. Lacan, "Variantes de la cure-type," *Écrits* (French), 354: "For it is fitting to reflect on the fact that it is not only through a symbolic assumption that speech constitutes the being of the subject, but that, through the law of the covenant whereby the human order is distinguished from nature, speech determines, from before its birth, not only the status of the subject but the coming-into-the-world of its biological being."

9. Cf. Joëlle Proust, *Comment l'esprit vient aux bêtes: Essai sur la représentation* (Paris: Gallimard, 1997), 150. This author does all she can to ensure that, in the case of the animal, the very word *response* signifies nothing more than a programmed *reaction*, deprived of all responsibility or even of any "intentional" responsiveness, if I can call it that—for the word *intentional* is used with a confidence and an imprudence, not to say phenomenological vulgarity, that is almost laughable. Concerning the syrphid, an insect that is "programmed to seek out females by automatically applying a pursuit trajectory in accordance with a given algorithm in order to intercept the pursued object," Joëlle Proust cites Ruth Millikan and comments thus: "What is interesting in this type of response is the fact that it is *inflexibly* provoked by certain precise characteristics in the *stimulus* (in the event, its size and speed). The insect cannot respond to other characteristics, neither can it exclude targets manifesting characteristics that are incompatible with the desired function. It cannot abandon its course by 'perceiving' that it is not following a female. This insect appears not to have any means of evaluating the correctness of its own perceptions. It would therefore seem *exaggeratedly generous* to attribute to it a *properly intentional* capability. It *responds to signs, but* these signs are not characteristic of an independent object; they are characteristic of proximate stimuli. As Millikan states, it follows a 'proximal rule.' However, the prewired response aims to bring about the fecundation of a female syrphid, that is to say, an object existing in the world" (228–29). I have italicized those words that, more than others, would call for a vigilant reading. The critical or deconstructive reading I am calling for would seek less to restitute to the animal or to such an insect the powers that it is not certain to possess (even if that sometimes seems possible) than to wonder whether one could not claim as much relevance for this type of analysis in the case of the human—with respect, for example, to the "wiring" of its sexual and reproductive behavior. Etc.

10. *pouvoir de tracer, de pister, de dé-pister, mais non de dé-pister le dé-pistage et d'*effacer *sa trace*: *Une piste* is a track and *pister* is sometimes used for "to follow (an animal's) tracks." However, *dépister*, which looks as though it has a privative sense, is the more usual word for "to follow tracks." Here Derrida is playing on that privative sense, following Lacan's usage as explained in n. 12 below.—Trans.

11. Allow me to refer the reader to my *Aporias*, trans. Thomas Dutoit (Stanford, Calif.: Stanford University Press, 1993), esp. 35–38 and 74–76.

12. In an important note in the "Seminar on 'The Purloined Letter,' " Lacan explains the original usage of the word *dépister* to which he is having recourse here: not "to track, follow a scent or tracks," but, on the contrary, as it were, "to confuse the issue [*brouiller la piste*] by covering one's tracks," *dé-pister*. In the same note he invokes at the same time Freud's famous text on the "antithetical sense of words, primal or not," the "magisterial rectification" that Benveniste contributed to it, and information from Bloch and Von Wartburg dating the second sense of the word *dépister* from 1975. The question of the antinomic sense of certain words, Lacan makes clear, "cannot be dispensed with [*reste entière*] if one is to bring out the instance of the signifier in all its rigor" (*Yale French Studies* 48 [1975], 51, translation modified).

Indeed, I would be tempted to add, in order to raise the stakes—especially if, as is the case here, we are to put to the test the axioms of a logic of the signifier in its double relation to the distinction between animal (capture by the imaginary) and human (access to the symbolic and to the signifier) orders, on the one hand, and to another interpretive implementation of undecidability, on the other. The supposedly assured difference between *pister* and *dé-pister*, or rather, between *dépister* ("track, or follow a track") and *dé-pister* ("cover one's tracks and purposely lead the hunter off the track") coalesces and underwrites the whole distinction between human and animal according to Lacan. It would be enough for this distinction to waver for the whole axiomatic to fall apart, in its very principle. That is what we are going to have to make clear.

13. *Écrits*, 305; italics are, of course, mine. Elsewhere I plan to analyze another text that, obeying the same logic ("the sexual instinct . . . crystallised in a relation of images") and concerning precisely the stickleback and its "copulation dance with the female," introduces the question of death, of the *being already dead*, and not just the being-mortal of the individual as a "type" of the species; not horses but the horse. Cf. Jacques Lacan, *The Seminar of Jacques Lacan, Book 1: Freud's Papers on Technique*, ed. Jacques-Alain Miller, trans. John Forrester (Cambridge: Cambridge University Press, 1988), 122–23.

14. "If instinct in effect signifies the undeniable animality of man, there seems no reason why that animality should be more docile for being incarnated in a reasonable being. The form of the adage—*homo homini lupus*—betrays its sense, and in a chapter from his *Criticon*, Balthazar Gracian elaborates a fable in which he shows what the moralist tradition means when it holds that the ferocity of man with respect to his fellow surpasses everything animals are capable of, and that carnivorous animals themselves recoil in horror from the threat to which he exposes all nature. But this very cruelty implies humanity. It is a fellow creature that he has in his sights, even in the guise of a being from a different species" ("Fonctions de la psychanalyse en criminologie," *Écrits* [French], 147).

15. Cf. "Le séminaire sur 'La Lettre volée'": "it was necessary to illustrate in a concrete way the dominance that we affirm for the signifier over the subject" (*Écrits* [French], 61 [not in the English translation—Trans.]); and "we have decided to illustrate for you today . . . that it is the symbolic order which is constitutive for the subject—by demonstrating in a story the decisive orientation [*détermination majeure*] which the subject receives from the itinerary of a signifier" ("Seminar on 'The Purloined Letter,'" 40).

16. Cf. "Le Facteur de la vérité," in Derrida, *The Post Card*, trans. Alan Bass (Chicago: University of Chicago Press, 1987).

17. Emmanuel Levinas, "Peace and Proximity," 168, cited and commented on in Derrida, *Adieu to Emmanuel Levinas*.

18. A study of the value of "fraternity," whose tradition and authority I have attempted to deconstruct (in *Politics of Friendship*, trans. George Collins [London: Verso, 1997]), should also be able to identify the credit given to it by Lacan, well beyond the suspicion in which the murderous and patricidal brothers are

held according to the logic of *Totem and Taboo*. In various places Lacan in effect dreams of *another fraternity*, for example, in these last words from "Aggressivity in Psychoanalysis": "it is our daily task to open up to this being of nothingness the way of his meaning in a discreet fraternity—a task for which we are always too inadequate" (*Écrits*, 29).

19. Lacan, "The Line and Light," in *The Four Fundamental Concepts of Psychoanalysis*, The Seminar of Jacques Lacan, Book XI, trans. Alan Sheridan (New York: W. W. Norton, 1998), 95. See also, esp., 75.

20. Lacan, "Situation de la psychanalyse et formation du psychanalyste en 1956," *Écrits* (French), 484.

21. *Écrits* (French), 345.

"I don't know why we are doing this"
NOTE: As mentioned in the Foreword, this last chapter is the transcription of a recording of Derrida's extempore lecture at the end of the colloquium.—Ed.

1. Martin Heidegger, *The Fundamental Concepts of Metaphysics: World, Finitude, Solitude*, trans. William McNeill and Nicholas Walker (Bloomington: Indiana University Press, 1995), 310. Further references will be given in the text.

2. Cf. *Aristotelis Metaphysica*, ed. W. Christ (Leipzig, 1886), A. 2, 983a 3f.

3. Martin Heidegger, *Being and Time*, trans. John Macquarie and Edward Robinson (New York: Harper and Row, 1962), §6, 41–49.

4. Ibid., 396.

5. Martin Heidegger, "On the Essence of Ground," trans. William McNeill, in Heidegger, *Pathmarks*, ed. William McNeill (Cambridge: Cambridge University Press, 1998), 97–135.

6. "Yet anyone who has never been seized by dizziness in the presence of a philosophical question has never asked the question in a philosophical way" (Heidegger, *The Fundamental Concepts of Metaphysics*, 180).

7. In French, *la prière*, also "prayer," "entreaty."—Trans.

8. Cf. *Aristotelis Organon*, ed. T. Waitz (Leipzig, 1844), vol. 1, *Hermeneutica (de interpretatione)*, chap. 4, 17a 1.

9. "When we say that the lizard is lying on the rock, we ought to cross out the word 'rock' [*so müssen wir das Wort "Felsplatte" durchstreichen*] in order to indicate that whatever the lizard is lying on is certainly given *in some way* for the lizard, and yet it is not known to the lizard *as* a rock [*nicht* als *Felsplatte*]. If we cross out the word . . . we imply that whatever it is is not accessible to it *as a being* [*Die Durchstreichung besagt . . . nicht* als Seindes *zugänglich*]. The blade of grass that the beetle crawls up, for example, is not a blade of grass for it at all" (Heidegger, *The Fundamental Concepts of Metaphysics*, 198).

10. "Every animal as animal has a specific set of relationships to its sources of nourishment, its prey, its enemies, its sexual mates, and so on. These relationships, which are infinitely difficult for us to grasp and require a high degree of cautious methodological foresight on our part, have a peculiar fundamental character of their own, the metaphysical significance of which has never properly been

perceived or understood before. . . . The animal's *way of being*, which we call '*life*,' is *not without access* to what is around it and about it, to that amongst which it appears as a living being. It is because of this that the claim arises that the animal has an environmental world of its own within which it moves. Throughout the course of its life the animal is confined to its environmental world, immured as it were within a fixed sphere [*in einem Rohr*] that is incapable of further expansion or contraction" (Heidegger, *The Fundamental Concepts of Metaphysics*, 198). Cf. §60b, "Animal behaviour as encircled by a disinhibiting ring" (ibid., 253ff.).